Gender and Sacred Textures

Comparative Research on Iconic and Performative Texts

Series Editor: James W. Watts, Syracuse University

While humanistic scholarship has focused on the semantic meaning of written, printed, and electronic texts, it has neglected how people perform texts mentally, orally and theatrically and manipulate the material text through aesthetic engagement, ritual display, and physical decoration. Ritualizing the material form of books – their iconic dimension – is to revere them as objects of power rather than just as words of instruction, information, or insight. Ritualizing books' expressive or performative dimension through song, artistic illustration and theater aims for inspirational effects.

This series encourages innovative research on the iconic and expressive/performative uses of written texts. It supports the activities of the Society for Comparative Research on Iconic and Performative Texts (SCRIPT), and also studies of these issues by other groups and individual scholars.

PUBLISHED

Books as Bodies and as Sacred Beings
Edited by James W. Watts and Yohan Yoo

How and Why Books Matter: Essays on the Social Function of Iconic Texts
James W. Watts

Iconic Books and Texts
Edited by James W. Watts

Korean Religious Texts in Iconic and Performative Rituals
Yohan Yoo

Miniature Books: The Format and Function of Tiny Religious Texts
Edited by Kristina Myrvold and Dorina Miller Parmenter

Reframing Authority: The Role of Media and Materiality
Edited by Laura Feldt and Christian Hogel

Sensing Sacred Texts
Edited by James W. Watts

GENDER AND SACRED TEXTURES

ENTANGLEMENTS OF MATERIALITY, EMBODIMENT, AND SACRED TEXTS IN RELIGIOUS IDENTITIES

EDITED BY MARIANNE SCHLEICHER

SHEFFIELD UK BRISTOL CT

Published by Equinox Publishing Ltd.
UK: Office 415, The Workstation, 15 Paternoster Row, Sheffield, South Yorkshire S1 2BX
USA: ISD, 70 Enterprise Drive, Bristol, CT 06010

www.equinoxpub.com

First published in Volume 14.1 of the journal *Postscripts*.

First published in book form 2025

British Library Cataloguing-in-Publication Data

A catalogue record for this book is available from the British Library.

ISBN-13	978 1 80050 551 3	(hardback)
	978 1 80050 552 0	(paperback)
	978 1 80050 553 7	(ePDF)
	978 1 80050 660 2	(ePub)

Library of Congress Cataloging-in-Publication Data (to follow)

Names: Schleicher, Marianne editor
Title: Gender and sacred textures : entanglements of materiality, embodiment, and sacred texts in religious identities / edited by Marianne Schleicher.
Description: Sheffield, UK ; Bristol, CT : Equinox, 2025. | Series: Comparative research on iconic and performative texts | Includes bibliographical references and index. | Summary: "This anthology asks how the handling, use, and embodied enactments of sacred texts regulate, entangle, occlude, tolerate, or even subvert religious and gendered identities"-- Provided by publisher.
Identifiers: LCCN 2025009642 (print) | LCCN 2025009643 (ebook) | ISBN 9781800505513 hardback | ISBN 9781800505520 paperback | ISBN 9781800505537 pdf | ISBN 9781800506602 epub
Subjects: LCSH: Sex role--Religious aspects | Gender identity--Religious aspects | Sacred books
Classification: LCC BL65.S4 G466 2025 (print) | LCC BL65.S4 (ebook) | DDC 200.81--dc23/eng/20250610
LC record available at https://lccn.loc.gov/2025009642
LC ebook record available at https://lccn.loc.gov/2025009643

Typeset by Sparks Publishing Services Ltd—www.sparkspublishing.com

Contents

List of Figures

Introduction

Gender and Sacred Text(ure)s: Extending the Field of Sacred Text Studies

Marianne Schleicher

This book focuses on the interaction of gender and sacred texts. Within the critical, comparative, and historical study of sacred texts, many excellent studies have been undertaken that offer close readings of sacred texts to retrieve information about their models of and for gender. In religiously engaged ways, religious specialists have produced highly systematic, literary, or creative rereadings of their foundational texts in order to reposition the gender norms of their tradition. What critical and religiously engaged scholarship still needs to ask is if or how the handling, use, and embodied enactments of sacred texts regulate, entangle, occlude, tolerate, or even subvert religious and gendered identities.

A primary motivation for juxtaposing gender and sacred texts in the book series *Comparative Research on Iconic and Performative Texts* already dedicated to interdisciplinary studies of diverse engagements with sacred texts, also as material objects, is to problematize some limitations that come with the concept of text in the term "sacred text". Most studies of sacred texts, whether as texts or material objects, focus on elite men's uses within official religion. This bias is explainable because men in patriarchal religions have held offices and privileges that would grant them direct contact with sacred texts in formal studies or liturgical use and because it is of their religiosity that most primary sources have kept records. Yet, as this book will argue, laymen and women in general have also associated their religiosity with sacred texts, even if their engagements were not direct and/or liturgical. To be able to understand lay religiosity dependent upon sacred texts, this book pursues a methodological focus on engagements with sacred texts in direct, yet non-liturgical as well as indirect ways. This focus brings to light activities such as production, ornamentation, aural reception, recitation, and in particular embodied enactments of sacred texts. To bolster this pursuit, this book introduces the analytical concept of "sacred texture".

My idea to introduce the concept of "sacred texture" was inspired by the philosopher Paul Ricoeur's *Interpretation Theory: Discourse and the Surplus of Meaning* (1976), where he distinguishes between speaking and writing. He argues that "all references in oral language rely on monstrations, which depend on the situation perceived as common by the members of the dialogue" (Ricoeur 1976, 35), whereas discourse, once it is fixed in writing, is freed from the limits of authorial intentions and of situational references. Instead, he speaks about the "semantic autonomy of the text" (Ricoeur 1976, 35), where internal references between the different parts enable a reader's reconstruction of a self-contained whole. Of relevance here is that Ricoeur mentions an exception to this dichotomy between oral and written communication: The concept of text

> combines the condition of inscription with the texture proper to the productive rules of literary composition. Text means discourse both as inscribed and wrought.
>
> [... Accordingly,] even oral expressions of poetic or narrative compositions rely on processes equivalent to writing. The memorization of epic poems, lyrical songs, parables and proverbs, and their ritual recitation tend to fix and even to freeze the form of the work in such a way that memory appears as the support of an inscription similar to that provided by external marks. (Ricoeur 1976, 33)

A text does not have to be inscribed. Its texture consists of letters, words, and sentences wrought and woven together as textile in a specific way that makes it recognizable as a particular text. According to Ricoeur, ritualized oral performances of a poetic or narrative kind qualify as texture, which makes both recitation, which repeats already produced texts, and the oral production of poems textural. Ricoeur's conception of text also as texture opens up the possibility of thinking about poetic and narrative performances in oral cultures as activities that may qualify as sacred texture. In Miriam Levering's pioneering anthology *Rethinking Scripture: Essays from a Comparative Perspective* (1989), she worried that an "emphasis on looking at religious achievements through texts privileges the literate over the oral, and the elite strands of a tradition over the folk or popular strands" (Levering 1989, 4), and that this would lead scholars to neglect the overall comparative insight that sacred texts as phenomena also have symbolic and mythic power providing knowledge about human religiousness.

Accordingly, many of the contributors to Levering's book focused on the aural aspects in scriptural use, but primarily with a focus on the praxis of recitation from a written copy.[1] With the concept of texture, I hope that it will be possible to speak not only about orality in literate culture, but also about textuality in oral cultures.

The concept of texture has another potential. The items within a texture are cohesive,[2] and their recognizability depends on a distinctive wreaking/weaving/sequencing of its items. Yet, if an oral repetition of a text, for example the *Shema* (Deut 6:4–9; 11:13–21; Num 15:37–41) opens with "Hear, O Israel! The Lord is our God," but then continues with fragments in the proper sequence, like "Take to heart these instructions ... Recite them ... when you lie down and when you get up ... scribe them on your doorposts" (Deut 6:4–9), the sequenced fragments will suffice to make them recognizable as belonging to the texture of the *Shema*. In cultures where only specialists have access to and are able to study physical copies of sacred texts – that is, the semantic whole – lay people will most likely know only fragments, to which contact is nevertheless important to establish and demonstrate their religiosity. In other words, monstration of fragmentary, yet sacred texture should also be included in sacred text studies as a practice that pertains to people's religious agency. Monstration is, according to Ricoeur, a characteristic of oral communication. However, in the hybrid phenomenon of sacred texture, monstration proves itself to be a resource, not only of oral communication, but fundamentally of mimetic communication[3] that enables religious people to point to what a word signifies, or to illustrate parts of a text with his or her bodily movements, or with art for that matter. Since a bodily or artful monstration, like an oral recitation, can omit parts, yet still fragmentarily manifest a sacred text by rendering parts of its texture, activities of many religious people will be recognizable as matters of sacred text use. I shall even argue that especially embodied enactment would serve as a means for a religious person to make an otherwise inaccessible sacred text accessible in the body. Terminologically, I suggest that "sacred text" refers to an inscribed text of a sacred status, directly accessible for hermeneutical and artefactual use,[4] whereas "sacred texture" refers

1. Cf. Smith 1989, 33-34; Coburn 1989, 104; Graham 1989 in its entirety.
2. On cohesion and texture in a linguistic perspective, see Halliday and Hasan 1976, 2-8.
3. For more on mimetic communication and its function in history of cultures, see Donald 2001.
4. I define hermeneutical use as a matter of deciphering a semantic whole, whereas artefactual use transforms a sacred text as a manipulable symbol that triggers all the senses and establishes transitivity between the individual and collective users, their

to its indirect manifestation, often as fragments or sequences in bodily enactments. Sometimes a use will imply both direct and indirect access and in such cases I suggest the graphic rendering "sacred text(ure)".

Going to these lengths to include oral production and fragmentary recitation and embodied enactment of sacred texture in sacred text studies pertains to representativity in our selection of source material to ensure that scholars of religion can document diverse forms of religious agency. The religious identity of many elite men has been indisputable because of their direct contact with something sacred, for example a sacred text. It is my hope that the concept of "sacred texture" will generate a methodological focus on hitherto overlooked ways for laymen and women in general to make their religious identities intelligible.

A couple of theories on identity formation inform this book. In *Gender Trouble: Feminism and the Subversion of Identity* (1990), philosopher Judith Butler presented her theory of performativity to explain the phenomenon of gender. Instead of perceiving any kind of identity as an essence, as something stable, Butler asserts that someone's identity is attained, but also becomes intelligible to others, through his or her participation in rule-generated practices within a culture (Butler 1990, 34, 185–6). Yet, not all people have equal agency, concretely understood as access to participating in cultural, rule-generated practices (Butler 1990, 198). This understanding offers itself to studies of religion as an emphasis on the importance of rituals or ritual-like acts for the intelligibility of religious identities, just as it invites the question of who has access to what rituals and ritual-like acts. The question of access has inspired the distinction in this book between direct and indirect access to sacred texts. If scholarship only focuses on people's direct access to sacred texts, it will mostly produce insights into elite male religious identity. If, however, access is qualified in a broad sense to include indirect and/or direct, non-liturgical engagements with sacred texts, it would also grant scholars insights into the formation of religious identities among laymen and women in general.

Another element in Butler's theory of performativity is her concept of "subversion" that offers a model for understanding what is required for a culture to accept significant variations in identities. When people have to engage in rule-generated practices to become intelligible, such engagements entail repetition. Yet, no repetition of a practice can be absolutely identical to the previous one, and incidental or deliberate variations will always occur. If outsiders try to affect identificatory norms, culture will

associations and cultural representations and the immediate context; cf. Schleicher 2017.

tend to be hostile, just as antinomian insiders will be met with some kind of violent/defensive regulation. However, if one participates in a culture's rule-regulated practices, even with some degree of variation, the culture will tend to interpret the participation as a matter of loyalty to culture and accordingly be tolerant and even acknowledge the varied element and thereby bestow on it intelligibility (Butler 1990, 191, 199). I mention this part of Butler's theory because it emphasizes how practices involving sacred texts will constantly transform or produce new religious identities and that culture will not necessarily be hostile to variation in practices as long as the impression of loyalty prevails.

One weakness in Butler's theory of performativity is that its underlying cultural constructionism fails to explain when physical matter comes to matter. For this reason, the book has taken inspiration from physicist and gender theoretician Karen Barad who adjusts Butler's theory of performativity to take account of the effects of materiality. One among many insights taken from quantum physics is that identities are constantly produced in processes of becoming when different phenomena meet and entangle. Identity is therefore not only the result of a person's participation in a rule-generated practice. Every material object involved in the practice will intra-act with things or people involved and be a co-producer of their identity (Barad 2007, 170–2). In a book that wants to take account of sacred texts not just as written discourse waiting to be interpreted, but also as material objects that intra-act with and contribute to people's religious identities, Barad's refinement of Butler's theory of performativity is important.

These theories of texture and performativity inspired the call for contributions sent out in July 2021. Half a year later, we held a three-day workshop, generously funded by the School of Society and Culture, Aarhus University, Denmark. People came from different fields with different specializations. Some knew about sacred texts and religion, others knew about gender and religion. The purpose of the workshop was not for participants to adopt specific theories, like those mentioned above, but to ensure that everyone was conscious of his or her understanding of gender, sacred, text, and sacred text. Accordingly, I gave a brief overview of existing research on these topics, leading to discussions where participants could position themselves and apply the favoured perspectives to their empirical material in a round of concluding presentations. The outcome was exhilarating and initiated the writing process leading first to a special issue of *Postscripts - The Journal of Sacred Texts, Cultural Histories, and Contemporary Contexts*, volume 14:1 (2023), and now to this book, published by Equinox.

The book opens with the chapter "Old Norse Women's Use of Sacred Textures in Crisis Situations" by Emma Cecilie Sørlie Jørgensen, trained in the comparative study of religion. Jørgensen sheds light on women producing sacred texture of an oral kind according to the imaginings of Icelandic saga literature in its portrayal of Old Norse religion. With Émile Durkheim's understanding of the sacred as numinous, protected, and set apart from the profane, with Ricoeur's abovementioned understanding of poetic or narrative texts as texture in oral culture, and various processual understandings of gendered identity, she brings her own translations and analyses of excerpts from *Njáls saga*, *Vǫlsa þáttr*, *Vǫluspá*, and *Eiríks saga rauða.* Jørgensen documents how literary female characters produced sacred textures in times of crisis with significant effect on their intelligibility as religious agents in Old Norse culture and with effects on their gender since their production of sacred texture implied an entrance into the domain of cultural defence otherwise associated with men's activities.

The second chapter, "Drinkable Ink or Womb-Destroying Words? A Solution for Suspected Adultery in Numbers 5:11–31," is written by Rosanne Liebermann, scholar of Old Testament Studies. Liebermann analyses the Book of Numbers on the so-called *sotah* ritual that was intended to determine the guilt or innocence of a woman suspected of adultery. Following James Watts's call to look beyond the semantic dimension of scripture and also reflect on the ritualization of scripture's iconic and performative dimensions, Liebermann focuses on the biblical description and prescription of how a text containing divine words is aurally performed, and how its iconic dimensions are transformed from the scroll format to a watery solution before the performance of the ritual requires the suspected woman to embody it through ingestion. Drawing upon R. W. Connell's theory of masculinities, she illustrates how the material object of a sacred text in this described and prescribed ritual sanctions and bolsters the hegemonic and complicit masculinities of the priest and the presumably cuckolded husband, when a woman does not handle, but is handled with a sacred text.

The third chapter, "Jewish Women and Sacred Text(ure)s: Making Women's Religious Agency in Jewish Book Culture Intelligible," is written by myself. I trained in the comparative study of religion with specialization in Jewish Studies. Inspired by the abovementioned theories on texture and identity formation I ask who has access when and where to which ritual or ritual-like activities that involve sacred texts or fragmentary parts of textures. In my search for source material, I begin in the Hebrew Bible and proceed to early Judaism, early rabbinic literature, and Ashkenazic Judaism in the Middle Ages, asking when texts were conceived as sacred in the first place, when and how access to them became regulated, and what effect this has on the intelligibility of religious identities, especially that of Jewish women. Drawing on my earlier distinction between hermeneutical and artefactual uses of sacred texts, I illustrate that in ascetic and/or pietistic contexts some elite women had direct access to sacred texts in the form of hermeneutical use and in the production of sacred and religious books as artefacts. For most other women, however, access to sacred texts was indirect, either through facilitating men's Torah studies or by bodily enacting textural fragments invoking commandments incumbent upon women or sequences from the lives of biblical or Talmudic heroes. A crucial finding is that women's embodied enactments of sacred textures, despite their lack of direct access to the sacred texts as objects, were as meritorious as elite men's direct access was, and the embodied enactments had great effect on the intelligibility of women's religious identity.

The fourth chapter, "The Gender of Purple Manuscripts and the Make-up of Sacred Scriptures," by art historian Thomas Rainer, analyses letters sent by the church father Jerome (fourth–fifth century) to Roman aristocratic women whom he warns against scriptural codices with purple-coloured parchment, gilt lettering, and precious covers. Simultaneously, Jerome encourages these Christian women to renounce any kind of bodily adornment, be it makeup or luxurious clothing. Rainer argues that the correspondence between Jerome's ideals for the materiality of Christian scriptures and for Christian women's education and appearance reflect a dualistic worldview that elevates the "naked" scriptural texts and Christian bodies in distanciation from this-worldly, distracting luxury and sensuality. Following James Watts's concept of scripture's iconic dimension, Rainer illustrates how asceticism necessitates not only an austere approach to the materiality of scripture to focus on the text itself, but also women's doffing of the sensuality that pre-Christian Roman culture associated with female identity. Instead, ascetic women had to approximate Jerome's ideals for male Christian scholars

The fifth chapter, "'Then Queen Esther Daughter of Abihail Wrote': Gendered Agency and Ritualized Writing in Jewish Scriptural Practice," is written by Joanna Homrighausen, a researcher in the Hebrew Bible and Jewish religion. She contextualizes and analyses the ritualized writings performed by four female ritual scribes in contemporary American Judaism: Nava Levine-Coren, Avielah Barclay, Jen Taylor Friedman, and Rachel Jackson. Based on Judith Butler's theory of performativity, Homrighausen illustrates how these women engage in the iterative act of copying the scroll of Esther within the halakhic framework, thus demonstrating loyalty to Jewish tradition and making themselves intelligible as Jewish ritual scribes. The religious agency that comes with ritual scripting has not been immediately available to Jewish women in pre-modern Judaism. However, Homrighausen illustrates how these scribes, with their iterative engagement in scripting, by adhering to the halakhic rules, and by bodily enacting the writing that the biblical figure of Esther engaged in herself, have subverted the normative expectations in modern American Judaism of a scribe's gendered identity.

The sixth chapter, "'I Left My Bible at Home…': Evangelical Women's Bodies as Biblical Text in the Workplace during the 1980s," is written by historian Rachel E. C. Beckley, who has specialized in Christianity in America. She makes the methodological choice of focusing on affiliated periodicals and not institutionally produced books and magazines to be able to access American Evangelical women's own writings in the 1980s. In an analysis of Shirley Schreiner Taylor's parable, "God Protects His Sheep among the Wolves," Beckley analyses the agency of an Evangelical woman upon entry into the workforce where her physical Bible had to be left at home. Beckley points to how the Bible, now inaccessible, became indirectly accessible by being ensconced in the Evangelical woman's body. Inspired by Judith Butler and Karen Barad's theories of performativity, Beckley argues that Evangelical women engaged in embodied mirrorings of biblical heroes' defence of their religiosity in hostile environments. Evangelical women like Taylor thereby replaced their material copies of the Bible with embodied enactments of biblical motifs and narratives as markers of their religious identity and as a means to continue the evangelization so seminal to Evangelical identity.

The seventh and last chapter, "Doing Piety through Care: Embodied Enactments of the Qur'an and Gender Perceptions in Muslim families in Contemporary Denmark," is written by Abir Mohamad Ismail who has specialized in Arab and Islamic Studies from an anthropological perspective. After introducing central passages in the Qur'an and the Ḥadīths that deal with *birr-al-wālidayn* (filial piety) and *'awra* (the intimate body parts that must be covered) and *'ayb* (shame/shamefulness), Ismail analyses two ethnographic cases from her fieldwork where she studied practices of elderly care in multigenerational Arab Muslim families living in Denmark. She documents how Um Ali, a 61-year-old woman, and Salim, a 57-year-old man, provide filial care for their parents as a matter of pious, bodily enactments as prescribed in Muslim sacred texts. It is, however, with inspiration from Judith Butler's theory of performativity that Ismail highlights that gendered expectations of who does what kind of care to whom complicates filial care due to clashes with scriptural commandments concerning the naked body. Here, men and women have different access to embodied enactments of sacred texts to such an extent that the entanglement of filial piety, nudity, and shame becomes a conflicted space where skilful navigation will decide whose Muslim and gendered identity will benefit the most.

Acknowledgments

I should like to thank all contributors for the time, efforts, and skills that they have invested in this book and for their accommodating, intelligent, and enthusiastic attitude whenever we have corresponded. I owe my gratitude to the School of Society and Culture, Aarhus University, Denmark for its trust and financial support in me and the project, which enabled the productive three-day workshop mentioned above. I thank Marianne Qvortrup Fibiger, head of my Department of the Study of Religion, also Aarhus University, for her continual support as well as generous funding of ensuing travel activities. Furthermore, I would like to express my warm thanks to Chief Editor of *Postscripts* Brad Anderson for letting me guest edit the special issue on Gender and Sacred text(ure)s, for his constant readiness to assist when questions arose, and for his insights and cogent comments and suggestions. Finally, I am indebted to James W. Watts for encouragement and advice over the years, also with regard to the planning of this book.

References

Barad, Karen. 2007. *Meeting the Universe Halfway: Quantum Physics and the Entanglement of Matter and Meaning*. Durham, NC: Duke University Press.

Butler, Judith. 1990 (1999). *Gender Trouble*. New York; Routledge.

Coburn, Thomas B. 1989. " 'Scripture' in India: Towards a Typology of the Word in Hindu Life." In *Rethinking Scripture: Essays from a Comparative Perspective*, edited by Miriam Levering, 102–28. Albany, NY: State University of New York Press.

Donald, Merlin. 2001. *A Mind So Rare: The Evolution of Human Consciousness*. New York: W. W. Norton & Co.

Graham, William A. 1989. "Scripture as Spoken Word." In *Rethinking Scripture: Essays from a Comparative Perspective*, edited by Miriam Levering, 129–69. Albany, NY: State University of New York Press.

Halliday, Michael Alexander Kirkwood, and Hasan, Ruqaiya. 1976. *Cohesion in English*. London: Routledge.

Levering, Miriam. 1989. "Introduction: Rethinking Scripture." In *Rethinking Scripture: Essays from a Comparative Perspective*, edited by Miriam Levering, 1-17. Albany, NY: State University of New York Press.

Ricoeur, Paul. 1976. *Interpretation Theory: Discourse and the Surplus of Meaning.* Fort Worth, TX: Texas Christian University Press.

Schleicher, Marianne. 2017. "Engaging All the Senses: On Multi-sensory Stimulation in the Process of Making and Inaugurating a Torah Scroll." *Postscripts* 8 (1–2): 39–65. https://doi.org/10.1558/post.32694

Smith, Wilfred Cantwell. 1989. "Scripture as Form and Concept: Their Emergence for the Western World." In *Rethinking Scripture: Essays from a Comparative Perspective*, edited by Miriam Levering, 29–57. Albany, NY: State University of New York Press.

About the Author

Marianne Schleicher is Associate Professor of Jewish Studies at Aarhus University, Denmark where she works on individual and collective uses of sacred texts, its materiality and intra-action with bodies, gender, and sexuality in both mainstream and mystical traditions. Her publications include the monograph *Intertextuality in the Tales of Rabbi Nahman of Bratslav* (Brill 2007), "Constructions of Sex and Gender: Attending to Androgynes and Tumtumim through Jewish Scriptural Use" (2011), "Attitudes to Deviation from Gender Norms in Israelite and Early Jewish Religion" (2018), and the co-edited volume *Entanglements and Weavings: Diffractive Approaches to Gender and Love* (2021). (ms@cas.au.dk)

1

Old Norse Women's Use of Sacred Textures in Crisis Situations

Emma C. Sørlie Jørgensen

Abstract

The purpose of this chapter is to identify Old Norse sacred texts and contribute to insights into the entanglements between Old Norse women's gender and their production and performance of sacred texts. By broadening the concept of text to include texture, the chapter proposes a definition that can identify some recorded Old Norse poetic speech acts as sacred textures. Empirically, the chapter analyses skaldic and eddic poetry composed by Old Norse women as a means to defend themselves and their communities against threats, and it examines how the production of sacred textures affected women's gender. The chapter conjoins theoretical reflections by Paul Ricoeur, Émile Durkheim, Rudolf Otto, Judith Butler, Karen Barad, and Gilles Deleuze and Félix Guattari, offering a platform for future analyses of sacred textures in other oral religious cultures.

Keywords: Old Norse religion, orality, gender, materiality, eddic poetry, skaldic poetry

Introduction

The purpose of this chapter is to identify and analyse sacred texts in an oral religious culture, namely Old Norse religion, as a contribution to this issue's attempt to broaden the concept of text to include texture, for example words woven together in ritual or ritual-like performances. Further, this chapter also seeks to contribute to insights into the entanglements of sacred texts and gender, and into how production and performance of sacred texts and Old Norse women's gender intra-acted.[1]

The chapter opens with a brief introduction to previous research that comments on the phenomena that I have decided to refer to as Old Norse sacred texture. Here, I shall bring out their contributions as well as the knowledge gaps that still need attention. To coin the concept of Old Norse sacred textures, I will draw upon insights from Paul Ricoeur, Émile Durkheim, and Rudolf Otto. To examine why Old Norse women produced sacred textures and how this production affected their gender, I will draw upon constructionist and new materialist theories by Judith Butler, Karen Barad, and Gilles Deleuze and Félix Guattari. Their theoretical insights will help me discuss the degree of agency attributed to the producers of sacred textures, address gender as processual, and examine how gender entangles with the effects of sacred textures.

Empirically, I shall analyse three accounts from the Icelandic saga literature, namely *Njáls saga* chapter 102, *Eiríks saga rauða* chapter 4, and the short story *Vǫlsa þáttr* which is a part of *Ólafs saga helga*, and I shall analyse stanzas 21 and 22 of the eddic poem *Vǫluspá*. These sources depict a woman poet, a housewife, and two prophetesses who produce and perform sacred textures. Based on close readings, including my own translation of specific passages, I will argue that some women produced sacred textures in crises as a means to protect Old Norse communities.

Previous Research on Old Norse Sacred Textures

Simon Nygaard is in my opinion the scholar who comes closest to identifying what I shall term Old Norse sacred textures. In his chapter "Being Óðinn Bursson" (2019), Nygaard analyses the eddic poem *Grímnismál* that tells the story of Grímnir who reveals himself to be the god Óðinn. Nygaard argues that oral, ritual performances of the poem created a transformational experience for the performer and the listeners through special metre, time perceptions, pronouns, adverbs of place, and the use of ritual props (Nygaard 2019, 59). By using the pronoun "I" (*ek*) and possibly also ritual props, the performer transformed into the god Óðinn in the ritual moment, something that is accepted by any audience present (Nygaard 2019, 63). I argue that the aural lyrical characteristics of the poem, for example, the *ljóðaháttr* metre with its alliteration, emphasizes the textual properties of the poem, and that the texture is treated as an artefact (Malley 2004, 70–2;

1. A term coined by Barad that "*signifies the mutual constitution of entangled agencies*" (Barad 2007, 33; Barad's italics).

Schleicher 2009, 50) that enables the transformation of the performer during the ritual. These traits lead me to suggest that *Grímnismál* could qualify as an oral, Old Norse sacred texture.

Previous scholarship has not really reflected on which genders had access to composing and performing the Old Norse poems. For instance, Nygaard assumes without reflection that the ritual specialist who performed *Grímnismál* is a man. Even though Nygaard does not reflect upon this, the poem itself indicates that his assumption is correct. *Grímnismál* unfolds the narrative of the man Grímnir, revealed to be the male god Óðinn,[2] supporting the notion that the pronoun "I" (*ek*), uttered by the ritual specialist, refers to a male narrator.

Since eddic poems are anonymous and written down after possibly many years of oral transmission, it does not make sense to look for an original composer of eddic poems (Gunnell 2013, 64). In contrast, skaldic poems are attributed to a single, often known, composer, who was most often male. Out of 448 known *skálds* (Wills n.d.), Sandra Ballif Straubhaar finds only fifty-four Old Norse women composing poetry (Straubhaar 2011). This unequal distribution of men and women *skálds* suggests that the art of poetry was a domain dominated by men, but not unfamiliar to women *skálds*. Most male *skálds* were attached to the courts of the Norwegian kings where they composed poems in the verse form *dróttkvætt* (courtly metre). John Lindow has suggested that *dróttkvætt* was a secret code language invented by the members of the king's courts, so that they could communicate without being understood by non-members, that is, the lower classes and women (Lindow 1975, 322–3). However, this suggestion seems doubtful. Straubhaar points out "then it is a particular credit to our *skáldkonur* [female *skálds*] here that they seem to have had no trouble with spontaneous composition in *dróttkvætt*, considering that they probably were not entitled to membership in one of these fraternities" (Straubhaar 2011, 11). An example of a female *skáld* is Steinunn Refsdóttir from *Njáls saga* whose poem I shall analyse below.

Another poem I shall turn to is perhaps the most famous eddic poem, *Vǫluspá*, narrated by a *vǫlva*, that is, an Old Norse prophetess with the abilities to see the past and future. The linguist Björn Collinder refers to the composer of *Vǫluspá* as "he" and "him", without reflecting upon why he makes this assumption (Collinder 1993, 21). Based on the limited and mostly negative representation of female humans and deities in the poem, Jenny Jochens writes that "to imagine that women formulated it strains

2. However, Óðinn's gender is not unambiguous, see Jørgensen 2020.

credibility" (Jochens 1989, 361–362). However, as eddic poems, including *Vǫluspá*, are anonymous and orally transmitted through hundreds of years, I do not think that it makes sense or is particularly interesting to speak of an original poet nor this person's gender. As Annette Lassen writes, "The poem presents itself as being the actual words of the prophetess" (Lassen 2013, 7). If we earlier accepted that the voice in *Grímnismál* is male because the poem presents itself as being the words of Óðinn, surely this argument could also be accepted in the case of *Vǫluspá.* The poem represents Old Norse notions of women's voices and women's access to trans-empirical knowledge that even the most powerful male gods did not have access to. Therefore, I argue that, when analysing the poem, we should take seriously that the poem claims to represent the voice of a woman and a social outcast, that her prophecy is imagined to stem from a woman's power and access to the numinous, that this power puts her in a position where men sought her advice, and that – if performed – the audience could have expected to hear one or more female voices.

Theoretical Framework

According to Paul Ricoeur, poems are texts that consist of dynamic entities that create unities of meaning. These compositions can be both oral and written (Ricoeur 1976, 32). Furthermore, he writes that discourse is produced "when a form is applied to some matter in order to shape it" (Ricoeur 1976, 33), emphasizing that texts are not mere inscriptions of words, but are shaped materiality. This understanding is consistent with the etymology of the word "text." "Text" derives from "texture," which means interweaving and connotes materiality, and as such, a text is woven words that rely on laws of composition that create discourses. Ricoeur argues that oral poetic and narrative expressions "rely on processes equivalent to writing" (Ricoeur 1976, 33) because the memorization of oral poems and narratives fixes their forms. To emphasize that oral Old Norse poetry consisted of dynamic connected entities that shaped and wove meanings, connoting materiality, I will henceforth use the word "texture" to describe Old Norse poetry. Based upon Ricoeur's understanding of texts, I suggest that a texture should be defined as the weaving of statements, whether oral or written.

To understand and define sacredness in relation to Old Norse religion, I combine the thoughts of Émile Durkheim and Rudolf Otto. Durkheim defines the sacred as "things set apart and forbidden" (Durkheim 1995, 44). Sacredness can be space, time, texts, humans, objects, set apart from the profane, and the sacred is thus always contrasted with the profane. Otto used the term "numinous" to refer to the irrational aspect of religion: a unique state of mind that cannot strictly be defined. It is a non-rational feeling of the *ganz Andere* (wholly other) that can only be evoked, not taught (Otto 1963, 7). According to Otto, the sacred is a *mysterium tremendum et fascinosum*: it is both terrifying and fascinating (Otto 1963, 13–14). Combining these two understandings, I define the sacred as that, which is set apart from the profane and is perceived to be surrounded with numinous power and accordingly provokes terror and fascination for those who accept it as sacred.

In the context of the study of Old Norse religion, Jens Peter Schjødt, also inspired by Otto, uses the term "numinous knowledge" in his habilitation thesis *Initiation between Two Worlds* (2008). Numinous knowledge has two constant aspects that makes it recognizable: it is considered to be of and about the trans-empirical world, and it is only known by special initiated individuals (Schjødt 2008, 78–80). In the analysis, I will draw inspiration from Schjødt's notion of numinous knowledge and consider Old Norse sacred textures as textures that claim access to trans-empirical, numinous knowledge. I will examine what kind of numinous knowledge the composers of sacred textures claim access to, how they use numinous knowledge, and how the access to numinous knowledge intra-acts with their gender.

To identify which Old Norse poems could be considered sacred, I offer the following working definition of Old Norse sacred textures: they are renderings of textures set apart and perceived to be shrouded in numinous power which makes them both terrifying and fascinating for those who accept them as sacred, mainly because they claim access to numinous knowledge.

To analyse how sacred textures were used in Old Norse religion I draw upon Gilles Deleuze and Félix Guattari's suggestion that everything is made up of segmentary, molecular, and experimental lines that forge identities. The lines are constantly established and broken in an everchanging process where they connect and disconnect from domains. The segmentary lines segment, territorialize, and stratify. They create binaries and hierarchies, and they regulate and divide phenomena into gender, sexuality, classes, races etc. (Deleuze and Parnet 1983, 69; 1987, 587–8). The molecular lines move in a constant flux where they deterritorialize and create passages between the segmentary lines in order to establish new connections (Deleuze and Parnet 1983, 69–70; 1987, 588). The experimental lines experiment and expand the territories of the other two lines. They are unpredictable and never permanent. Experimental lines try out new, unknown and possibly dangerous connections before they either break off or, if they establish a successful connection, turn into molecular lines (Deleuze and Guattari 1987, 589). Because identities are made up of these dynamic lines, the domains that the lines connect to and disconnect from affect the individual's identity, making identities constantly changing, but always domain dependent. A part of the methodology inspired by Deleuze and Guattari is therefore to map the lines and their connections and examine how they affect identity. In the context of the usage of sacred textures, this methodology lends itself to examining how the access to the production of sacred textures affected gender and social status and vice versa. A further consequence of Deleuze and Guattari's thinking is to examine how segmentary and molecular lines defend and establish cohesion in the Old Norse culture. Based on this theoretical point of departure, I will map which types of lines are being established when sacred textures are produced and pay attention to how and in what way the lines intra-act with the sacred texture and the composer's gender and social status.

To understand Old Norse gender, I synthesize constructionist and new materialist insights. My constructionist and processual insights are inspired by Judith Butler's theory of performativity. Butler argues that gender is constructed by repeated performances of rule-regulated acts (Butler 1999, 45). It is the acts that subjects perform and the activities they participate in that govern the intelligibility of someone's identity and gender. A subject's agency depends on the subject's access to participation in the rule-regulated iterative acts (Butler 1999, 198). Butler, being a representative of the linguistic turn, argues that access to objects is always-already embedded in discourse. Consequently, because matter can only be perceived through a prism of linguistic categories, Butler's constructionist paradigm cannot explain the effects of materiality.

Sharing Butler's processual understanding of gender, Karen Barad rehabilitates Butler's concepts of performativity and agency in a new materialist context by insisting that matter is agentive and intra-active (Barad 2007, 170). Intra-action is a term coined by Barad that "*signifies the mutual constitution of entangled agencies*" (Barad 2007, 33, Barad's italics). Barad defines agency as "'*doing' or 'being' in its intra-activity. It is the enactment of iterative changes to particular practices* [...] *through the dynamics of intra-activity*" (Barad 2007, 178, Barad's italics). Barad thus insists that gender should be viewed in a mutual entanglement with materiality, acts, activities, and so on. These new materialist insights are compatible with Deleuze and Guattari's three lines that I mentioned above. The segmentary, molecular, and experimental lines are entangled and intra-act with both the material and the immaterial.[3]

By combining the constructionist and new materialist insights from Butler and Barad, I define Old Norse gender as processual, domain dependent, and as something that is constructed through repeated performances of rule-regulated acts. Furthermore, I argue that bodily materiality activates associations and expectations to a certain kind of identity that we understand as gender. The methodological consequences of these insights are to investigate the degree of agency attributed to the producers of sacred textures. I will investigate which rule-regulated acts the producers of sacred textures get access to, and how the domains within which they produce their textures intra-act with their gender.

Analysis

Since it is impossible to gain access to Old Norse poetry performed orally thousand years ago, the source material I shall analyse consists of renderings of oral textures that have been fixed in medieval Icelandic manuscripts.[4] Even though the textual renderings are from the thirteenth century, they testify to an oral tradition of poetry that derives from the tenth century (Sapp 2022, 202). There is no visual distinction between prose and poetry in the manuscripts, and it is thus necessary to recite the texts to recognize auditive markers of their poetic form. In addition, they contain many aural sense impressions. For instance, Terry Gunnell brings an example from *Grímnismál* stanza 19 where the r-sound resembles the growling of wolves (Gunnell 2016, 102). These features emphasize that, even when fixed on vellum, the texts were never meant to be read silently. As John Miles Foley states, they are "textual shards of a once-living work of verbal-art" (Foley 2002, 45).

As a starting point of my analysis, I shall take the *nornir* (sg. *norn*). *Nornir* are a collective of female supernatural beings who live by and tend to the world tree Yggdrasill, the centre of the cosmos. Their topologically central position correlates with the importance of their function in the Old Norse worldview: they determine the fates of both gods and humans.

3. That Deleuze and Guattari's methodology is useful to explain and analyse gender is also a point that Elizabeth Grosz (1993) and Marianne Schleicher (2020) have brought out.

4. The analysis contains quotes and names from Old Norse literature. Without getting into the debate about the pronunciation of Old Norse, for accessibility here is how certain Old Norse characters are pronounced: ð "th" as in "that"; þ "th" as in "thorn"; æ "a" as in "cat"; œ a diphthong of "o" and "e," pronounced similarly to the "u" in "burn"; ǫ: "o" as in "bought."

The etymology of *norn* is unclear, but it has been suggested that it is related to "whispering" and "communicating secretly" (Pokorny 1959–69, 975; Ström 1985, 202; Bek-Pedersen 2020). In the source material, *nornir* are rarely represented as individuals, and they rarely speak or appear in physical form. Instead, they feature as intangible, but present figures in the Old Norse people's conceptual world, usually appearing only in references to their deeds. In *Helgakviða Hundingsbana in fyrri* stanzas 3 and 4 it is told that *nornir* determine the course of a hero's life by binding and fastening strands.[5] With their silent bodily acts, the *nornir* produce and convey powerful messages, effectively determining and shaping the fate of humans and gods. These activities correspond with the etymological suggestion of *norn* meaning "communicating secretly." With bodily acts they produce messages and shape fates in secret and in the periphery where humans cannot access them. I do not focus on the *nornir* because I believe that their shaping of fate can be classified as sacred textures. Instead, I argue that their weavings of fate originate in a trans-empirical world and therefore become similar to speech acts of a numinous kind.[6] By binding threads, they silently form and produce textures of meaning that intra-act with the lives of humans and gods in ways that are both terrifying and fascinating. The presence of *nornir* and their activities in the Old Norse sources show that the sources are situated in a context where it is known that women's bodily acts can change the course of events and affect human lives.

In *Njáls saga,* ch. 102, the female *skáld* Steinunn Refsdóttir spontaneously composes two near-perfect *dróttkvætt* stanzas. The Christian missionary Þangbrandr has arrived in Iceland from Germany to convert the Icelandic people to Christianity. He succeeds in converting several prominent Icelanders, and he kills those who refuse to convert. After his ship has sunk

5. Karen Bek-Pedersen notes that it is a common motif in many European traditions that fate and textile work is connected, and that textile work can be perceived as metaphors for speech acts (Bek-Pedersen 2020, 1508; 2011, 150). Bek-Pedersen writes that textile work can be seen as the equivalent of a silent, but nevertheless effective female voice that conveys messages and meanings, and that might even be more effective than the spoken word (Bek-Pedersen 2011, 156). I agree with Bek-Pedersen that textile work may function as an effective voice, but I will not use the *nornir*'s activities as an example of texture. The *nornir* are silent, and their textile work does not rely on laws of composition that create discourse.

6. It says in *Vǫluspá* stanza 20 that the *nornir* carved on wood, which could indicate that they carved runes. However, deeper investigation needs to be conducted to determine whether this activity qualifies as a matter of writing and/or the production of sacred textures.

during a storm, he encounters Steinunn and tries to convert her to Christianity. To defend herself and Old Norse religion, she composes the two stanzas and successfully fends him off (my translation follows):

10. Braut fyrir bjǫllu gæti
bǫnd ráku Val strandar,
mǫgfellandi mellu,
móstalls, Vísund allan;
hlífðit Kristr, þá er kneyfði
knǫrr, málmfeta varra;
lítt ætla ek, at guð gætti
Gylfa hreins at einu.
[...]

11. Þórr brá Þvinnils dýri
Þangbrands ór stað lǫngu,
hristi búss ok beysti
barðs ok laust við jǫrðu.
Muna skið um sjá síðan
sundfœrt Atals grundar,
hregg því at hart tók leggja,
hánum kennt, í spánu.
(*Brennu-Njáls saga* 1954, 265–6)

10. In front of the bell-keeper,[7]
the slayer of the *jǫtunn*[8]'s son[9]
crushed completely the Bison of the gull-perch;[10]
The bonds[11] drove the Falcon[12] ashore.
Christ did not protect
when the merchant ship,
the metal-treader[13] of oar-strokes, was crushed.
Little, I think, did God protect
Gylfi's reindeer.[14]
[...]

---

7. Þangbrandr.
8. *Jǫtnar* (sg. *jǫtunn*) are otherworldly Old Norse beings who are both the enemies and lovers of *Æsir* (the principal Old Norse gods). In English they are known as giants.
9. Þórr.
10. Gull-perch is a *kenning* (figure of speech) for sea and Bison is the name of Þangbrandr's ship.
11. Meaning "binding gods."
12. A *heiti* (synonym) for ship.
13. A *heiti* for a shod horse that is a *kenning* for a ship.
14. Ship.

11. Þórr shoved Þangbrandr's long beast of Þvinnill[15]
out of its place
shook the ship and beat
the prow and struck it against the earth.
Henceforth, the ski-of-Atall's-ground[16]
will not be able to swim,
because a fierce storm
caused by him[17]
has hewn it in fragments.

Steinunn's poem qualifies as an oral sacred texture because it consists of weavings of statements that rely on laws of composition equivalent to writing. The poem has an evocative rhythm with alliterations (e.g., ***b**raut fyrir **b**jǫllu gæti | **b**ǫnd*) and assonances (for example, *br**au**t fyrir bjǫllu gæti | bǫnd*). The *kennings* (Old Norse figures of speech) and *heiti* (synonyms) are creative, lively, and complex, and they testify to Steinunn's extensive knowledge of the sea, sailing, and the art of poetry. For instance, *málmfeta varra* (metal-treader of oar-strokes) is a *kenning* within a *kenning*; *málmfeta* is a *heiti* for a shod horse, a horse wearing shoes, which is a *kenning* for ship. When it comes to the poem's sacredness, Steinunn claims to have numinous knowledge about the Old Norse gods' activities in the trans-empirical sphere, and how these doings affect the empirical world. She reveals to Þangbrandr that the Norse god Þórr caused a storm and crushed Þangbrandr's ship, and that Christ was not able to protect the ship. The poem thus questions the alleged almightiness of the Christian god: if God was omnipotent, would he not then have prevented Þórr from smashing his priest's ship? Steinunn's poem establishes that the Old Norse gods are superior to the Christian god, and since it is so, then why should she convert to Christianity? By drawing upon numinous knowledge in her poem, Steinnun claims to have privileged access to sacred insights. Þangbrandr is unable to deliver a counterattack to her poem, revealing that he does not share Steinunn's access to numinous knowledge. He has no knowledge of Christ's engagements with the Norse gods, and thus, he cannot argue against Steinunn's claims and must see himself defeated. When Steinunn performs her poem, she creates a situation that is set apart and shrouded with numinous power. By performing her poem, she transforms their encounter from an ordinary discussion to an experience that is set apart from

15. Þvinnill is a sea-king, and Þvinnill's beast is a *kenning* for ship.

16. Atall is the name of a sea king, Atall's ground is a *heiti* for the sea, and ski is a *heiti* for ship. The ski-of-Atall's-ground is thus a *kenning* for a sailing ship.

17. Þórr.

the ordinary. The texture she performs inspires awe, fascinates, and, perhaps most of all, terrifies. *Njáls saga* does not tell how Þangbrandr reacts to Steinunn's poem. It only says that "*Eptir þat skilðusk þau*" (after that, they parted). Since Þangbrandr sees no other way out of the situation than to leave, it is plausible that he felt defeated. After all, a woman has just revealed her access to the sacred sphere and revealed that the Norse gods are superior to the Christian god by using his lived experience, his shipwreck (which must have been a terrifying experience in itself), as supporting evidence. Furthermore, *Njáls saga* does not state how Steinunn knows about Þangbrandr's shipwreck. It is not accounted for whether Þangbrandr told her himself. It is thus possible that Steinunn gained this information through her access to the trans-empirical sphere, emphasizing that Þangbrandr indeed must have found himself in a situation set apart from the ordinary, that would have been both terrifying and fascinating.

Drawing upon Deleuze and Guattari's lines, I suggest that Steinunn in her performance of the sacred texture forges segmentary lines. She uses the sacred texture to territorialize the space around her and to form a defence against Christianity, something that threatens not only her, but the culture, religion, and traditions that she represents. The segmentary lines, forged as she performs the sacred texture, proves to be an effective defence. Þangbrandr is unable to deliver a counterattack, he is unable to convert her to Christianity, and he is unable to kill her as he did four Icelandic men prior to his meeting with Steinunn. By performing her poem, the sacred texture materializes through Steinunn's body. Her body and the sacred texture become entangled, they intra-act, and through a metonymic relation between Steinunn's body performing the sacred texture and the numinous knowledge she gains from her performance, we can say that Steinunn's body becomes sacred in the moment she recites her poem. While Steinunn performs the poem (and not before nor after her recitation), the sacred texture is embodied in Steinunn, which affects and transforms her body to a sacred space. Her body becomes set apart and forbidden, which effectively prevents Þangbrandr from converting her to Christianity or killing her.

The sacred texture also affects her gender. The act of composing and performing poetry, and especially *dróttkvætt*, was related to a domain dominated by elite men (Frank 1978, 24; Lindow 1975, 322). Straubhaar, who has detected thirteen women producing *dróttkvætt*, writes that her book illustrates that "men did not have a monopoly over its [dróttkvætt's] production" (Straubhaar 2011, 5). This is indeed true, but with hundreds of preserved *drottkvætt* stanzas and only thirteen women producers, it still stands that *dróttkvætt* was primarily a masculine genre. The production of *dróttkvætt* is thus a rule-regulated act that evokes connotations to and establishes and maintains masculinity – and perhaps also high social status since *dróttkvætt* poetry was closely linked to the kings' courts. Steinunn has no official authority, yet she fearlessly confronts the Christian priest by producing a poem in an elitist, masculine metre. In addition, she creates flawless *kennings* related to sailing, an activity which is also a male-dominated domain. In the saga literature, it is a common motif that Icelandic men sail to the Norwegian kings' courts to gain fame, whereas women are typically portrayed only on ships going West for the purpose of establishing settlements with their families. When Steinunn composes her sacred texture in a *dróttkvætt* metre while referencing the domain of sailing, she participates in a rule-regulated act that constructs her gender towards the masculine and a type of masculinity that is associated with the power of the elite. She performs as a powerful man, giving her the needed authoritarian position to fend Þangbrandr off without being hurt. It is interesting that Þangbrandr prior to his meeting with Steinunn killed four men, but he is unable to kill Steinunn. It thus seems that Steinunn, a woman performing as a man and drawing upon male-dominated milieus, is more powerful than Þangbrandr and the men whom Þangbrandr killed. The encounter between Steinunn and Þangbrandr thus demonstrates how a woman could compose an Old Norse oral sacred texture and contribute to the protection of the Old Norse community against Christianity.

Njáls saga is not the only account of a woman using the sacred texture as a defence against Christianity. This is also depicted in the chapter of *Ólafs saga helga* titled *Vǫlsa þáttr*. The short story of *Vǫlsa þáttr* takes place at a farm in Norway during autumn. The housewife of the farm has embalmed the penis of a butchered horse and given it the name Vǫlsi. When she holds Vǫlsi, it becomes full of power so that it can stand erect by itself. Before dinner, the housewife holds Vǫlsi in her hands and composes a stanza over it. After she has composed the stanza, she passes Vǫlsi to her husband, who takes it and then he too composes a stanza. Every evening during autumn, Vǫlsi is passed around at the dinner table to every member of the household who each composes a stanza. One evening, the Christian King Óláfr, later known as St Óláfr, and two of his men visit the household in disguise, and they too must obey the housewife and hold Vǫlsi and compose a stanza. The thirteen stanzas in *Vǫlsa þáttr* are composed in eddic style, and many of them have a sexual content. All the stanzas composed around the dinner table contain the verse "*þiggi Mǫrnir þetta blœti*" (may *Mǫrnir* receive this sacrifice). The first stanza that is composed by the housewife and which initiates the ritual goes like this (my translation follows):

Aukinn ertu Uolse
ok vpp vm tekinn
lini gæddr
en laukum studdr
þiggi Maurnir þetta blœti
en þu bonde sealfr
ber þu at þer Uolsa
(*Vǫlsa þáttr* 1862, 333)

You are enlarged, Vǫlsi
and lifted up
provided with linen
and supported by leeks
may Mǫrnir receive this sacrifice
and you, the farmer himself,
you take Vǫlsi to yourself

Composed in eddic style, the stanzas in *Vǫlsa þáttr* do not share the elegance and complexity of Steinunn's *dróttkvætt* stanzas. They have no *kennings* or *heiti* and they do not follow strict metric rules that continue throughout every stanza. However, I suggest that the stanzas qualify as texture, because they consist of statements woven together that rely on laws of composition, loose as they may be. For instance, the stanza contains poetic devices such as alliteration (***l**ini gæddr* / ***l**aukum studdr*), internal alliteration (*lini gæ**ddr*** / *laukum stu**ddr***), and assonance (*þiggi M**au**rnir þetta blœti*). The recurring verse "*þiggi Mǫrnir þetta blœti*" weaves all the stanzas together into one coherent texture.

The texture is an important part of a ritual where the housewife has the role of a ritual specialist who urges everyone present to participate. During the ritual, the members of the household recite the verse "may *Mǫrnir* receive this sacrifice", indicating that they are partaking in a sacrificial ritual. However, *Vǫlsa þáttr* does not make clear what the sacrificial object is. Schjødt suggests that it could be the spoken stanzas or, more likely, Vǫlsi (Schjødt 2020, 801). These suggestions follow a definition of sacrifice in which sacrificial objects are set apart and offered to other-worldly beings, but not necessarily destroyed or consumed.[18] I agree with Schjødt that Vǫlsi is most likely the object that is sacrificed to the *mǫrnir*.

Because *mǫrnir* can be understood in either a masculine singular or feminine plural form, we do not know for sure who or what *mǫrnir* refers to.

18. Following e.g. *Encyclopaedia Britannica* (Faherty 2022).

Olof Sundqvist suggests that we should understand *mǫrnir* in the masculine singular form, meaning "sword" – a phallic symbol also in the Old Norse culture (Sundqvist 2020, 1227). In previous scholarship, it has often been argued that the god of fertility, Freyr, was related to a phallic cult, and thus, Sundqvist argues that Vǫlsi may be a representation of Freyr. This interpretation suggests that the sacrificial object (Vǫlsi) and the recipient of the sacrifice (*mǫrnir*) are both Freyr (Sundqvist 2020, 1227). Gro Steinsland and Kari Vogt suggest that *mǫrnir* should be understood in the feminine plural form, meaning "women *jǫtnar*" (giantesses) (Steinsland and Vogt 1981, 97). *Jǫtnar* (sg. *jǫtunn*) are otherworldly Old Norse beings who are both the enemies and lovers of *Æsir* (the principal Old Norse gods). Given that Freyr had *jǫtnar* as (sexual) partners, Steinsland suggests that the ritual is a *hieros gamos*, a sacred marriage, between women *jǫtnar* (*mǫrnir*) and Freyr, embodied in Vǫlsi (Steinsland 2005, 350). No matter which translation we choose, it emphasizes Vǫlsi as a phallic symbol related to fertility and sex. This corresponds with the semantic content of most of the other stanzas in *Vǫlsa þáttr* which also revolve around fertility and sex.

During the ritual, two women of the household play the most active and dominating parts.[19] The housewife is the one who initiates the ritual and urges everyone to participate. The servant maid tenderly accepts Vǫlsi, and her stanza explicitly states that she would like Vǫlsi to penetrate her, showing that she is favourably disposed towards Vǫlsi and the ritual. Women are the ones who benefit from the fertility of the phallus, which may explain why these women are particularly interested in participating in and maintaining the fertility ritual every evening. If we accept Steinsland's interpretation that *mǫrnir* means women *jǫtnar*, then it also makes sense that the women are the eager recipients of the sacrifice, mirroring that the sacrifice is dedicated to female trans-empirical beings. Scholars do not agree whether *jǫtnar* were receivers of worship, but some suggest that the *jǫtnar* Skaði and Gerðr (the wives of Freyr's father, Njǫrðr, and Freyr) had status as goddesses and received worship (Steinsland 1986, 213–15; Lindow 2002, 269). Whether *mǫrnir* refers to Freyr or women *jǫtnar*, it no doubt refers to deities who possess numinous power that the housewife can access when she performs her texture. The housewife thus actively uses texture to invoke a numinous power that materializes in and intra-acts with the erect horse penis that becomes a sacred object. By dedicating the sacrifice to the *mǫrnir*, the housewife uses texture and Vǫlsi as hubs[20] to chan-

19. Except the daughter of the family, who is sympathetic towards Christianity and the Christian King Óláfr.

20. A term lent from Schleicher 2017, 42.

nel a molecular line between her household and the trans-empirical world. Since Vǫlsi fills with numinous power and becomes erect in her hands, the housewife shows the household that through her texture she can successfully gain access to a sacred, numinous sphere that is set apart and both terrifying and fascinating, which qualifies the texture as sacred.

The men of the household do not share the women's enthusiasm over the ritual. All men reluctantly accept Vǫlsi, and their stanzas make it clear that they would rather leave this ritual to the women. The farmer says in his stanza "If I were in charge, | this offering | would not be presented this evening" (*Vǫlsa þáttr* 1862, 334, my translation). This statement emphasizes that it is the woman of the house who is in charge at dinner time. The ritual takes place in a private sphere, at home, which is a female-dominated domain where the men have limited power. Old Norse women knew this, and they actively used dinnertime to implement and enforce actions that their male relatives otherwise did not want to engage in (Borovsky 1999, 17). The housewife in *Vǫlsa þáttr* uses her power in the private sphere to demand everyone in the household participate in her ritual. But why does the housewife insist that everyone, including the men of the household and foreign guests, participate in the ritual, if it is only beneficial to women and if the men clearly feel uncomfortable during the ritual?

Vǫlsa þáttr stipulates the year 1029 as the time of the incident. During this time gradually more people converted from Old Norse religion to Christianity. The old religion, its traditions, values, and worldview were threatened and taken over by a foreign religion with its different worldview. When the housewife insists on performing her Norse fertility ritual every evening, she maintains a ritual that has its roots in the old, endangered religion. A horse phallus may have been used in a number of Old Norse rituals (see Hultgård 2003), and thus, Vǫlsi may not only represent fertility, but also be symbolic of Old Norse religion and culture in its entirety. By obliging her household to hold Vǫlsi in their hands and then pass it to the next member of the household every evening, the housewife forces her household to remind themselves of their Old Norse heritage and reflect upon the importance of holding on to this heritage in a time of change. With Vǫlsi, the members of the household embody Old Norse religion and culture, and it is up to them to preserve and maintain it to secure its survival.

Not only does the housewife oblige them to hold Vǫlsi; she also commands them to compose a texture which dedicates a sacrifice to Old Norse deities. Thus, the members of the household must formulate and shape oral textures that protect and preserve Old Norse religion, and they have to listen to other textures that do the same. The preservation of Old Norse religion is thus materialized in both a horse penis and in the oral sounds of textures shrouded with numinous power. By performing this ritual every evening, the housewife uses Vǫlsi and the texture to draw molecular lines between every member of the household and their guests. These lines connect everyone present with each other, which is important at a time where Christianity threatened to tempt some of the members away from the household practices and beliefs. The daughter of the family is sympathetic towards Christianity while the men are dangerously passive and indifferent. This means that the household is at risk of being divided, but the housewife takes action. By having everyone perform the same Old Norse ritual every evening, the housewife attempts to strengthen and preserve the coherence of the household members. The ritual also establishes segmentary lines. By performing the ritual, the housewife draws segmentary lines that establish a defence against Christianity. We saw with Steinunn how powerful a sacred texture is when it is used as a means against Christianity, and the same thing happens in *Vǫlsa þáttr*. The sacred texture creates a situation that is set apart, prohibiting the household from converting to Christianity.

The last person to hold Vǫlsi and perform a stanza is the disguised King Óláfr. The first part of his stanza is about sailing, then he too dedicates Vǫlsi to the *mǫrnir,* and lastly, he utters "and you, dog of the house, you take care of this monster" (*Vǫlsa þáttr* 1862, 335, my translation). Before anyone can stop him, the king throws Vǫlsi to the dog who quickly snatches and swallows it. The hub that channelled a molecular line to a sacred sphere and that, along with the sacred texture, established segmentary lines functioning as a shield against Christianity, disappears. The housewife gets upset and composes a stanza saying: "lift me over door-hinges | and onto door-beams | to see if I can retrieve | the sacred sacrifice" (*Vǫlsa þáttr* 1862, 335, my translation). The word "see" is a translation of the Old Norse *vita* which is related to divination. In this texture, the housewife thus claims to have access to numinous insights that can inform her whether Vǫlsi can be saved. This stanza is often compared to an account by the Arabic diplomat Ibn Fadlan who encountered in 922 by the river Volga what are often believed to be Old Norse settlers from Sweden. Ibn Fadlan witnesses a funeral in which a slave woman is lifted above a doorframe, enabling her to see into another world (Ibn Fadlan 2000, 17). It seems that the housewife in *Vǫlsa þáttr* does the same when she is lifted above a doorframe, emphasizing that she indeed has access to trans-empirical knowledge. This suggests that Old Norse women with access to trans-empirical knowledge knew of different techniques that allowed them to access and produce numinous knowledge. Production of sacred textures was one technique, and to be lifted above a doorframe was another. However, even though the housewife with her last sacred stanza gains access to numinous knowledge, Vǫlsi cannot be retrieved. The damage has already been done. The numinous power and the segmentary lines – created from the speech acts of the sacred texture and materialized in the horse penis – all disappear along with Vǫlsi. The defence against Christianity has gone and the household is exposed to conversion. King Óláfr seizes this opportunity and converts the household to Christianity.

Both in *Njáls saga* and *Vǫlsa þáttr* women stand up against Christianity, while men either are not capable of doing so (in *Njáls saga*) or are passive observers who seem indifferent towards the new religion that threatens Old Norse culture (in *Vǫlsa þáttr*). Zoe Borovsky notes that with the introduction of Christianity, Old Norse women's rights were reduced. It was in the interest of the church to reduce the family-based power in the private domain. Thus, the male-dominated public social-legal domain was valued over the private female-dominated domain (Borovsky 1999, 26). Consequently, the conversion to Christianity had a negative impact on Old Norse women's access to power, and it was in the interest of women to preserve the Old Norse worldview and not implement Christian customs. This may explain why we see women using sacred textures as defences against Christianity in the source material.

Another explanation may be that what we see is a literary device where women are praised for performing the tasks of men in order to bring the male audience's attention to men's passivity and encourage them to act.[21] Whereas Steinunn succeeds in fending Þangbrandr and Christianity off by engaging in rule-regulated acts that evoke connotations to masculinity, the housewife in *Vǫlsa þáttr* does not enjoy the same success, even though she, like Steinunn, uses a sacred texture. She composes a poem which is a rule-regulated act within a male-dominated domain, but it is not composed in the *dróttkvætt* metre. This means that the housewife's poem does not evoke connotations to high social status and power. Instead, to strengthen her defence, the housewife uses a horse penis as a hub representing Old Norse religion. The penis exemplifies how matter activates associations and expectations to masculinity, and when the housewife holds Vǫlsi, she is able to make it erect. The housewife thus equips herself with an erect penis that together with her sacred texture transforms her household from a woman-dominated domain into a domain of defence associated with the

21. Following Schleicher 2000, 163–4, 169.

responsibility of men. This proves to be a successful defence against Christianity until her opponent reveals himself as the king. King Óláfr's stanza mirrors the eddic style of the housewife, and thus he does not compose his stanza in the courtly metre *dróttkvætt*. Yet, because he has been appointed King of Norway, he already connotes the highest social and elitist status of the society. He does not need a *dróttkvætt* stanza to do so. As king, he has access to more power than anyone else, and unlike Þangbrandr, he accepts the housewife's challenge and composes a sacred texture that matches her verbal competence. King Óláfr's power exceeds the housewife's, which he demonstrates when he throws Vǫlsi to the dog and destroys the phallic sacred object. The material penis that intra-acted with the housewife's gender disappears. King Óláfr has emasculated and exposed her so that he is free to convert her and her family to Christianity.

Steinsland and Vogt suggests that the housewife might be a *vǫlva*, a prophetess with the abilities to see the past and future (Steinsland and Vogt 1981, 103–4). When she orders to be lifted above the doorframe to see if Vǫlsi can be saved, she is able to perform divination which is a knowledge associated with the practices of *vǫlur*. Furthermore, Steinsland and Vogt argue that the names Vǫlsi and *vǫlva* derive from *vǫlr* meaning staff, a tool used by *vǫlur* to practice *seiðr* (*Eiríks saga Rauða*, ch. 4). However, most sources describe *vǫlur* as isolated, nomadic women who have no relations to their family homestead, and their relations to the trans-empirical is connected to the trans-empirical sphere in general and not specific beings. Thus, Steinsland and Vogt acknowledge that the housewife does not fit the typological traits of the *vǫlur*, but she does have features that evoke associations to the *vǫlur*. Whether or not the housewife is a *vǫlva*, she uses sacred textures as a means to gain access to numinous insights, which, as we will see below, was a technique also known and used by *vǫlur*.

In the eddic poem *Vǫluspá*, the king of the gods, Óðinn, has asked and paid a *vǫlva* to reveal numinous knowledge about the creation, destruction, and recreation of the world. Knowing that the world is soon to be destroyed in *ragnarǫk*[22] Óðinn finds himself in a crisis situation, and he needs to know what is to happen. The *vǫlva* reveals her numinous insights through a poem with more than 60 stanzas. Two of the stanzas are as follows (with my translation):

22. The eschatological event in Old Norse mythology.

21 Þat man hon fólcvíg
fyrst í heimi,
er Gullveigo
geirom studdo
oc í hǫll Hárs
hána brendo;
þrysvar brendo,
þrysvar borna,
opt, ósialdan,
þó hon enn lifir

22 Heiði hana héto,
Hvars til húsa kom,
Vǫlo velspá,
Vitti hon ganda;
seið hon, hvars hon kunni,
seið hon hug leikinn,
æ var hon angan
illrar brúðar
(*Vǫluspá* stanzas 21–2)

21 She remembers
the first war in the world
when the gods pierced[23] Gullveig
with spears
and in Hár[24]'s hall
burned her;
thrice burned,
thrice born,
often, unseldom,
though she still lives.

22 Heiðr they called her
when she came to houses
a *vǫlva* skilled in prophecy
she practised magic with staffs
she practised *seiðr* wherever she could
she bewitched minds with *seiðr*
she was always a delight
to wicked women

23. *Studdo* means "supported," meaning that the gods threw so many spears at Gullveig that her body is held upright by spears.

24. Hár is another name for Óðinn.

In these stanzas, the *vǫlva* describes the practices of the *vǫlur* and how *vǫlur* were treated badly by the gods.[25] The stanzas in *Vǫluspá* consist of statements woven together that rely on laws of composition. For instance, the stanzas above have elegant alliterations throughout almost every verse (***Heiði*** ***h****ana* ***h****éto* / ***H****vars til* ***h****úsa kom*), as well as anaphoras (***þrysvar*** *brendo* / ***þrysvar*** *borna*). Keeping in mind the indicators outlined above, *Vǫluspá* would qualify as a texture.

The *vǫlva* utters in her first stanza that Óðinn has asked her to share ancient stories. To do so, she needs everyone to listen and be quiet. She then initiates her visionary revelation of numinous knowledge about the primeval times, how the world will perish into the ocean, and how the world will rise again with a new generation of gods and humans. The numinous power she gains access to is inaccessible to Óðinn, despite him being a powerful god who also practises *seiðr*. This indicates that the knowledge that the *vǫlva* reveals is the most sacred, forbidden, and set apart in the Old Norse cosmos, and that it requires tremendous skills to access. *Seiðr* was dangerous and also shameful for men to practise (*Ynglinga saga*, ch. 7), because it was associated with femininity. Even though Óðinn practices *seiðr* (and perhaps alters his gender in doing so),[26] he still has many connections to domains dominated by men (for instance the domain of war), limiting his access to the most sacred numinous knowledge. *Vǫlur* were strongly tied to the domain of *seiðr* that was dominated by women, to such an extent that the *vǫlur*'s connections to other domains were limited. The identity and position of the *vǫlur* in the Old Norse society were tied to their knowledge and practice of *seiðr*. Because *seiðr* in Old Norse religion was tied to femininity, I argue that the *vǫlva*'s female gender intra-acts with her magical skills and practice, enhancing the reach of her vision and allowing her access to the outermost corners of possible knowledge. This allows the *vǫlva* to establish lines to numinous power that no one else can access, not even Óðinn. The vision she reveals about the world's horrible destruction is terrifying and fascinating, leaving the listener and Óðinn horrified at what is to come. We can thus posit that the texture of *Vǫluspá* is sacred because it claims access to numinous knowledge and is shrouded in numinous power which makes it both terrifying and fascinating.

Vǫlur practised magic, performed divination, and composed sacred textures on the request of others who paid them. One of the techniques used

25. It is speculated that it may be the speaker of *Vǫluspá* who refers to her own life and work (Straubhaar 2011, 72), and it is believed among scholars that Gullveig and Heiðr are names for the same woman (Lindow 2020, 1036).

26. See Jørgensen 2020.

to access numinous knowledge is magic with staffs (*Vǫluspá* 22), another is composing a sacred texture, and we know from *Vǫlsa þáttr* and Ibn Fadlan that a third technique is to see above a doorframe. Stanza 21 of *Vǫluspá* describes how marginalized *vǫlur* were in the Old Norse society, and how their skills were considered dangerous. The gods threw so many spears at Gullveig that the spears supported her standing body, and afterwards they burnt her thrice. Still, this did not kill her. The torturous attempts to kill Gullveig show how powerful the *vǫlur* were believed to be. Their connections to sacred and incomprehensible knowledge and power made the *vǫlur* invincible, and consequently, they were perceived as threats to the Old Norse community. The *vǫlur* were women set apart and thus excluded from access to rule-regulated acts such as marriage and the ties, responsibilities, and safety that comes from being part of a family and community. Their access to powerful and dangerous numinous knowledge, for instance through the production of sacred textures and magic with staffs, marginalized and alienated them from the Old Norse community.

Another account of a *vǫlva* using sacred textures is from *Eiríks saga rauða* ch. 4. Because of a shortage of food, a settlement in Greenland pays a *vǫlva*, Þorbjǫrg, to find out when there will be food again. Þorbjǫrg prepares to perform a *seiðr* ritual and asks if any woman present knows the chants required for the ritual. These chants are called *varðlokkur*. *Varð* can be translate as "ward" and *lokkur* as "lure", and *varðlokkur* could then have been chants that should attract the spirits to the ritual. A Christian woman, Guðriðr, admits that she was taught the chants as a child, and after some persuasion, she agrees to sing the *varðlokkur*. Þorbjǫrg then places herself in a high seat, which evokes associations to the women lifted above doorframes in *Vǫlsa þáttr* and Ibn Fadlan. It seems that divination works best when the practitioner is lifted and has an overview of both the immanent and the trans-empirical world. The other women in the settlement form a ring around the *vǫlva*, and Guðriðr begins to speak the *varðlokkur*. She does so beautifully, and many spirits are lured to the *vǫlva*. The *seiðr* ritual is successful, and Þorbjǫrg reveals that soon the times of hardship will end. Unfortunately, we have no accounts of what is sung in the *varðlokkur*, and thus an analysis of the texture is impossible. Nevertheless, the *varðlokkur* has an effect. It functions as one of the *vǫlva*'s means to gain access to numinous knowledge. Þorbjǫrg reveals that the spirits at first refused to do her biddings, but that Guðriðr's chants charmed them, allowing Þorbjǫrg to see the future. The chant established temporary access, an experimental line, to the numinous, shrouding the ritual with numinosity and allowed Þorbjǫrg to retrieve the information she needed. Even though the description of the *varðlokkur* is scarce, the saga tells us that Guðriðr *kvað* (spoke/uttered) the chant, which is the same verb used in the source material when anyone performs a poem. This suggests that *varðlokkur* were not just melodic sounds that formed a song, but that they were spoken weavings of words that formed an effective texture.

Eiríks saga rauða emphasizes that the practice of *seiðr* relies on women's agency. It is a woman, the *vǫlva*, who sits on a high seat and sees into the future. For the ritual to work, the person who sings the *varðlokkur* must be a woman. Before the *varðlokkur* is sung, the other women gather around the *vǫlva*, creating an apotropaic ring around her. This ring of women might both protect the *vǫlva* from outside interruptions, as well as the community from the spirits who are lured into the circle. Just as in the case of Steinunn in *Njáls saga*, the housewife in *Vǫlsa þáttr*, and Óðinn in *Vǫluspá*, the sacred texture in *Eiríks saga rauða* is performed in a context of crisis. This suggests that Old Norse women produced and used sacred textures in ad hoc crisis situations. Steinunn and the housewife needed to act in masculine ways to match and beat their male opponents. In the case of *Eiríks saga rauða*, the threat is a lack of food, and it seems that to solve the crisis, an increase of masculinity does not work. Because *seiðr* is tied to femininity, the ritual requires the presence of many women. The women's participation in the ritual strengthens the *vǫlva*'s abilities and the effect of the ritual. This will benefit the whole settlement, because their access to food will return and their survival will be secured.

The accounts of Steinunn in *Njáls saga*, the housewife in *Vǫlsa þáttr*, and the *vǫlur* in *Vǫluspá* and *Eiríks saga rauða* thus demonstrate how women produced and used Old Norse sacred textures in crisis situations as means to ward off threats and protect Old Norse communities.

Conclusion

Motivated by my wish to examine sacred textures as a religious phenomenon in Old Norse religion and how they relate to gender, I have put forward a definition that can capture Old Norse sacred textures. This definition relied on Ricoeur's understanding of textures, written and oral, as weavings of words and statements, which enables us to identify textures in an oral, religious culture. Drawing upon insights from Durkheim and Otto, I defined Old Norse sacred textures as Old Norse textual renderings of textures set apart and shrouded in numinous power which makes them both terrifying and fascinating, mainly because they claim access to numinous knowledge. Wanting to examine why Old Norse women produced sacred textures and how this production affected their gender, I synthesized constructionist and new materialist insights in order to address the agency of these women and how the domains within which they produced their textures intra-acted with their gender. I analysed four accounts from the Icelandic saga literature of Old Norse women who produced and performed Old Norse sacred textures. Two of them, Steinunn from *Njáls saga* and the housewife from *Vǫlsa þáttr*, were facing the arrival of a new religion, Christianity, that threatened the continued existence of Old Norse religion and culture. To fend off this threat, the women produced sacred textures. To strengthen their defences, Steinunn composed her texture in the *dróttkvætt* metre, and the housewife equipped herself with a horse penis, both evoking connotations to masculinity. The women thus gained access to a domain of defence associated with the responsibility of men. The third account I analysed was the eddic poem *Vǫluspá* where the powerful male god Óðinn in the midst of a crisis turns to a marginalized *vǫlva* to ask for information about the beginning and end of the world. The *vǫlva* is closely tied to the female-dominated domain of magic. I argued that the *vǫlva*'s femininity strengthens her *seiðr* magic in such a way that she can access the outermost corners of knowledge. *Vǫluspá* is thus a sacred texture that reveals numinous knowledge only accessible to the *vǫlur*. In the fourth account, I analysed a *vǫlva* who performs a ritual of *seiðr* in a crisis where an Old Norse settlement lacks food. Because *seiðr* was tied to femininity, she needs a woman to perform and sing a sacred texture that allures spirits and she needs the presence of many women to strengthen the effect of the ritual.

Based upon these analyses, I find that these four sources reflect how Old Norse women produced and performed sacred textures in ad hoc crisis situations as a means to ward off threats and protect Old Norse communities. Furthermore, it seems clear that the production of sacred textures was a technique, among others, that Old Norse women could use, as portrayed in these sources, to claim numinous insights. A crucial finding is that by expanding the concept of text to texture, Old Norse women's productions and performances of sacred textures represented a kind of women's religious agency that scholarship cannot afford to overlook.

Acknowledgments

I would like to thank the participants of the Gender and Sacred Text workshop in Rebild 2022 for engaging in discussions and sharing their ideas at the initial stage of this chapter. An earlier version was presented at the Performing Magic in the pre-Modern North Conference 2023, and at the UCL Medieval Scandinavia Seminars in 2023. I thank the participants of both events for their valuable feedback. I owe thanks to Simon Nygaard, Liv Köhne Lind, and Brad Anderson for discussing my ideas and commenting on drafts. I also owe a note of thanks to Catharina Raudvere for appreciated comments and suggestions at an early stage of the chapter's creation. A very special thank you is due to Marianne Schleicher for detailed comments and feedback on many aspects of this chapter.

Primary Sources

Brennu-Njáls saga. 1954. In *Íslenzk fornrit; 12*, edited by Sveinsson Einar Ól. Reykjavík: Hið íslenzka fornritafélag.

Edda: Die Lieder des Codex Regius nebst verwandten Denkmälern. 1983. In *Germanische Bibliothek*, edited by Gustav Neckel and Hans Kuhn. Heidelberg: Carl Winther Universitätsverlag.

Eyrbyggja saga. Brands þáttr ǫrva. Eiriks saga rauða. Grœnlendinga saga. Grœnlendinga þáttr. 1935. In *Íslenzk fornrit* 4, edited by Einar Ól Sveinsson and Matthías Þórðarson. Reykjavík: Hið íslenzka fornritafélag.

Flateyjarbók: En samling af norske konge-sagaer med indskudte mindre fortællinger om begivenheder i og udenfor Norge samt annaler. 1862. edited by Guðbrandur Vigfússon and C. R. Unger. Christiania: Malling.

Grímnismál see *Edda: Die Lieder des Codex regius*.

Heimskringla I. 2002 [1941]. In *Íslenzk fornrit, 26*, edited by Bjarni Aðalbjarnarson. Reykjavík: Hið íslenzka fornritafélag.

Helgakviða Hundingsbana I (in fyrsta), II (ǫnnur) see *Edda: Die Lieder des Codex regius*.

Ibn Fadlan. 2000. "Ibn Fadlan and the *Rusiyyah*." Translated by James E. Montgomery. *Journal of Arabic and Islamic Studies* 3: 1–25.

Vǫlsa þáttr see *Flateyjarbók*.

Vǫluspá see *Edda: Die Lieder des Codex regius*.

Ynglinga saga see *Heimskringla*.

References

Barad, Karen. 2007. *Meeting the Universe Halfway: Quantum Physics and the Entanglement of Matter and Meaning*. Durham, NC: Duke University Press.

Bek-Pedersen, Karen. 2011. *The Norns in Old Norse Mythology*. Edinburgh: Dunedin Academic Press.

——— 2020. "Norns." In *The Pre-Christian Religions of the North: History and Structures*, edited by John Lindow Jens Peter Schjødt, and Anders Andrén, 1501–12. Turnhout: Brepols.

Borovsky, Zoe. 1999. "Never in Public: Women and Performance in Old Norse Literature." *Journal of American Folklore* 112(443): 6–39. https://doi.org/10.2307/541400

Butler, Judith. 1999. *Gender Trouble*. New York: Routledge.

Collinder, Björn. 1993. "Inledning." In *Den Poetiska Eddan*, 11–41. Stockholm: Forum.

Deleuze, Gilles, and Claire Parnet. 1983. "Politics." In *On the Line*, edited by Gilles Deleuze and Félix Guattari, 69–115. New York: Semiotext(e).

——— and Félix Guattari 1987. *A Thousand Plateaus: Capitalism and Schizophrenia*. London: Bloomsbury Academic.

Durkheim, Emile. 1995. *The Elementary Forms of Religious Life*, translated by Karen E. Fields. New York: Free Press.

Faherty, Robert L. 2022. "Sacrifice." *Encyclopedia Britannica*. Accessed 17 Nov. 2022. https://www.britannica.com/topic/sacrifice-religion/Time-and-place-of-sacrifice.

Foley, John Miles. 2002. *How to Read an Oral Poem*. Urbana, IL: University of Illinois Press.

Frank, Roberta. 1978. *Old Norse Court Poetry: The Dróttkvætt Stanza*. Islandica 42. Ithaca, NY: Cornell University Press.

Grosz, Elizabeth. 1993. "A Thousand Tiny Sexes: Feminism and Rhizomatics." *Topoi* 12(2): 167-79. https://doi.org/10.1007/bf00821854

Gunnell, Terry. 2013. "Vǫluspá in Performance." In *The Nordic Apocalypse: Approaches to Vǫluspá and Nordic Days of Judgement*, edited by Terry Gunnell and Annette Lassen, Acta Scandinavica 2, 63–77. Turnhout: Brepols.

———. 2016. "Eddic Performance and Eddic Audiences." In *A Handbook to Eddic Poetry: Myths and Legends of Early Scandinavia*, edited by Brittany Schorn, Carolyne Larrington, and Judy Quinn, 92–113. Cambridge: Cambridge University Press.

Hultgård, Anders. 2003. "Phallusverehrung." In *Reallexicon der germanischen Altertumskunde*, 135–9. Berlin: De Gruyter.

Jochens, Jenny. 1989. "Vǫluspá: Matrix of Norse Womanhood." *Journal of English and Germanic Philology* 88(3): 344–62. https://www.jstor.org/stable/27710187

Jørgensen, Emma C. Sørlie. 2020. "Óðinn: sejdmester uden paradoks." In *Religion. Tidsskriftet for Religionslærerforeningen for Gymnasiet og HF* (2): 18–26.

Lassen, Annette. 2013. "The Early Scholarly Reception of Vǫluspá from Snorri Sturluson to Árni Magnússon." In *The Nordic Apocalypse: Approaches to Vǫluspá and Nordic Days of Judgement*, edited by Terry Gunnell and Annette Lassen, Acta Scandinavica 2, 3–22. Turnhout: Brepols.

Lindow, John. 1975. "Riddles, Kennings, and the Complexity of Skaldic Poetry." *Scandinavian Studies* 47(3): 311–27. http://www.jstor.org/stable/40917528

———. 2002. *Norse Mythology: a Guide to the Gods, Heroes, Rituals, and Beliefs*. Oxford: Oxford University Press.

———. 2020. "Vanir and Æsir." In *The Pre-Christian Religions of the North. History and Structures*, edited by John Lindow Jens Peter Schjødt, and Anders Andrén, 1033–50. Turnhout: Brepols.

Malley, Brian. 2004. *How the Bible Works: An Anthropological Study of Evangelical Biblicism*. Walnut Creek, CA: AltaMira Press.

Nygaard, Simon. 2019. "Being Óðinn Bursson: The Creation of Social and Moral Obligation in Viking Age Warrior-Bands through the Ritualized, Oral Performance of Poetry: The Case of Grímnismál." In *Social Norms in Medieval Scandinavia*, edited by Jakub Morawiec, Aleksandra Jochymek, and Grzegorz Bartusik, 51–74. York: Arc Humanities Press.

Otto, Rudolf. 1963. *Das Heilige. Über das Irrationale in der Idee des Göttlichen und sein Verhältnis zum Rationalen.* Munich: C. H. Beck (originally published 1917).

Pokorny, Julius. 1959–69. *Indogermanisches etymologisches Wörterbuch.* Vol. 2. Bern: Francke.

Ricoeur, Paul. 1976. *Interpretation Theory: Discourse and the Surplus of Meaning.* Fort Worth, TX: Texas Christian University Press.

Sapp, Christopher D. 2022. *Dating the Old Norse Poetic Edda: A Multifactorial Analysis of Linguistic Features.* Studies in Germanic Linguistics 5. Amsterdam/Philadelphia, PA: John Benjamins Publishing Co.

Schjødt, Jens Peter. 2008. *Initiation between Two Worlds: Structure and Symbolism in Pre-Christian Scandinavian Religion.* Odense: University Press of Southern Denmark.

———. 2020. "Cyclical Rituals." In *The Pre-Christian Religions of the North: Histories and Structure*, edited by John Lindow Jens Peter Schjødt and Anders Andrén, 797–823. Turnhout: Brepols.

Schleicher, Marianne. 2000. "Døtre, skøger og mødre i Jahves hænder." *Dansk Teologisk Tidsskrift* 63(3): 161–80.

———. 2009. "Artifactual and Hermeneutical Use of Scripture in Jewish Tradition." In *Jewish and Christian Scripture as Artifact and Canon*, edited by Craig A. Evans and H. Daniel Zacharias, 48–65. New York: Bloomsbury Academic.

———. 2017. "Engaging All the Senses: On Multi-Sensory Stimulation in the Process of Making and Inaugurating a Torah Scroll." *Postscripts: The Journal of Sacred Texts, Cultural Histories, and Contemporary Contexts* 8(1-2): 39–56. https://doi.org/10.1558/post.32694

———. 2020. "Effects of Materiality in Israelite-Jewish Conceptions of Gender and Love: On a Necessary Synthesis of Constructionist and New Materialist Approaches." In *Entanglements and Weavings: Diffractive Approaches to Gender and Love*, edited by Deirdre C. Byrne and Marianne Schleicher, 11–33. Leiden: Brill. https://doi.org/10.1163/9789004441460_003

Steinsland, Gro. 1986. "Giants as Recipients of Cult in the Viking Age?" *Words and Objects: Towards a Dialogue between Archeology and History of Religion* B71: 212–22.

———. 2005. *Norrøn religion: myter, riter, samfunn.* Oslo: Pax.

——— and Vogt, Kari. 1981. "'Aukinn ertu Uolse ok vpp vm tekinn': En religionshistorisk analyse av Vǫlsþáttr i Flateyjarbók." *Arkiv för nordisk filologi* 97: 87–106.

Straubhaar, Sandra Ballif. 2011. *Old Norse Women's Poetry: The Voices of Female Skalds.* Woodbridge: Boydell & Brewer.

Ström, Folke. 1985. *Nordisk hedendom: Tro och sed i förkristen tid.* 3rd ed. Göteborg: Akademiförlaget-Gumpert.

Sundqvist, Olof. 2020. "Freyr." In *The Pre-Christian Religions of the North. Histories and Structure*, edited by Anders Andrén, John Lindow, and Jens Peter Schjødt, 1195–1246. Turnhout: Brepols.

Wills, Tarrin. N.d.. "Skaldic Project: Statistics." Skaldic Poetry of the Scandinavian Middle Ages. Accessed 2 June 2025. https://skaldic.org/m.php?p=skpstatstable

About the Author

Emma C. Sørlie Jørgensen is a PhD fellow at the Department of the Study of Religion at Aarhus University, Denmark. She works within the field of Old Norse religion and her research interests include literature, oral performances of poetry, gender, magic, and war. So far, she has published three articles in Danish on Óðinn, masculinity and feasts, and gender as domain dependent. (ej@cas.au.dk)

2

Drinkable Ink or Womb-Destroying Words? A Solution for Suspected Adultery in Numbers 5:11–31

Rosanne Liebermann

Abstract

The biblical text of Numbers 5:11–31 describes a ritual designed to determine the guilt or innocence of a woman suspected of adultery: she must drink a mixture of water, dirt, and the ink of written curses given to her by a priest. This article analyses how the ritualized use of a material sacred text as described in Numbers 5:11–31 – and the ways it interacts with the bodies of the people involved – impacts the biblical construction of gender identities. Using concepts introduced by R. W. Connell, I argue that the ritual makes use of a material sacred text to reinforce a hegemonic masculine identity for the Israelite priesthood, while encouraging the complicit masculinity of laymen and the subjugated feminine identity of women. In doing so, the ritual of Numbers 5:11–31 bolsters the hierarchy of gender identities constructed by the book of Numbers and the Pentateuch more broadly.

Keywords: Hebrew Bible, book of Numbers, sotah, priesthood, adultery, Pentateuch

Introduction

An Israelite priest transcribes a short list of curses onto a piece of parchment. Before the ink has dried, he blots out the freshly written words into a mixture of holy water and dirt from the floor of the tabernacle – the deity's portable sanctuary carried by the Israelites as they wander through the Sinai desert. The priest passes the watery solution to an Israelite woman with dishevelled hair standing in front of the altar. She is a *sotah,* a woman who has "turned aside" into the house of a man to whom she is not married – or at least, she is suspected of having done so by her husband, who has initiated the ritual. The priest recites the curses to the woman, who agrees to their terms, and then he and the husband watch carefully as the liquified text enters her body. Soon, it will reveal whether the woman has been unfaithful. If guilty, she is expected to suffer severe harm to her reproductive health: probably a miscarriage or prolapsed uterus. If innocent, her fertility will be intact; any future child she bears is identified as her husband's.

This strange ritual, described in Numbers 5:11–31, is the only one in the Hebrew Bible in which a priest makes and handles a sacred text in material form. I understand sacred text to consist of a series of words – written, spoken, or otherwise made material – held by a religious community to contain revealed, trans-empirical knowledge and therefore attributed with the characteristics of holiness (see Levering 1989, 58). What distinguishes a sacred text from non-sacred texts is that it is ritualized: adopted and used by a religious community in ways that draw attention to it (Watts 2006, 140, 145, 155; following Smith 1987, 109).[1] The curses recited and then written down by the priest in Numbers 5:19–23 consist of a designated series of words revealed to Moses by the deity Yhwh, according to Numbers 5:1. Moreover, the curses are made in and include Yhwh's divine name (5:21), which rabbinic commentators considered decisive for the power of the text (see, for example, Haberman 2000, 32). The *sotah* account confirms the curse text's sacred status by describing multiple ways in which it is ritualized: it is created and manipulated by a religious professional (the priest) in a sacred space (the tabernacle) in the context of an offering to the deity. The bodies of the people involved must move through the sacred space and cause other ritualized things (holy water and dirt from the tabernacle) to interact with the text. These details draw attention to the text and connect it to other things recognized as sacred by the religious community.

There is no evidence regarding the historical practice of this ritual, meaning that the only way the text containing the curses is known to exist is via its inclusion in the Pentateuch, canonized as scripture in both Jewish and Christian traditions. The description of the ritual in Numbers 5:11–31 thus puts words from a larger sacred text into the hands and mouth of the priest. It is not in the remit of this article to examine the many interacting

1. While many scholars (including Miriam Levering and James Watts, whose definitions I have drawn from) tend to use the term "scripture" to refer to what I have just described, this word has connotations of written-ness that do not necessarily apply to all materializations of sacred texts.

sources of the Pentateuch; for the current purpose, I largely take a canonical approach towards the Masoretic Text of the Pentateuch as a body of scripture intentionally edited into this form. However, Christian Frevel (2020, 293, 306) has convincingly argued that the *sotah* passage is a late Pentateuchal text, because it meets a need not fulfilled by the laws about adultery in other legal codes (Lev 20:10; Deut 22:22) – that is, what to do if there is insufficient evidence concerning the suspected adultery. This indicates that whoever edited the *sotah* tradition into the Pentateuch did so with the intention of it forming part of the canonical religious law of Israel. If this was the case, including the words written and spoken by the priest in Numbers 5:19–23 ensured their status as scripture as well.

Not only is the creation of a material sacred text as part of a ritual unusual in the Hebrew Bible, but it is also rare for women to handle sacred texts, as the *sotah* does in Numbers 5:24–7. Women are rarely described as having close contact with sacred texts in the Hebrew Bible: it is men who write them down (e.g. Exod 24:4; Deut 17:18; 31:9; Josh 8:32; Jer 36:2–4), keep them (e.g. Deut 31:9; Ezra 7:14), rediscover them (e.g. 2 Kgs 22:8), read them aloud (e.g. Exod 24:7; Deut 31:11; Josh 8:34–5; 2 Kgs 22:10; 23:2; Jer 36:6, 10, 15, 21; Neh 8:1–5), interpret them (e.g. Neh 8:7–8[2]), and occasionally destroy them (e.g. Exod 32:19; Jer 36:23). Sometimes, women are specified (alongside men, children, and resident aliens) as those who listen to sacred texts being read aloud (e.g. Deut 31:11; Josh 8:35; Neh 8:2). In contrast to women's passive and generalized experiences of sacred texts elsewhere in the Hebrew Bible, Numbers 5:11–31 instructs that a woman who may be in a state of ritual impurity (*tame'*) due to having committed adultery should be brought into the closest possible contact with a material sacred text by consuming it.

Numbers 5:11–31 therefore raises several questions: why is a husband's suspicion of his wife's unfaithfulness the only occasion that prompts a priest's creation of a material sacred text in the biblical canon? And why is it the only one where a woman comes into close contact with a sacred text? Because the ritual involves a strict delineation of roles determined in large part by the gendered identities of the people involved – the masculine

2. One exception may be the prophetess Huldah in 2 Kgs 22:14–20, who is consulted by the priest when a neglected "book of the law" is discovered in the Jerusalem temple. Yet while Huldah claims that the words of the book will be fulfilled, she is not said to interact with the physical book itself. Moreover, as Esther Fuchs (2001, 62–4) has pointed out, this rare example of a female prophet's words in the Hebrew Bible also constitutes an unfulfilled prophecy, since Huldah claims that King Josiah will have a peaceful death (2 Kgs 22:20), and yet Josiah is killed by a foreign enemy in the book's very next chapter (23:29).

priest, the masculine husband, and the feminine wife – answering these questions requires an analysis of how the material sacred text interacts with the genders of these three actors. Despite the large amount of scholarly attention devoted to Numbers 5:11–31, such an analysis has not yet been conducted. I will provide a brief overview of the text's interpretational difficulties and some of the main trends in reading it before suggesting how material-focused approaches might provide new insights.

Previous Literature on Numbers 5:11-31

There are several ambiguities in Numbers 5:11–31 that require some discussion in order to determine the basic procedure of the ritual. First, it is unclear exactly which circumstances cause the ritual to take place. Verses 12–13 state that this is a case where a woman "turns aside and conducts unfaithfulness against [her husband], so that a man lies with her sexually, but it is hidden from her husband's eyes, and she is undetected, but she is defiled, and there is no witness against her." This describes a situation in which a woman has committed adultery, and there may be evidence pointing towards it, such as time spent alone with another man.[3] According to other legal codes in the Hebrew Bible, a wife committing adultery is a crime that requires the deaths of the woman and her male lover (Lev 20:10; Deut 22:22). Yet in the case described in Numbers 5:12–13, the woman cannot be tried according to the regular legal proceedings for adultery, because the two witnesses required for a conviction cannot be produced.

However, Numbers 5:14 describes a potentially different case, describing a situation whereby a "spirit of jealousy" (*ruach qin'ah*) comes over the husband so that "he is jealous regarding his wife" whether or not she is actually "defiled." This suggests that a husband's unfounded suspicions are reason enough for the ritual to take place. Due to this discrepancy, scholars previously assumed that Numbers 5:11–31 was comprised of two or more originally separate sources (see discussion in Brichto 1975, 55; Milgrom 1989, 350; Britt 2007, 7). Yet most now regard the text as a unified whole intentionally outlining two cases that should be resolved by the same ritual (following Fishbane 1974, 35). The circumstance uniting them is that a man's honour as a husband is under threat, but there is not sufficient evidence to convict his wife of wrongdoing and thereby restore social equilibrium in the normal manner.

3. In the Mishnah and Tosefta's interpretations of Num 5:11–31, the woman must be proven to have "turned aside" into another man's house in order for her husband to initiate the ritual (see Levine 1993, 202; Haberman 2000, 23–4).

A second interpretive problem is that it is not at all clear what would happen to a guilty woman once she has drunk the mixture. The curse section can be translated as follows:

> The priest will make her swear, and he will say to the woman: "If a man has not lain with you, and if you have not turned aside [to] defilement under your husband, may you be shown innocent by these bitter waters[4] that curse. [20]But as for you who did turn aside under your husband and who is defiled, and a man has lain with you (aside from your husband)" – [21]and the priest will make the woman swear with the oath of the curse, and the priest will say to the woman – "May Yhwh set you as a curse and an oath in the middle of your people, when Yhwh makes your thigh falling and your stomach swollen, [22]and may these waters that curse come into your bowels to swell a stomach and make a thigh fall." Then the woman will say, "Amen, amen." [23]Then the priest will write these curses in the book and wipe (them) out in the bitter waters. [24]He will make the woman drink the bitter waters that curse, and the waters that curse will enter her as bitterness. (Num 5:19–24)[5]

The priest then takes the grain offering from the woman's hands and burns part of it on the altar before making the woman drink the watery mixture. All of this action takes place in front of Yhwh's altar inside the tabernacle's sanctuary (Num 5:16, 18), meaning the woman would be acutely aware of her position so unusually close to the Holy of Holies as she drank the words of the curses. The text repeats from the priest's curses the anticipated results if she is guilty or innocent, with the addition that if she is innocent, she will have a child.[6]

Exegetes have long debated the meaning of the fallen thigh and swollen stomach. The juxtaposition of this outcome with that of the *sotah* conceiving if innocent suggests that it involves a negative effect on her reproductive health. This is further indicated by the parts of the woman's body affected: the Hebrew word for "thigh" (*yarek*) can be a euphemistic term for the reproductive organs,[7] while the word for "stomach" (*beten*) can refer to the uterus. Based on this evidence, scholars most often conclude that the woman is expected to suffer a miscarriage and/or uterine prolapse,

4. The Septuagint has "waters of reproof," here and in every other instance in Num 5.
5. All translations are my own.
6. Some argue that this means she will retain the child she is already carrying, while others suggest that she would conceive after previously having been infertile (see Frymer-Kensky 1984, 18–19; Levine 1993, 182, 201).
7. Though *yarek* more commonly refers to the male reproductive organ, leading some to suggest that it functions here as a reference to the husband's potential loss of the ability to have children through his wife if she is guilty (e.g. Haberman 2000, 33; Camp 2015, 113–14).

perhaps caused by edema (hence the "swelling" of the uterus).[8] The miscarriage explanation would suggest that the woman had been pregnant, which some commentators assume to be the cause of her husband's suspicion that she has been unfaithful (e.g. McKane 1980, 474; Levine 1993, 181; Haberman 2000, 32).[9] Although there is no explicit mention that the woman in the ritual is pregnant, the ritual's concerns with her reproductive capacity suggest that this might be the case.

It is also unclear whether the bodily effects of the ritual constitute the entirety of the guilty woman's punishment. Even though the punishment for adultery is death elsewhere in the Pentateuch (Lev 20:10; Deut 22:22), Numbers 5 does not mention what should happen to the woman after the ritual if it reveals her guilt. This is further complicated by the lack of an anticipated timeline: the text does not specify whether the negative effects on the *sotah's* body should be immediately visible, or if they could take place some months into the future, as in the case of a positive outcome (childbirth). Some scholars suggest that the ravaging of the woman's body if she is guilty stands in lieu of any punishment enacted by human hands (e.g. Frymer-Kensky 1984, 22–3; Milgrom 1989, 350; Ellens 2009, 72–73). But what would happen to the woman if she lived on in this condition? Her husband might have the legal right – or even duty – to divorce her on the grounds of her defiling unfaithfulness (e.g. Deut 22:20–1; 24:1–4; see Levine 1993, 199).

The Book of Numbers is primarily concerned with maintaining the purity of the Israelite camp. Numbers 5 opens with a command to remove from the camp people who have become ritually impure (*tame'*) due to skin disease, discharge, or contact with the dead, so that they may not defile the area where Yhwh dwells among the Israelites (verses 1–4). Since Numbers 5:11–31 mentions seven times that a woman who has committed adultery is defiled (*tame'*; verses 13–14, 20, 27–9), it is unlikely that the writers of this passage envision her remaining in the community should she be proven guilty. In that case, the loss of her reproductive health and banishment from the Israelite camp (and therefore from Yhwh's presence) would be a fate so dreadful from the perspective of the Book of Numbers that death would almost be preferable. The text's lack of specification regarding the

8. The latter interpretation goes back at least as far as Josephus (*Ant.* 3.11.6; see Levine 1993, 201; Frymer-Kensky 1984, 19). The verb associated with the stomach/uterus, *tsavah,* is a *hapax legomenon* in the Hebrew Bible, and its meaning is unclear. Since the Septuagint uses the Greek verb *pretho* here, meaning "to swell," most commentators accept this meaning.

9. Others disagree, e.g. Frymer-Kensky 1984, 18–19.

woman's punishment suggests that the sole purpose of the ritual is to identify her as either guilty or innocent. If Numbers 5:11–31 is a late addition to the Pentateuchal texts, as Frevel (2020, 293, 306) has suggested, its writer would likely expect the existing Pentateuchal laws regarding capital punishment for adultery (Lev 20:10; Deut 22:22) to come into play if the woman's guilt were confirmed.

There is a great deal more scholarly discussion concerning the details of Numbers 5:11–31, but for the purpose of the present study, I will mention just two relevant trends in the interpretation of the ritual as a whole. The first is that many scholars emphasize its purpose of removing a husband's right to punish his wife if he suspects her of unfaithfulness (e.g. Brichto 1975, 66–7; Milgrom 1989, 350; Haberman 2000, 34; Britt 2007, 6; Frevel 2020, 306). He is not allowed to act upon his jealousy alone, but rather must undertake a specified procedure to determine whether his wife is guilty. Some point out that the priest's mixture of water, dirt, and ink would not, biologically speaking, cause a woman any real harm, meaning that, if the ritual were ever carried out, it would inevitably "prove" her innocence and save her life even if she *had* committed adultery (e.g. Brichto 1975, 65–7; Frevel 2020, 309). Any unborn child she was carrying would be born into her husband's household without further suspicion. Other commentators speak of the inevitable humiliation that would accrue to the husband if his wife should be proven unfaithful in such a public manner, suggesting that the ritual was designed to act as a deterrent to any husband tempted to raise accusations against his wife (e.g. Britt 2007, 14; Camp 2015, 125). From this point of view, the *sotah* ritual protects women from the potentially life-threatening danger of masculine jealousy.

A second dominant strand of interpretation does not necessarily dispute this point but focuses instead on how the ritual exists to validate a husband's feelings of jealousy, regardless of whether they are founded in reality. According to this view, the ritual serves to uphold a patriarchal society in which a husband can put his wife through a degrading trial without any evidence (e.g. Bach 1999; Haberman 2000, 18; Ellens 2004, 55, 79; Stiebert 2019, 86, 95–9; Scholz 2021). There is no gender-reversed version of the ritual, in which a woman who suspects her husband of being unfaithful can bring him to trial. This is because, while sexual intercourse with any man other than her husband was a capital crime for married women according to the laws of the Pentateuch, a man was only guilty of adultery if he had intercourse with another man's wife (Lev 20:10; Deut 22:22). Though not encouraged in biblical texts, a married man could have intercourse with women outside of his marriage, provided they did not belong to another man's household (e.g. slaves or sex workers: Lev 19:20; cf. Prov 6:26), or he could take a second wife. (Though polygamy was not widely practised in ancient Israel or Judah, it is permitted according to Exod 21:10; Deut 21:15–17; see Frevel 2020, 305). Feminist scholars therefore argue that the very existence of the ritual described in Numbers 5:11–31 confirms a system of marriage in which women's sexuality was controlled by men.

Both interpretational trends just summarized demonstrate that gender concerns have been at the centre of reading Numbers 5:11–31 for decades. A specific construction of gendered identities clearly underlies the *sotah* ritual: not only that a feminine identity necessitates sexual fidelity to one's husband and a masculine identity includes the unrequited expectation of sexual fidelity from one's wife, but also that masculine priests protect the purity of the Israelite camp and of Yhwh's dwelling place. These concepts of gender are prevalent throughout the Pentateuch, but what is unique about Numbers 5:11–31 is how they are ritually reinforced via the use of a material sacred text.

It may seem paradoxical to focus on the material aspects of this ritual when there is no material evidence that it was ever conducted. However, if Numbers 5:11–31 is read not as a record of a historically enacted ritual, but rather as part of what makes up the literary world of the Book of Numbers, its references to a sacred text and to human bodies can be seen as structuring elements of the religious order created by the text.[10] The Book of Numbers does not reflect a historical reality. It is a post-exilic Judean composition (e.g. Frevel 2013, 22), yet it describes the Israel of an imagined "wilderness period" many centuries before: the twelve tribes travelling through the Sinai desert prior to settling in the land of Canaan. Therefore, examining how material sacred texts interact with gendered identities in the *sotah* ritual of Numbers 5 cannot necessarily provide information about this system in ancient Judaean or Israelite society, which historically never bore much resemblance to what the Book of Numbers depicts. But it does reveal how the writers of Numbers believed sacred texts and gendered identities *should* function in an ideal religious community of Yhwh worshippers (see Frevel 2018, 72; 2020, 291). Since the Book of Numbers is part of Jewish and Christian canonical scripture, its ideology has been influential in both religions (see Camp 2015, 125; Scholz 2021). It is therefore

10. For this reason, the present study does not include the extensive Mishnaic and rabbinic discussion of the *sotah* ritual, except where it might shed light on ambiguous aspects of Num 5:11–31, because these belong to different literary worlds.

important to understand the internal logic of the text as well as how it legitimizes its own authority.

Focusing on the material aspects of sacred texts mentioned within the Hebrew Bible draws attention to who produces, accesses, and handles physical sacred texts and how this engenders power within the religious community. Although a few studies along these lines have been conducted (e.g. Watts 2015, 2018; Frevel 2018), they have not considered how uses of material sacred texts interact with biblical constructions of gendered identities, even though hierarchies of gender and power are inextricably entwined (Connell 2005, 71).

Claudia Camp's 2015 study of the *sotah* ritual partially addresses this gap by examining the interplay between sacred text, religious authority, and gender. She argues that the priest's privileged relationship to text enables him to demonstrate his control over reproduction ("biological as well as cultural"), undermining the authority of both the family and of competing oral traditions surrounding fertility and childbirth, which were likely primarily preserved and used by women (Camp 2015, 128). Camp's approach additionally considers how the priest's use of sacred text influences the masculine and feminine identities of lay people by moving a man's control over his patrilineage and a woman's control over her fertility into the priestly jurisdiction (Camp 2015, 128). Yet Camp does not focus on how the interactions between the material sacred text and each of the differently gendered bodies involved in the ritual reinforces the hierarchies of gender and power she accurately identifies. Theoretical models of both the materiality of sacred texts and of gender have the potential to open up new questions regarding how these material things function in the ritual described in Numbers 5:11–31.

Theoretical Approaches to Sacred Text and Gender

The "material turn" in religious studies has recognized the significant role played by physical things – including bodies – and their interactions with one another; for example, how a sacred space is arranged, furnished, and decorated; how people move their bodies in and through that space; how they are dressed; what they hold and touch; what they can sense and what phenomenological effects this has on them; which cultural memories this triggers; and how this affects people's sense of individual and group identities, including gendered identities (e.g. Morgan 2010, 2021; Hazard 2013). An examination of the material elements of religion reveals that people generally do not consider their bodily actions and interactions in the context of religion as merely symbolizing something sacred, but rather as embodying the sacred (and its associated hierarchies) itself (Morgan 2016, 273). This realization can shed light on the use of sacred things, including a text, in response to a suspicion of adultery in the ritual of Numbers 5:11–31.

Sacred text is a category of things that have special agency within religious traditions. While religious communities and the scholars who study them tend to attribute to the verbal contents of sacred texts significant meaning beyond their physical form, the material creation, properties, and uses of sacred texts can also reveal information about how a religion is structured and practised (Malley 2004; Watts 2006, 2013, 2015, 2018; Schleicher 2017). For example, James Watts (2006) has distinguished three dimensions of sacred text: semantic, performative, and iconic. The semantic dimension includes interpreting a text's meaning, analysing its composition, tracing its process of canonization, and other tasks relating to the contents of the text (Watts 2006, 136, 141) – this approach to sacred text tends to dominate studies of the Hebrew Bible. But the other two dimensions Watts identifies open new paths of inquiry into Numbers 5:11–31, where a sacred text takes on an unusual material form. Since Watts focuses only on written scripture (and not other material forms), he classifies a "performative" dimension – including private or public reading, dramatization, and other such activities (Watts 2006, 141, 149) – distinct from an "iconic" dimension – the physical form taken by a written text (Watts 2006, 142). However, the sacred text described in Numbers 5:11–31 is given both a written and an oral form within the same ritual, suggesting that performance and icon can work together. Watts's terminology is a helpful starting point for considering how sacred texts can function as things in conjunction with the contents of their words. This is even more relevant when studying societies with high rates of illiteracy, such as ancient Israel and Judah, where most lay people's engagements with sacred texts would have involved the texts' material, rather than semantic, features.[11]

Watts has demonstrated that one of the things material sacred texts can do is legitimize the religious authority of the person using them (Watts 2006, 148–50).[12] The Pentateuch reveals that this is the case in the religious world it constructs, since some of its texts refer to themselves as those

11. Schleicher (2011, 49; 2017, 42) argues this is true of all societies regardless of literacy rate.

12. Watts identifies three functions of sacred texts corresponding to his three dimensions: the semantic dimension gives authority, the performative dimension inspires, and the iconic dimension legitimizes. However, he acknowledges that these terms and functions overlap, and that each dimension is reinforced by the ritualization of the others (Watts 2006, 150).

given material form through engraving, writing, and public reading. For example, Deuteronomy 31:9–13 states that Moses wrote down "this law" (the book of Deuteronomy) and gave it to the Levitical priests, commanding them to read it aloud to all of Israel as part of the Sukkot festival every seven years (Frevel 2018, 57). This demonstrates that those who wrote down the Book of Deuteronomy already conceived of it being ritualized in a material way (Watts 2015), storing and reinforcing Israel's shared memory (Frevel 2018, 58; cf. Deut 17:18).[13] The task of looking after this written law and enforcing its commands is given to the priesthood (Deut 31:9–13; cf. Lev 10:8–11).[14] Thus, any ritualization of material texts described in the Pentateuch legitimizes not only the religious traditions the text contains but also the authority of the priesthood associated with and confirmed by that text (Watts 2015). Examining texts like this can reveal how the writers of the sacred text envisaged its use as a material thing that could help bring their worldview into effect.

Since the expression and experience of gendered identities also takes place within the material realm, it follows that physical interactions with sacred texts influence and are influenced by the religious community's concepts of gender. Constructions of gender are related to who has control of a society's material assets and how they maintain that control; gendered identities are not as simple as being either masculine or feminine (Connell 2005, 82). The text from Numbers 5:11–31 describes two very different masculine figures – the priest and the husband – one of whom creates and manipulates the material sacred text and one who does not. R. W. Connell's model of a hierarchy of masculinities could therefore assist in understanding how gendered identities, both masculine and feminine, affect and are affected by the *sotah* ritual. Connell identities a "hegemonic masculinity," which is an embodiment of the ideals of a patriarchal society and therefore holds institutional power within it (Connell 2005, 76–7). She also categorizes a "complicit masculinity" held by those who do not fully meet all the standards of hegemonic masculinity and thus do not hold the

13. A similar situation can be observed regarding the "Book of the Covenant" (Exod 20:22–23:33) as described in Exod 24:4–8 and the Ten Commandments in Exod 24:12. For examples from outside of the Pentateuch, see Josh 8:30–5; 2 Kgs 23:2; Neh 8:1–3 (cf. Ezra 7:14).

14. Pentateuchal texts disagree about the composition of the priesthood: while texts usually attributed to the "Priestly" source (including the book of Numbers) limit the priesthood to the male descendants of Aaron, other Pentateuchal texts consider all male members of the tribe of Levi to be priests. On the complex relationship between the book of Numbers, the "Priestly" source, and the Pentateuch as a whole, see e.g. Frevel 2013.

same amount of power, yet still benefit from the patriarchal system and so do not challenge it (Connell 2005, 79).

While helpful for understanding the different masculine identities evident in Numbers 5:11–31, Connell's model is based on the concept of social agency (Connell 2005, 81). New materialists have problematized constructionist assumptions such as this, arguing that the physical nature of bodies influences how they are interpreted (e.g. Haraway 1988; Grosz 1993; Barad 2003; Sencindiver 2017; Schleicher 2021). This is evident in the *sotah* ritual, which is motivated by the nature of the wife's body as one that has the potential to bear children, both legitimate and illegitimate. The gendered features and practices of the human bodies participating in this ritual dictate how they interact with the sacred text, while the sacred text and its use within the ritual act to confirm the participants' distinct gendered identities. Analysing this example of an interaction between bodies and text from a material perspective reveals how the Hebrew Bible makes rhetorical use of material sacred texts to enforce, maintain, or even potentially challenge hierarchies of power and gender.

Analysis: The Priestly Use of Sacred Text in Numbers 5:11–31

Beginning with the priest's creation of a material sacred text in the *sotah* ritual, it is worth investigating whether the theories just discussed can provide insights into this unique set of instructions in the Hebrew Bible and their connection to suspected adultery. The ritual involves a priest applying a sacred text to the interpretation of a dispute in which opposing truth claims (the wife committed adultery or she did not commit adultery) cannot otherwise be solved. A similar situation is evident in Deuteronomy 21:1–9, which describes what to do when a murder has been committed but there is no obvious culprit. The Pentateuch views murder as such a disruptive and defiling act that, like adultery, the impurity it creates can only be resolved by putting the offender to death (Exod 21:12; Lev 24:17; Num 35:30–4). If there is no offender, the community must deal with the impurity in another way.[15] Thus, Deuteronomy 21:1–9 dictates that the elders of the city nearest to where the dead body is found must sacrifice a heifer and wash their hands over it. While doing so, they must recite the specified words of an oath stating that they did not commit or witness the murder and asking Yhwh to remove its blood guilt from their community. As in Numbers 5:11–31, men with an elevated social role (though here elders and not priests) are attributed with the authority to apply a sacred

15. The parallel situations in Deut 21:1–9 and Num 5:11–31 have been noted by e.g. Fishbane 1974; Frymer-Kensky 1984; Haberman 2000.

text to a situation of potential dispute. Watts has demonstrated that people who have the greatest exegetical influence in determining which text applies to which situation possess the most authority to direct the religious community's beliefs and practices. This is because communities tend to privilege the ritualized interpretation of sacred text (its semantic dimension) as the means by which conflicts should be settled (Watts 2006, 148–9). Therefore, the priest's semantic use of sacred text in the *sotah* ritual, like the elders' use in the case of an unknown murderer, confirms his authority to wield sacred text as a means of resolving disputes that would otherwise be unsolvable due to lack of evidence.

Unlike the elders in Deuteronomy 21:1–9, the priest in Numbers 5:11–31 also gives the sacred text a physical form by writing it down on parchment and then blotting the words into a mixture of water and dirt from the tabernacle (Num 5:23). By writing with ink on a scroll (*sefer*), the priest recalls the form taken by Yhwh's written law elsewhere in the Hebrew Bible (Deut 31:9–13; Exod 24:7; Josh 8:34–5; 2 Kgs 23:2; Neh 8:1–3). Marianne Schleicher (2017, 47) has pointed out that the Mishnah (*m Yadayim* 4:5) states that the Torah's sacred status depends on it being written in "Assyrian script" (meaning the Aramaic writing system adopted by Hebrew) on parchment and in ink, thereby establishing a "visual norm" for scriptural texts. The description of the written sacred text in Numbers 5:23 recalls this visual norm, associating the priest with the divine authority of Yhwh's law and with the priestly role of safeguarding, interpreting, and copying that law (as dictated, for example, by Lev 10:8–11 and Deut 31:9–11).[16] This idea is supported by Watts's theory that people who produce and use sacred texts in their iconic dimension (as material things) are legitimized through their visual connection with a central symbol of their religious tradition (Watts 2006, 149). It is then difficult for other members of the religious community to challenge their authority without seeming to be challenging core principles of the religion itself.

While the three dimensions of sacred text Watts identifies – semantic, performative, and iconic – may not be entirely distinct in Numbers 5:11–31 (the semantic application of the text and its transformation into iconic form are themselves performances), Watts's theory is still useful for understanding why the priest is instructed to use sacred text in such unique ways in the *sotah* ritual. Ritualizing the iconic dimension of a sacred text in

16. Although Num 5:23 does not specify that the priest should write on parchment, Frevel (2018, 73–4) has demonstrated that this is most likely to have been the intended material, since papyrus was not common in the southern Levant before the fourth century BCE.

addition to its semantic elements has a more powerful effect than ritualizing it in only one dimension (Watts 2006, 150; cf. Schleicher 2017, 42) and it legitimizes the privileged religious authority of the priesthood.

The priestly authority evoked by the priest's use of sacred text in Numbers 5:11–31 is that constructed in the Pentateuch, where it is closely linked to concepts of masculinity. For example, priestly men are described as being able to assert physical dominance when their authority is challenged. David Clines (2010, 55–6) has suggested that the Levites are attributed with a warrior masculinity in Exodus 32:26–9, when they massacre their fellow Israelites as punishment for worshipping a golden calf instead of Yhwh.[17] Meanwhile, in Numbers 25:6–8, Aaron's grandson Phinehas protects the purity of the Israelite camp by running a spear through an Israelite man and the foreign bride he has brought within the camp's borders. The priests also protect their bodily integrity to a greater extent than laymen by being stricter about what enters their bodies (e.g. Lev 6:18–22 [MT]; 7:6–10, 31–5; 10:9; Num 18:8–19; Deut 18:1–5); what their bodies may touch (e.g. Lev 21:1–4); and their permitted sexual partners (e.g. Lev 21:7). They exert control over female sexuality, not only of their own wives and daughters (e.g. Lev 21:9), but also of all women in the Israelite community via their administration of religious law, thereby also curtailing the sexual and reproductive actions available to other men. Yet priests themselves must be virile so that they may produce sons to continue their priestly line: men with priestly heritage whose genitals are damaged may not take up priestly office (Lev 21:20). Priests provide for their households materially by virtue of their genealogy and not via the hard labour of their bodies, which laymen conduct on their behalf to support them (e.g. Num 18:10-24; Deut 18:1–2). Finally, priests exert their energies in the public sphere due to their role of ministering in the tabernacle.[18]

When compared to Connell's (2005, 76–7) definition of hegemonic masculinity, the Pentateuch's presentation of the priesthood can be seen as a means of legitimizing their institutional power by depicting priests as

17. This event also involves subjugation via the forced drinking of a watery mixture (this one made with the dust of the ground-up statue worshipped by the Israelites; Exod 32:20).

18. Howard Eilberg-Schwartz (1994) argued that in a society where masculinity is a common representation of power, Yhwh must have been perceived as the most masculine in order to be the most powerful. Similarly, Alan Hooker (2014, 24–7) suggested that the masculinity of the priests must be subordinate to that of Yhwh, which is why they must cover up the masculine elements of their bodies in deference to him when serving at the altar. While these are important observations that challenge the priests' ultimate hegemonic masculinity in relation to the deity, they do not affect the hegemonic nature of the priests' masculinity in terms of their relationship to other humans.

fulfilling all aspects of the masculine ideal. Cross-cultural studies of patriarchal societies have identified several components of hegemonic masculinity that are usually present to varying extents, including military might, close control of the boundaries of one's body, honour (largely based on controlling female sexuality against the advances of other men), virility, ability to provide for one's household, and exerting one's energies in public spaces outside of the home (Haddox 2016, 179–181). The examples above reveal how Pentateuchal descriptions of priests fulfil all these categories. Thus, priestly authority as constructed by the Pentateuch is inextricable from gendered identities. In legitimizing a hegemonic masculine identity for the priesthood, the Pentateuch creates a hierarchy of gendered identities that also includes laymen and all women. This hierarchy is evident in and confirmed by the ritual described in Numbers 5:11–31.

The Textual "Solution" to the Problem of Suspected Adultery

Unlike the priest conducting the *sotah* ritual, the jealous husband does not come into physical contact with the sacred text. Yet by initiating the ritualization of this text, he identifies himself with the concepts of masculinity it encodes. For example, control of material possessions is at stake. The Pentateuchal system of inheritance dictates that sons inherit from their fathers (e.g. Num 27:1–11), with women being unable to own property outside of exceptional circumstances (e.g. Num 27:8, but see Num 36:6–12 for how the text mitigates the unusual situation). This masculine control of material wealth ensures continued masculine dominance, so laymen were unlikely to challenge it, even if it meant providing for the priesthood by donating some of their own property as cult offerings (e.g. Num 18:8–24; Deut 18:1–2). In Connell's (2005, 79) terms, laymen as they are constructed by the Pentateuch can therefore be said to have a complicit masculine identity, whereby they support the hegemonic masculinity of the priests because it allows them to maintain patriarchal control over property.

However, if a man's wife were unfaithful and bore another man's son into his household, potentially undetected, the husband would risk his property becoming alienated from his paternal line. In this inheritance system, therefore, it was vital for men to ensure that their wives were not having sexual intercourse with anyone else (Haddox 2016, 181). A male lover would present a direct challenge to the husband's masculine control over his household – both its possessions and its people. Such a challenge could not go unaddressed without compromising the husband's masculine identity. Erin Villareal has demonstrated, based on a study of the term "jealousy" (*qin'ah*) in the Hebrew Bible, that the experience of the husband described in Numbers 5:14 is not a feeling occasioned by romantic attachment to his wife, but rather a culturally conditioned sense that his rights to relational exclusivity within his marriage have been compromised (Villareal 2022, 50; cf. Haberman 2000, 30; Ellens 2009, 76). Therefore, if a husband experiences *qin'ah,* regardless of his wife's actions, he has experienced a threat to his masculine social and economic status (Villareal 2022, 58), and this perception must be addressed to restore the correct order of things. Because it is the husband who experiences the *qin'ah,* he is the one who must bring the offering and initiate the ritual that will allow his issue to be resolved (Villareal 2022, 61, 68). Villareal points out that, when used elsewhere in the Pentateuch, the term *qin'ah* often refers to Yhwh's sense of a violation of his covenantal agreement with his people (a covenant that includes a prohibition of adultery, e.g. Exod 20:14; Deut 5:24–6). Thus, the use of the term *qin'ah* to describe the husband's experience in Numbers 5 points to an even more serious circumstance than a dispute between a married couple (Villareal 2022, 62–70). This is why the issue must be resolved in the tabernacle in the presence of Yhwh as opposed to anywhere else (see Frevel 2020, 303).

In addition to being a breach of the covenant with Yhwh, the Pentateuch also presents adultery as something that causes impurity. If a woman commits adultery, not only is her husband's certainty of paternity under threat, but the purity of his body and of the entire camp would also be compromised (Milgrom 1989, 351; Haberman 2000, 19). The Holiness Code identifies adultery as one of the sexual acts so impure that it would result in the Israelites being expelled from their land (Lev 18:20). More specifically, Deuteronomy 24:1–4 states that a man who divorces his wife cannot have intercourse with her again later if she has been with another man in the interim, because this would be impure. Tikva Frymer-Kensky suggests that the same principle might apply to a man whose wife had been unfaithful during their marriage, especially since Numbers 5:13 describes her as impure (*tame'*). Therefore, the Pentateuch may have imposed upon the husband the duty of bringing his wife to the ritual, even if he were inclined to forgive her infidelity. This could be the meaning of Numbers 5:31, which states that the jealous husband must bring his wife to trial "so that the man is innocent of iniquity" (Frymer-Kensky 1984, 18). The *sotah* ritual therefore reinforces the complicit masculine identity of non-priestly men envisaged by the Pentateuch: they must guard their wives' sexuality in order to maintain masculine control of property, but their duty and method of doing so is controlled by the more powerful masculine priests.

The interaction between the sacred text materialized in Numbers 5:11–31 and the body of the *sotah* herself asserts her gender identity in the most powerful way of all three people involved. This is necessary because the very nature of the feminine-identified body as penetrable poses a threat to the hierarchical structure of gender envisaged by the Book of Numbers. The text preferences the hegemonic masculine body epitomized by the priests; that is, a body "intact, enclosed, boundaried, and ordered" (Haberman 2000, 32). The rest of the community is modelled after this body: the Israelite camp has a clear boundary keeping impurity out (e.g. Num 5:1–4); the tabernacle in its centre is bounded by the priestly families who surround it and protect its heightened level of purity (Num 1:47–53; 3:5–39); and the households camped around them are organized according to tribe, each one constituting the boundaries of the patriarch's family and property (e.g. Num 2:1–32; Haberman 2000, 20). By contrast to the idealized masculine body, the feminine body has unstable boundaries: it can be penetrated. A wife's body constitutes a potential opening for the progeny of an outsider to enter her husband's household, disrupting the careful lines of genealogy and property ownership constructed by the Book of Numbers. If the wife of a priest committed adultery undetected, the consequences could be even more disastrous, as she could give birth to a boy without the requisite priestly heritage, who would then be raised to hold priestly office, bringing him into improper contact with Yhwh (see Num 3:10). Thus, an adulterous woman undermines the Pentateuch's entire hierarchy of gendered identities and religious authority (Haberman 2000, 30).

Connell has demonstrated that a structure of gender inequality involving a massive dispossession of resources – such as a system in which women cannot own or inherit property – usually implements violence to enforce itself when crises in the gender order arise (Connell 2005, 83–84; see also Ellens 2009, 76, 80). Although the *sotah* ritual circumvents the worst violence that could be enacted on the woman's body by prohibiting her death without trial, it does violence to it in a different way: stripping her of her head covering, manoeuvring her around the tabernacle, and forcing her to ingest a mixture that she is to believe can cause severe bodily harm. The forcefulness of the ritual supports the interpretation that the *sotah* has caused a crisis in the gender order.

However, the situation described in Numbers 5:11–31 is one of ambiguity. In this case, it has not yet been determined whether the *sotah* has actually done anything to disrupt the gender hierarchy. Her body therefore poses a second material problem for the Priestly writers: it is potentially polluting and clean at the same time. Her body may carry a child who will be a legitimate member of her husband's household, or it may carry an illegitimate child who cannot be accepted into the community of Israel – until the tenth generation, according to Deuteronomy 23:3 (see Levine 1993, 204; Haberman 2000, 16; Destro 2020, 132). This ambiguity challenges the Pentateuchal organization of society even more than a proven case of adultery would, since the latter could be promptly and legally dealt with by the capital punishment of both offenders. Yet the *sotah* cannot simply be put to death or banished from the community, even as a precaution. Not only would this contradict the Book of Numbers' insistence upon more than one witness for capital convictions (Num 35:30), but it would also undermine the book's project of an enclosed Israelite community relying on reproduction for its continued survival.

A community with such an exclusive worldview depends upon fertile female members for its continued existence. Given the high rates of infant and maternal mortality in the ancient world, the text must acknowledge Israelite women and babies as resources that could not be wasted. Therefore, the writers of the book of Numbers could not advocate for risking the unnecessary death or banishment of a fertile woman and any potential legitimate child she was carrying. Not only would this have put the physical survival of the Israelite community at risk, but it also would have been highly objectionable to other community members who cared for the woman: if not her husband, then presumably her parents, siblings, any existing children, and so on. Putting the *sotah* through an ordeal attributed with the divine power to detect infidelity, the ritual of Numbers 5:11–31 provides a way for her and any unborn child she is carrying to be reintegrated into her husband's household (presuming the ritual has no damning effects). Yet it also protects the Pentateuchal hierarchy of gender identities by demonstrating that unfaithfulness in marriage is unacceptable for women. But the situation is a delicate one: for the ritual to work as intended, it cannot seem as if the *sotah* can get away with the challenge she poses to the existing order. The material nature of the problems posed by her body – the possibility of its defilement and of an illegitimate child – means the ritual must present these problems as resolved on a material level.

Several different ritualized materials are involved in the procedure described in Numbers 5:11–31. The grain presented in offering to Yhwh, the holy water, and dirt from the tabernacle all function to confirm the holiness and authority of the sanctuary and its priesthood. Yet, as already demonstrated, it is the material sacred text that reinforces the priests' control over Yhwh's law and the hierarchy of gendered identities it inscribes. The importance of this textual element of the ritual over all others is indicated by its central location in the chiastic movement of bodies and things. Jacob Milgrom has demonstrated how the grain offering moves from the *sotah* to the priest to Yhwh, while the watery mixture moves from Yhwh to the priest to the *sotah*. The reader's attention is drawn to the middle of this movement (verses 19–23), where the words of the oath are spoken and written down (Milgrom 1989, 351–2; see also Ellens 2009). By physically interacting with the sacred text, the *sotah* aligns herself with its principles, including the patriarchal system it encodes (see Watts 2018, 173–5).

First, the accused woman binds herself to the words of the text orally by replying "Amen, amen" to the priest's recitation (verse 22). There are other examples in the Hebrew Bible where saying "Amen" in response to a spoken sacred text constitutes a sign act placing the speaker under the conditions of that text (e.g. Deut 27:15–26; see Levine 1993, 198). Yet the woman's verbal consent is not sufficient for the purpose of the *sotah* ritual. One reason for this may be that touch is a more powerful indication of alignment with a sacred text than speaking it. Consumption is the most intimate action of all because it indicates an internalization of the text, making it part of oneself (Watts 2018, 176–8). Prior to its liquefaction, the sacred text in Numbers 5:11–31 visually resembles the written law of Yhwh as it is described elsewhere in the Hebrew Bible. A woman would be dissuaded from thinking she could exert manipulative control over such a text – for example, by safely undergoing the ritual in the knowledge that she was guilty – because this would constitute a dangerous desecration of something iconically associated with Yhwh's law (see Watts 2018, 178–80). By consuming the text, the woman indicates that her body is under the jurisdiction of Yhwh's written law and the priesthood who has exclusive access to it.

There may be another reason why the woman's spoken assent to the oral form of the sacred text is insufficient for the *sotah* ritual. Brian Britt (2007, 9) has pointed out that Numbers 30:3–16 states that women may swear binding oaths, but that these can be nullified by their male head of household if he does not approve. Therefore, in the textual world of the Book of Numbers, a woman's spoken word was not as powerful as a man's. The ritual described in Numbers 5:11–31 can be contrasted to the previously mentioned case in Deuteronomy 21:1–9, in which a murder has been committed without a culprit to punish. Here, the male elders of the community take a spoken oath stating that they did not commit or witness the murder (v. 7), and their words, along with the sacrifice of a heifer, effect the cleansing of the community. Yet in the case in Numbers 5, when a woman is the only one who knows whether adultery has been committed, an additional step beyond her verbal oath is required to submit her fully to its terms. This reveals the paradoxical nature of the situation, whereby the feminine-coded body has sufficient agency to disrupt the hierarchical system of gendered identities, but a feminine identity precludes being able to swear a fully binding oath that she has not done so.

The laws in Numbers 5:1–10 specify that they apply to both men and women as moral agents (see Frevel 2020, 302, 308; Rees 2013, 30), and yet in verses 11–31, the woman is most often the object of a man's actions: for example, it is a man who lies with her and not the other way around (v. 13). This reinforces the idea that in the case of suspected adultery, it is first and foremost the feminine-coded body and what can be done with it – rather than the woman's real actions or intentions – that pose a challenge to the Pentateuchal hierarchy of gendered identities (cf. Britt 2007, 3; Scholz 2021, 280–1). Thus, the *sotah* ritual provides a means by which a threatening feminine body can be brought back into alignment with Pentateuchal law. This is achieved not by speaking, but by ingesting the relevant part of that law.

By applying a sacred text directly to the woman's body, the priest makes use of its semantic dimension at the same time that he materializes it in its iconic dimension. Watts suggested that, especially in situations of dispute, the interpretation of a sacred text is often considered a method of determining the divine will; that is, a form of divination (Watts 2006, 141). Several biblical scholars have indeed proposed a possible divinatory function for the watery mixture in Numbers 5. For example, Adriana Destro has suggested that the symbology of the materials involved alludes to divination (Destro 2020, 115), while Herbert Chanan Brichto (1975, 59, 66) has attributed an "oracular" quality to the liquid. Philo interpreted the mixture as the "waters of proof/testing," possibly reflecting a reading of the Hebrew *marim* (usually translated "bitter") as *morim,* "oracle" (Milgrom 1989, 303). Britt (2007, 4) stated that the ritual "reduces the woman's body to a sign, a text of divination that must be read to determine her guilt or innocence." Yet none of these commentators expands upon this intriguing divinatory function of the text except Destro, whose interpretation focuses on the Mishnaic and rabbinic versions of the ritual rather than the biblical one. In some of these later retellings, the various possible effects the solution might have on the *sotah*'s body are described in detail; for example, the different colours the woman's skin might turn. Destro (2020, 129) considers these the oracular "signs" that are then deciphered by the priest. However, the biblical version of the ritual does not describe the woman's symptoms beyond the potential effects on her reproductive system. What requires deciphering is not what happens to the woman after she has drunk the potion, but whether she has committed adultery and is defiled, possibly pregnant with the child of a man who is not her husband. The oracular sign to be interpreted is inside the body of the *sotah*.

The use of a divinatory text to decipher the meaning of things inside the body can be compared to the Mesopotamian tradition of omen discernment. Internal organs such as the lungs and livers of sheep, as well as new-born human and animal babies, were seen as bearing messages from the divine. These could only be interpreted by religious professionals with the use of specific texts. In the case of the Mesopotamian birth omens, the interpretations of the physical features of new-borns (and, occasionally, of events during pregnancy such as miscarriages) usually concerned the fate of the king or of the household into which the child or animal was born. However, there are several that reveal information about the behaviour or destiny of the mother. For example, one reads: "If a woman gives birth to a giant, either male or female – a sinful man impregnated that woman in the street" (Leichty 1970, 38). Another predicts the mother's future infertility (Leichty 1970, 58). Although these examples constitute only a small percentage of the vast collections of Mesopotamian omens, they attest to the idea that pregnancy and childbirth could be "read" as messages from the divine concerning the people involved.[19]

The Akkadian textual reference for decoding these messages, titled *Shumma izbu* ("If an abnormal birth..."), was in use from the early second to the late first millennium BCE. In theory, someone who witnessed anomalies related to pregnancy and birth would report them to their local priest. The priest would then use a copy of the *Shumma izbu* catalogue to interpret what divine message might have been sent via the anomaly. He would write up his findings in a report including all the possible omens relevant to the case at hand. All such written reports that exist today come from Ashurbanipal's library, meaning that they were archived centrally by the Neo-Assyrian administration (Leichty 1970, 8). The authority of local priests was therefore established via their privileged access to written texts containing supernatural information, such as *Shumma izbu*; their ability to read and interpret those texts; and their access to the central administration in the form of written reports filed for posterity in the king's library. It is evident that, as in the case described in Numbers 5, the ability to read, interpret, and create texts granted priests religious and social power.

---

19. Erle Leichty (1970) pointed out that cases involving the pregnant woman's own actions and health overlap with magico-medical texts diagnosing symptoms suffered during pregnancy and childbirth, which specialists often attributed to demonic attacks or sorcery (see e.g. Scurlock 1991). This again demonstrates that characteristics associated with women's pregnancies and childbirth experiences were considered signs that could relay messages from the supernatural realm.

In the textual world of the Book of Numbers, the entirety of Israel dwells in one camp, and there is no king. The priests in the central tabernacle are the only priests. Therefore, they do not need to make written reports of their findings for anyone else's benefit. The situation also differs from what is described in *Shumma izbu* because the biblical priest needs to interpret what is inside the woman's body before a child is potentially born into the wrong household. Since the priest is unable to inspect the signs hidden inside of her without harming her, he copies out the relevant text and applies it directly to those signs by having her consume it in liquid form. The text itself then interprets what is inside the woman's body as either clean or defiled; legitimate or illegitimate; making the signs visible to human eyes in the form of the woman's fertility or loss of fertility.

The power attributed to the text enhances that of the priest, who knows the correct combination of words; can materialize them orally and in the iconic form of a *sefer*; and holds an institutional position that allows him to apply these interpretive words to the enigmatic body of the *sotah*. It also reinforces the subordinate status of feminine identity by placing feminine-coded bodies under the control of masculine priests, nullifying their ability to challenge the masculinity of their husbands and the patriarchal structure of society.

Conclusion

One of the observations I made at the start of the present enquiry was how unusual it is in the world of the Hebrew Bible for a woman to come into close contact with a written sacred text, as the *sotah* does. But my analysis has shown that she does not so much handle the sacred text as she is handled with it; she does not interpret it, but her body is interpreted by it. Examining how the writers of the Book of Numbers imagined that a material sacred text could nullify the material threat posed by the body of a potentially adulterous woman has revealed how they reinforced the connection between the power of Yhwh's written law and the embodied masculine authority of the priesthood at the expense of a subjugated feminine identity.

Evoking the priesthood's exclusive ability to access, read, interpret, create, copy, and handle sacred texts is one of the ways the Pentateuch legitimizes their power. But the priesthood's maintenance of their location at the top of the hierarchies of both gender and religious authority, even within a literary construction, also requires the complicity of non-priestly men. The masculinity of laymen does not reach the hegemonic priestly standard established by the Pentateuch, but nevertheless allows them to benefit from the subjugation of women.

Examining how this ideology is manifest in the *sotah* ritual reveals the impact that priestly hegemony has on both masculine and feminine identities as presented by the Book of Numbers. This hegemony is severely threatened by feminine-coded bodies that can diverge or "turn aside" (*sotah*), potentially bringing another man's child into their husbands' households, and disrupting patriarchal lines of inheritance. The material threat posed by such bodies requires a material response employing the most convincing legitimization of priestly power available. Understanding how the priest uses a sacred text to bring an unruly feminine-coded body back into the religious order during the *sotah* ritual reveals how sacred texts and gender can impact one another in the material realm: a relationship that requires greater recognition in studies of religion.

Acknowledgments

I would like to thank Marianne Schleicher for inviting me to contribute to this special issue and for her expert advice when writing and editing this article. Any shortcomings of course remain my own.

References

Bach, Alice. 1999. "Good to the Last Drop: Viewing the Sotah (Numbers 5.11–31) as the Glass Half Empty and Wondering How to View it Half Full." In *Women in the Hebrew Bible: A Reader*, edited by Alice Bach, 503–22. New York: Routledge.

Barad, Karen. 2003. "Posthumanist Performativity: Toward an Understanding of How Matter Comes to Matter." *Signs* 28(3): 801–31. https://doi.org/10.1086/345321

Brichto, Herbert Chanan. 1975. "The Case of the *Śōṭā* and a Reconsideration of Biblical 'Law.'" *Hebrew Union College Annual* 46: 55–70. https://www.jstor.org/stable/23506866

Britt, Brian. 2007. "Male Jealousy and the Suspected Sotah: Toward a Counter-Reading of Numbers 5:11–31." *The Bible and Critical Theory* 3(1): 5.1–5.19. https://doi.org/10.2104/bc070005

Camp, Claudia V. 2015. "Numbers 5:11–31: Women in Second Temple Judah and the Law of the Controlling Priest." In *Celebrate her for the Fruit of her Hands. Essays in Honor of Carol L. Meyers*, edited by S. Ackerman, C. E. Carter, and B. A. Nakhai, 111–32. University Park, PA: Pennsylvania State University Press.

Clines, David J. A. 2010. "Dancing and Shining at Sinai: Playing the Man in Exodus 32–34." In *Men and Masculinity in the Hebrew Bible and Beyond*, edited by Ovidiu Creangă, 54–63. The Bible in the Modern World 33. Sheffield: Sheffield Phoenix Press.

Connell, R. W. 2005. *Masculinities*. 2nd edition. Berkeley, CA: University of California Press.

Destro, Adriana. 2020. *The Law of Jealousy: Anthropology of the Sotah*. 2nd edition. Brown Judaic Studies 181. Atlanta, GA: Scholars Press.

Eilberg-Schwartz, Howard. 1994. *God's Phallus and Other Problems for Men and Monotheism*. Boston, MA: Beacon Press.

Ellens, Deborah L. 2009. "Numbers 5:11–31: Valuing Male Suspicion." In *God's Word for Our World*, edited by D. L. Ellens, J. H. Ellens, I. Kalimi, R. Knierim, and D. J. H. Ellens, 1: 55–82. London: Bloomsbury.

Fishbane, Michael. 1974. "Accusations of Adultery: A Study of Law and Scribal Practice in Numbers 5:11–31." *Hebrew Union College Annual* 45: 25–45.

Frevel, Christian. 2013. "The Book of Numbers: Formation, Composition, and Interpretation of a Late Part of the Torah. Some Introductory Remarks." In *Torah and the Book of Numbers*, edited by Christian Frevel, Thomas Pola, and Aaron Schart, 1–38. Tübingen: Mohr Siebeck. https://www.jstor.org/stable/23506847

———. 2018. "On Instant Scripture and Proximal Texts: Some Insights into the Sensual Materiality of Texts and their Ritual Roles in the Hebrew Bible and Beyond." In *Sensing Sacred Texts*, edited by James W. Watts, 57–79. Comparative Research on Iconic and Performative Texts. Sheffield: Equinox.

———. 2020. *Desert Transformations: Studies in the Book of Numbers*. Forschungen zum Alten Testament 137. Tübingen: Mohr Siebeck.

Frymer-Kensky, Tikva. 1984. "The Strange Case of the Suspected Sotah (Numbers V 11–31)." *Vetus Testamentum* 34(1): 11–26. https://doi.org/10.1163/156853384x00025

Fuchs, Esther. 2001. "Prophecy and the Construction of Women: Inscription and Erasure." In *Prophets and Daniel: A Feminist Companion to the Bible*, edited by Athalya Brenner, 54–69. The Feminist Companion to the Bible (2nd ser.) 8. London: Sheffield Academic Press.

Grosz, Elizabeth. 1993. "A Thousand Tiny Sexes: Feminism and Rhizomatics." *Topoi* 12: 167–79. https://doi.org/10.1007/bf00821854

Haberman, Bonna Devora. 2000. "The Suspected Adulteress: A Study of Textual Embodiment." *Prooftexts* 20(1–2): 12–42. https://doi.org/10.1353/ptx.2000.0004

Haddox, Susan E. 2016. "Masculinity Studies of the Hebrew Bible: The First Two Decades." *Currents in Biblical Research* 14(2): 176–206. https://doi.org/10.1177/1476993x15575496

Haraway, Donna. 1988. "Situated Knowledges: The Science Question in Feminism and the Privilege of Partial Perspective." *Feminist Studies* 14(3): 575–99. https://doi.org/10.2307/3178066

Hazard, Sonia. 2013. "The Material Turn in the Study of Religion." *Religion and Society: Advances in Research* 4: 58–78. https://doi.org/10.3167/arrs.2013.040104

Hooker, Alan. 2014. "'Show me Your Glory': The Kabod of Yahweh as Phallic Manifestation?" In *Biblical Masculinities Foregrounded*, edited by Ovidiu Creangă and Peter-Ben Smit, 17–34. Hebrew Bible Monographs 62. Sheffield: Sheffield Phoenix Press.

Leichty, Erle. 1970. *The Omen Series Šumma Izbu*. Texts from Cuneiform Sources. Locust Valley, NY: J. J. Augustin.

Levering, Miriam. 1989. "Scripture and its Reception: A Buddhist Case." In *Rethinking Scripture: Essays from a Comparative Perspective*, edited by Miriam Levering, 58–101. Albany, NY: State University of New York Press.

Levine, Baruch A. 1993. *Numbers 1-20*. The Anchor Bible 4A. New York: Doubleday.

Malley, Brian. 2004. *How the Bible Works: An Anthropological Study of Evangelical Biblicism*. Cognitive Science of Religion Series. Walnut Creek, CA: Altamira Press.

McKane, W. 1980. "Poison, Trial by Ordeal and the Cup of Wrath." *Vetus Testamentum* 30(4): 474–92. https://doi.org/10.1163/156853380x00434

Milgrom, Jacob. 1989. *The JPS Torah Commentary: Numbers*. Philadelphia, PA: Jewish Publication Society.

Morgan, David. 2010. "Introduction: The Matter of Belief." In *Religion and Material Culture: The Matter of Belief*, edited by David Morgan, 1–17. London: Routledge.

———. 2016. "Materiality." In *The Oxford Handbook of the Study of Religion*, edited by Michael Stausberg and Steven Engler, 271–88. Oxford: Oxford University Press.

———. 2021. *The Thing about Religion: An Introduction to the Material Study of Religions*. Chapel Hill, NC: University of North Carolina Press.

Rees, Anthony. 2013. "Toward an Ecological Reading of the Sotah Ritual." *Pacific Journal of Theology* 2(50): 28–37.

Schleicher, Marianne. 2011. "Artefactual and Hermeneutical Use of Scripture in Jewish Tradition." In *Jewish and Christian Scripture as Artifact and Canon*, edited by C. A. Evans and H. D. Zacharias, 48–65. London: Bloomsbury.

———. 2017. "Engaging All the Senses: On Multi-Sensory Stimulation in the Process of Making and Inaugurating a Torah Scroll." *Postscripts* 8(1–2): 39–56. https://doi.org/10.1558/post.32694

———. 2021. "Effects of Materiality in Israelite-Jewish Conceptions of Gender and Love: On a Necessary Synthesis of Constructionist and New Materialist Approaches." In *Entanglements and Weaving: Diffractive Approaches to Gender and Love*, edited by Deirdre C. Byrne and Marianne Schleicher, 11–33. Leiden: Brill Rodopi.

Scholz, Susanne. 2021. "Dismantling the Phallic Economy with a Hermeneutics of Reproductive Justice: A Reconsideration of the Sotah in Numbers 5:11–31." *Journal of Religious Ethics* 49(2): 270–89. https://doi.org/10.1111/jore.12351

Scurlock, J. A. 1991. "Baby-Snatching Demons, Restless Souls and the Dangers of Childbirth: Medico-Magical Means of Dealing with Some of the Perils of Motherhood in Ancient Mesopotamia." *Incognita* 2: 135–83. https://data.isiscb.org/isis/citation/CBB000029070

Sencindiver, Susan Yi. 2017. "New Materialism." In *Oxford Bibliographies: Literary and Critical Theory*, edited by Eugene O'Brien. Oxford: Oxford University Press. https://doi.org/10.1093/obo/9780190221911-0016

Smith, Jonathan Z. 1987. *To Take Place: Toward Theory in Ritual*. Chicago: University of Chicago Press.

Stiebert, Johanna. 2019. "Divinely Sanctioned Violence Against Women: Biblical Marriage and the Example of the Sotah of Numbers 5." *The Bible and Critical Theory* 15(2): 83–108.

Villareal, Erin. 2022. *Jealousy in Context: The Social Implications of Emotions in the Hebrew Bible*. Siphrut: Literature and Theology of the Hebrew Scriptures. University Park, PA: Pennsylvania State University Press.

Watts, James W. 2006. "The Three Dimensions of Scriptures." *Postscripts* 2(2–3): 135–59.

———. 2013. "Disposing of Non-Disposable Texts: Conclusions and Prospects for Further Study." In *Death of Sacred Texts*, 147–59. Farnham: Ashgate.

———. 2015. "Iconic Scriptures from Decalogue to Bible." *Studies in Book Culture* 6(2): 1–12. https://doi.org/10.7202/1032712ar

———. 2018. "Scriptures' Indexical Touch." In *Sensing Sacred Texts*, edited by James W. Watts, 173–84. Comparative Research on Iconic and Performative Texts. Sheffield: Equinox.

About the Author

Rosanne Liebermann is Associate Professor of Old Testament at Aarhus University in Denmark. She holds a PhD in Near Eastern Studies from Johns Hopkins University. Her research primarily focuses on the body and embodiment in the Hebrew Bible. This includes rhetorical uses of the body and closely related items, such as clothing, to construct ethnic identities, gender, and religious authority. Liebermann's publications include "Clothing and Body Modification in the Hebrew Bible" (2021); "Unravelling the Scarlet Thread: Women and Ritual Binding in the Hebrew Bible" (2023), and the monograph *Exile, Incorporated: The Body in the Book of Ezekiel* (Oxford University Press, 2024). (rosanne.liebermann@cas.au.dk)

3

Jewish Women and Sacred Text(ure)s: Making Women's Religious Agency in Jewish Book Culture Intelligible

Marianne Schleicher

Abstract

This chapter argues that the concept of "sacred texture" is a necessary supplement to standard understandings of sacred texts in Jewish religion to capture lay people's, especially women's, material-embodied acts as aspects of sacred text use. Such acts may include spoken or performed fragments or sequences from a sacred text that activate associations to it and thereby make the acts intelligible as representations of the sacred text, be it up close or at a distance. The chapter draws upon, but also expands perspectives on sacred texts as material objects (Malley, Watts, and Schleicher) by including theories by Halliday and Hasan, and Ricoeur on texture, by Deleuze and Guattari on processes of becoming, and by Butler on identity as something emerging from engagements in a culture's iterative acts. The theoretical underpinnings beg the question of who has access when and where to which particular iterative acts that involve sacred texts and textures? The analysis begins with the Hebrew Bible to find out when texts were conceived as sacred in the first place and when and in what way access to them became regulated. The analysis continues into early Jewish sources, rabbinic literature, and Ashkenazic Jewish sources from the Middle Ages to reflect on Jewish women's involvement with sacred texts and textures in ways that broaden our knowledge of how they made their religious identity intelligible.

Keywords: texture, gender, Hebrew Bible, rabbinic literature, Ashkenaz, embodiment, performativity

Introduction

Many people's activities in Jewish book culture have so far been unrecognizable as matters of religious agency because of too narrow understandings of "sacred text" and its ritualizations. Since Talmudic times, Torah study has been considered a commandment incumbent upon men, which is why studies of Jewish uses of sacred texts have focused mostly on literate, elite men's readings, literary reuses, and interpretations of sacred texts – uses that I have classified as hermeneutical (Schleicher 2009, 50). However, sacred texts are not just containers of words waiting to be read or interpreted. Sacred texts are also phenomena of a sacred status within the world of religions. Here, I limit myself to Durkheim's technical definition of sacred as that which is set apart, "that which the profane must not and cannot touch with impurity. ... Sacred things are things protected and isolated by prohibitions; ... rites and rules of conduct ... [that] prescribe how man must conduct himself with sacred things" (Durkheim 1995, 39–40). Because of their sacred status, sacred texts as artefacts require a special handling and/or invite performances in ritualized ways, as argued by Malley (2004), Watts (2008), and Schleicher (2009, 2017). Yet, hardly any publications have applied a material-embodied approach to sacred texts to see if women, and laymen for that matter, engage with sacred texts outside religious institutions in regulated, yet hitherto overlooked, ways that could add to our understanding of how one can "do" one's religious identity in interaction with sacred texts. This chapter intends to help close this knowledge gap.

As a historian of Israelite-Jewish religion, I shall select my empirical data from pre-modern Israelite-Jewish religion. Ideally, I would have liked to analyse both men and women's non-hermeneutical uses, but I shall prioritize sources that provide insights into women's alternative ways of engaging with sacred texts as a first step. Because I problematize conceptualizations of sacred texts, I need to begin the analysis in the Hebrew Bible to find out when texts were conceived as sacred in the first place and when and in what way access to them became regulated. I shall continue this investigation into early Jewish sources and from there to early rabbinic literature before I proceed to medieval Jewish sources from the Northern part of the Carolingian Empire, a region known in Hebrew as *Ashkenaz*. I close the analysis with the Ashkenazic sources because they offer varied and rich information about women's non-hermeneutical involvement with sacred texts in ways that, as I shall argue, can broaden our knowledge of how Jewish women made their religious identity intelligible.

Theoretically, to capture the varied material-embodied uses of sacred texts, I draw primarily on my previous characterization of artefactual uses of sacred texts (Schleicher 2009, 2017). I argue that artefactual uses position the sacred texts as symbols, onto which users can "project their needs, experiences, and hopes ... [making] sacred texts serve as a hub that establishes connections in all directions ... tying them together with collective and cultural representations due to cues in the immediate surroundings" (Schleicher 2017, 42). In this chapter, I want to expand the focus to how embodied enactments of sacred texts, such as reciting or performing even tiny parts of a sacred text, contribute to establishing someone's religious identity. James W. Watts has previously written about the intrinsic performative dimension of sacred texts. Watts addresses how scriptural words can be publicly or privately read, recited, memorized, chanted/sung in ritualized ways, or artistically displayed through calligraphy and inscriptions. With less influence from religious authorities, scriptural words or scenes can be dramatized through bodily performances or artistically illustrated as a way to attain merit (Watts 2008, 141–2, 148). Watts's eye for the semantic, performative, and iconic dimensions as intrinsic to scripture has been groundbreaking in sacred text studies. However, given my Deleuzian approach to identity as a process of becomings emerging from the interacting phenomena in whatever is entangled (Deleuze and Guattari 1987), I want to avoid conceptions of "sacred text" as a definite object, a unitary whole. Instead, I shall theorize the embodied enactments of sacred texts in a way that sheds light on uses that render the sacred texts as fragmentary, porous, composite, dynamic, and processual. I therefore suggest supplementing the notion of "sacred text" with the concept of "sacred texture." The idea of speaking of sacred texture derives from linguistics (Halliday and Hasan 1976: 1–6) and literary theory (Ricoeur 1976, 33). Here, "texture" signifies the ties within a text that in a sequential way creates cohesion between its parts. I shall argue that spoken or performed fragments of such texture suffice in a religious context to activate associations to prescribed or narrated acts in sacred texts and thereby make them recognizable as representations of the sacred text, be it up close or at a distance from the sacred text itself. I believe that such enactments or embodiments of sacred textural fragments suffice to make one's religious identity intelligible and should be considered an integral part of studies in sacred texts. Below, I therefore distinguish between hermeneutical and artefactual uses of sacred texts based on direct access to a text and on sacred textures where embodied enactments invoke textural fragments or sequences from the sacred text without requiring its presence. Sacred texts and sacred textures sometimes exist side by side in the same context, and in such situations, I shall employ "sacred text(ure)s."

Finally, to strengthen the analytical focus on uses of sacred text(ure)s in interaction with gender, I include Judith Butler's theory of performativity (Butler 1990). Butler argues that people's participation in iterative acts within a culture enable their identity to become intelligible, for example as male or female. Participation in such acts marks one's cultural loyalty and yet allows for variation and development because no iterative doing can ever be identical to previous ones. Identity is thus something processual. An analytical consequence of this cultural dynamic is always to ask who has access when and where to which particular iterative acts within a culture. In a religious context, it follows that rituals and ritual-like acts, including hermeneutical and artefactual uses and embodied enactments of sacred textures, become hubs that contribute efficiently to someone's religious and gendered identity.

Sacredness of Texts in the Hebrew Bible?

Humans and artefacts of the Israelite cult had to be sanctified in order to be in the presence of the already sacred; in this case, Yahweh (Exod 40:10–15). While Moses and the stone tablets were not sanctified in a technical sense, they were chosen or made by Yahweh in the first place (Exod 3:12; 31:18) and thus compatible with the sacred. However, in the biblical descriptions of how the tabernacle is to be inaugurated, nothing indicates that human agents had to handle objects, once they had been divinely made or sanctified, in a regulated way. This pertains to the stone tablets with the Ten Commandments that God writes with his own finger (Exod 31:18; 32:16; Deut 4:13; 9:10). The divine origin of this writing does not prevent Moses from carrying the tablets in his bare hands, nor from smashing them in anger when he sees the Israelites dancing around the golden calf (Exod 32:19; Deut 9:17). The second set of stone tablets that Moses writes on God's dictation (Exod 34:27–9) and places inside the Ark (Exod 25:16; 40:20; 1 Kgs 8:9) are not handled in any regulated way either. Once placed inside the Ark, this unhandleable text only seems to serve as a hidden testimony to the covenant.[1] It is not to be handled, seen, or read, not even by the high priest on the Day of Atonement when he enters the Holy of Holies to purify the inner sanctuary (Lev 16).

1. See Watts 2015 for more on the stone tablets as relic texts.

According to another biblical passage, Moses wrote down the Torah on a scroll and presented it to the Levitical priests (Deut 31:9). He commanded them to read it on the Feast of Tabernacles at the end of every seventh year to the entire "people – men, women, children, and the strangers in your communities – that they may hear and so learn to revere the LORD your God and to observe faithfully every word of this Teaching" (Deut 31:12).[2] Here, Moses makes the Levites responsible for disseminating God's words to all of the people, emphasizing that everyone should hear in order to learn. Hearing and learning are not restricted to a specific group. On the contrary, the correct way of life among the Israelites depends on everyone's access to hearing all the words of the Torah every seventh year. In the intervening seven years, the Torah scroll should be placed next to the Ark as a testimony, a reminder to the people of how they should live (Deut 31:26). Physical access to such a mnemotechnical aid is, however, extremely limited due to its neighbour, the Ark, inside the Holy of Holies.

To be a king required reading and writing skills. According to the Law of the King, a king should "write for himself a copy of this torah on a scroll before the Levitical priests. It shall be with him, and he shall read in it all the days of his life to study and fear all the words of this torah of Yahweh, his god, and to enact these laws" (Deut 17:18–19; my translation[3]). The passage informs us that either the Levites had an authoritative copy of the relevant parts of the Torah, from which they could read aloud, or they could recite it from memory for the king to copy. Still, no requirements are mentioned vis-à-vis the king's descent or state of purity when writing and handling the Torah copy.[4] Understanding is once again prioritized.

The special skills of the Levites and the importance of understanding are also emphasized in the Book of Nehemiah. On the people's request, "Ezra the priest brought the Teaching before the congregation, men and women and all who could listen with understanding" (Neh 8:2). At this first recorded word-based service of God in the history of religion, Ezra reads from the Torah in a public square, standing on a simple platform of wood constructed for the occasion so that everyone can hear his voice.

2. All translations of the Hebrew Bible stem from *The Jewish Study Bible* 2004, unless otherwise stated. Note that *The Jewish Study Bible* renders *torah* as "Teaching."

3. I chose my own translation here, because the Hebrew allows for the understanding that not only should he read the Torah, but he should actually write it himself.

4. Joshua also writes a copy of Moses' Torah on the stones of the altar on Mount Ebal (Josh 8:32). While Joshua was appointed by God to lead the people (Josh 1:2), nothing in Josh 8:32 indicates that the chiselling of the Torah is regulated.

Ezra reads from early morning until midday. The Levites, standing with the Israelites, then read the Torah again or perhaps translate it into Aramaic to make sure that everyone understands what has been read. Here, the people can request that the Torah be brought close to them, into a profane square. The text does not mention that the people need to prepare or even be sanctified prior to the listening. Once again, it is everyone's understanding of the content of the Torah that is emphasized and presented as a premise for the continued divine blessings. Ezra, the priest and scribe, along with the Levites, performs the very reading from the Torah scroll, probably because only male specialists like priests and scribes knew how to read.[5]

The understanding of the entire people is also central in two more or less identical narratives in 2 Kings 22 and 2 Chronicles 34 where the high priest Hilkiah finds a Torah scroll in the temple. Hilkiah passes on the scroll to Shaphan the scribe who reads it first before he takes the scroll to King Josiah and reads it to him. Here, it is surprising that only the scribe seems literate. Once the king realizes that the people of Judah were unaware of or did "not obey the words of this scroll" (2 Kgs 22:13), the king sends a delegation, including the high priest and the scribe, to ask the prophetess Huldah for advice on how to ward off God's impending wrath. In these passages, nothing indicates that the scroll passed from one person to another in a particularly regulated way. In addition, the king not only needs a scribe to read the scroll to him; he also requests a woman to interpret how to react to its content. The king consults Huldah because she is a prophetess and in this narrative, nothing prevents God from sending divine words through the mouth of a woman.

Descriptions that indicate that a text is sacred in the technical sense – as requiring users to be in a sanctified state or handling it in a regulated way – stem from some of the prophetic books where prophets transmit the words of Yahweh. In the call narrative of Isaiah, the seraphs announce the advent of something sacred with the *kedushah*: "Holy, holy, holy! The LORD of Hosts" (Isa 6:3). The problem is, as Isaiah states: "I am a man of unclean lips" (Isa 6:5). The impure state of the lips is a hindrance to transmitting the words of God. One of the seraphs knows the remedy. It takes a glowing piece of coal from the altar to touch Isaiah's lips, upon which it announces: "Your guilt shall depart and your sin be purged away" (Isa

5. Hezser 2001, 496, discussing literacy among Jews some centuries later in Roman Palestine, estimates the literacy rate to fluctuate between 3 and 15 per cent, depending on the ability of the readers to read long documents or just decipher single words or sentences.

6:7). From here, Isaiah can serve and disseminate God's words. God himself touches the face of the prophet Jeremiah with his hand before he places divine words in Jeremiah's mouth (Jer 1:9). In a similar way, God orders Ezekiel to eat a sweet-tasting scroll with words of lamentations, moaning, and woe prior to his dissemination of God's words (Ezek 2–3:3). Ingestion of divine words is addressed in Numbers 5 on the suspected adulteress. It describes words of divine origin as potentially dangerous to the consuming individual. It says, "The priest shall write these curses on a scroll and blot them out into the water of bitterness. He is to make the woman drink the water of bitterness" (Num 5:23–24; my translation).[6] Here, the water contains the ink from a curse on a scroll. The content of this scroll contains the words of God, just as it transmits the insight of God into the woman's guilt or righteousness. The narrative portrays a righteous woman as invulnerable to the bitter water and explains that her worth as a woman would be restored thanks to her bodily contact with the remains from the ink of the scroll. Yet, to the guilty woman it would be dangerous. "[H]er belly shall distend and her thigh shall sag" (Num 5:27).[7] A similar notion of a dangerous scroll reflecting God's insights into people's guilt is seen in the Book of Zechariah, where the prophet has a vision of a flying scroll that God has sent. It is "the curse which goes out over the whole land" (Zech 5:3) to punish theft and false oaths. In other words, scrolls and/or words of God in these texts require protection through special handling and behaviour similar to what was required when handling sacred artefacts in the sanctuary. Still, none of these prophetic texts indicate that ritual laws regulated the handling of scrolls.

Incipient Sacredness of Texts in Early Judaism

In early Judaism, the assumption that certain texts, especially the Torah, were of divine origin gained currency. The *Letter of Aristeas* from c. 200 BCE speaks of Jewish books, especially the Law of the Jews, that are considered of a "divine nature ... sacred and hallowed" (Aristeas vv. 30–1).[8] By the end of the first century CE, the Jewish historian Josephus mentions in *Against Apion* (*C.Ap.*) that Jews consider twenty-two books credible with regard to accounts of time from the beginning of creation until Persian dominance of the Ancient Near East. The twenty-two books were the five books of

6. The *Jewish Study Bible* omits that the curses are to be written on a scroll.
7. For more on Num 5 as a matter of priestly handling of sacred texts, see Liebermann in this book.
8. Quotations from the *Letter of Aristeas* are taken from Shutt's translation, cf. Charlesworth (ed.) 1985.

Moses, thirteen books by prophets, and four collections of hymns and advice. Josephus explains that the credibility of these books prevented people from changing their content because "it is an instinct with every Jew ... to regard them as the decrees of God, to abide by them, and, if need be, cheerfully to die for them" (*C.Ap.* 1.37–42).[9]

A novelty emerges in the second century BCE as an effect of a growing dualistic worldview; that is, the phenomenon of esoteric texts. In the Book of Daniel, God grants Daniel insights into some kind of judgement day in the near future where King Antiochus IV Epiphanes shall be punished for his persecution of the Jews and where his dominion shall be replaced by God's dominion over all peoples, administered by "one like a human being" (Dan 7:13). A divine voice tells Daniel to guard the words he has heard and "seal the book until the time of the end" (Dan 12:4) where "the knowledgeable will understand" (Dan 12:10). In this apocalypse, insights into the future are not to be shared with the majority, only the knowledgeable. Similarly in *The Book of 4 Ezra* (first century CE), Ezra, the fifth-century BCE priest and scribe, reappears as the protagonist who is to sit forty days with God, just like Moses, to transmit God's dictation to his five scribes, which results in 94 books. God instructs Ezra to make "public the twenty-four books that you write first, and let the worthy and the unworthy read them; but keep the seventy that were written last, in order to give them to the wise among your people" (*4 Ezra* 14:45–6).[10] The twenty-four exoteric books are close in number to the twenty-two books mentioned by Josephus (*C.Ap.* 1.37–42).[11] However, the seventy books enjoy an esoteric status; that is, for the select few in the future whenever that will be. In the Syriac manuscript version of *The Book of 4 Ezra*, Ezra transcends after the stay with God "to the place of those who are like him". In the Latin manuscripts, two chapters follow that describe a kind of judgement day. In other words, it is likely that the esoteric content of *The Book of 4 Ezra's* seventy books similar to Daniel's visions is associated with salvation to the world-to-come, after which they can be shared.

---

9. Quotations from *Against Apion* are taken from Thackeray's translation, cf. Josephus 1926.

10. Quotations from *The Book of 4 Ezra* are taken from B. M. Metzger's translation; cf. Charlesworth (ed.) 1983.

11. According to Sid Z. Leiman, Josephus' list of thirteen prophetic books would include Joshua, Judges+Ruth, Samuel, Kings, Isaiah, Jeremiah+Lamentations, Ezekiel, Twelve Minor Prophets, Job, Daniel, Ezra+Nehemiah, Chronicles, and Ezra. The hymns and advice would be Psalms, Proverbs, Ecclesiastes, and Song of Songs. In 4 Ezra, Ruth and Lamentations were probably counted independently, thus explaining the difference between the total number of twenty-two and twenty-four. For more, see Leiman 1989.

It goes for both Daniel and Ezra that they purify themselves/are purified prior to their visionary states where they receive insights from God. At the beginning of the Book of Daniel, it says, "Daniel resolved not to defile himself with the king's food or the wine he drank" (Dan 1:8). Here, Daniel sanctifies himself by combining Torah observance, including the dietary laws, and piety, for example through prayer and absolute faith in God in his Babylonian exile, far away from the Israelite cult. Ezra is made compatible with the divine in a more prophetic way when a trans-empirical being purifies his mouth: "a full cup was offered to me; it was full of something like water, but its color was like fire. And I took it and drank; and when I had drunk it, my heart poured forth understanding, and wisdom increased in my breast, for my spirit retained its memory" (*4 Ezra* 14:39–40). In the case of *the Book of 4 Ezra*, the purification alters his cognitive abilities to prepare him to sit with God for forty days, but also to prepare himself and others for salvation to a world-to-come through the transmitted words. What we witness in late antiquity is that, just as the entire ontology becomes dichotomized into an immanent and a transcendent world, so do sacred texts. At this stage, the distinction is set up between exoteric and esoteric books. The esoteric books require the scribes to be in some kind of purified state before they can produce the books that may serve as a means to assist readers to salvation to the transcendent world.

At this point in Jewish history, also under the influence of a dualistic worldview, sects emerge to establish cooperation toward a group's salvific goals. The reading and interpretation of sacred texts are central and esoteric activities where the interpretative techniques and results are for members only. In the *Community Rule* (1QS) from among the Dead Sea Scrolls, members were not allowed to discuss the Torah or a rule with outsiders (1QS 5:15–16).[12] Other texts and fragments from the Judaean desert mention that Torah instruction was important for all children. Accordingly, both boys and girls were taught how to read and study the Torah from

12. Geza Vermes (2004) has the translation that "No member of the Community shall follow them in matters of doctrine and justice." I consulted Dr Søren Holst who is a Danish specialist on the Dead Sea Scrolls and asked him about the exact wording in the extant manuscript, cf. http://dss.collections.imj.org.il/community. He replied that it is: "ואשר לוא ישיב איש מאנשי היחד על פיהם לכול תורה ומשפט" [*ve-asher lo yashiv ish me-anashei ha-yachad al paihem le-kol torah u-mishpat*] (1QS 5:15–16). If one takes into account that the surrounding sentences focus on how members should not interact with non-sect members, I should argue for the translation: "just as no man of the congregation should answer them concerning matters of Torah and ruling."

the age of 10 until 20.[13] Age or gender does not seem to have been an obstacle to Torah study, as long as one submitted to the ascetic way of life within the sectarian community.

Another sect, permeated by a dualistic worldview, was that of the Therapeutes. Some scholars doubt that the sect ever existed;[14] yet I include it here because at least the descriptions in *On The Contemplative Life or Suppliants* (*Cont.*) reflect what one Greek-speaking Jew, Philo, considered an ideal religious community in 41 CE. He narrates how male and female Therapeutes in the Northern part of Egypt secluded themselves for six days during the week to study. From dawn until dusk, without any food or drink, they engaged in composing their own hymns and psalms and in allegorical interpretations of "laws and oracles delivered through the mouth of prophets, and psalms and anything else which fosters and perfects knowledge and piety" (*Cont.* 25).[15] Perfect knowledge and piety depend on allegorical interpretation of what is now directly referred to as "Holy Scriptures" (*Cont.* 28, 75). In focus is "the allegory, since they think that the words of the literal text are symbols of something whose hidden nature is revealed by studying the underlying meaning" (*Cont.* 28). Sect members engage individually in allegoresis on weekdays and collectively on Sabbaths and feast days (*Cont.* 30–2, 78). When they meet for a general assembly, they gather in a "common sanctuary ..., one portion set apart for the use of men, the other for the women. For women too regularly make part of the audience with the same ardour and the same sense of their calling" (*Cont.* 32–3). Later, Philo explains:

> The feast [of Shavuot] is shared by women also, most of them aged virgins, who have kept their chastity not under compulsion, ..., but of their own free will in their ardent yearning for wisdom. Eager to have her for their life mate they have spurned the pleasures of the body and desire no mortal offspring but those immortal children which only the soul that is dear to God can bring to the birth unaided because the Father has sown in her spiritual rays enabling her to behold the verities of wisdom. (*Cont.* 68)

The Therapeutes do not distinguish between exoteric and esoteric books, but between literal and allegorical meanings of sacred texts. This dualistic conception of sacred texts mirrors its dualistic anthropology, where the body with its gender characteristics is part of the immanent, transient world. If men and women, however, engage in asceticism to cultivate the soul, the soul would evolve and eventually enable the ascetic's access

13. Cf. J. Baumgarten 1983, 125–35; 1992, 170–2; Schuller 1994, 118; Crawford 2003, 178–80.

14. Cf. Engberg-Pedersen 1999.

15. Quotations are taken from Colson's translation, cf. Philo 1954.

to the world-to-come.[16] This marks two important developments in the history of religion. First, asceticism seems to have replaced ritual purification as a preparation for being close to and for handling something sacred. Second, ascetic cultivation of the soul in these traditions makes gender irrelevant. Once an ascetic, a woman's female body is no obstacle for handling, performing, and studying sacred texts.

In the early Jewish material it is worth noticing that the concept of "sacred texts" is applied only in Greek-Jewish sources either of a diaspora context far away from the Jerusalem Temple or of the period after the Temple was burned down and the temple cult brought to an end. The sources analysed indicate that the idea of the sacred somehow moved from the Temple to texts and that iterative acts associated with the cult of Yahweh and its objects were transferred to the ritual or ritual-like handling of texts with reference to the notion that certain texts contained the words of God. Metonymically, God's words enabled the continued presence of God in exile.[17] Furthermore, as the remaining analysis will show, any relation to this divine presence in the sacred texts would have an effect on any Jew's religious identity.

Rabbinic Reflections on Sacred Texts and Access

Around 200 CE, the rabbis also speak about "sacred writings" and stress that they impart uncleanness to the hands: "כָּל כִּתְבֵי הַקֹּדֶשׁ מְטַמְּאִין אֶת הַיָּדַיִם" [*kol kitvei ha-qodesh metammein et ha-yadayim*]; that is, "all the sacred writings defile the hands" (mYad 3:5; my translation). Following this statement in the Mishnah, tractate Yadayim (mYad), the rabbis discuss whether the Song of Songs and Ecclesiastes defile the hands too. Many scholars have interpreted the statement to reflect Jewish concerns about canonization without really being able to explain the logic of how something sacred can defile the hands. Here, I shall disregard canonization and concentrate instead on how this rabbinic discussion sheds light on what exactly would set certain texts apart as sacred. Michael J. Broyde has suggested that a common denominator for the Song of Songs and Ecclesiastes, as well as Esther in a later rabbinic discussion (bMeg 7a), is that none of them contains the Tetragrammaton.[18] Since early Judaism, use of the Tetragrammaton was regulated. Only utterances of God's name in the Temple were allowed, and they required prior purification. Blasphemous

16. For more on Philo's complex approach to gender, see Harrison 1994, 1995.

17. For more on the Torah as a metonymy/representation of God, see Stern 1987, 619; Holdrege 1989, 227.

18. Broyde 1995, 66.

or untimely utterances could elicit the death penalty.[19] The Dead Sea Scrolls include examples where the Tetragrammaton is rendered in paleo-Hebrew script or sometimes with four dots or dashes. In other words, early Judaism already treated the Tetragrammaton as something sacred both in oral and written form. When Abba Shaul in the Mishnah (Sanhedrin 10:1) adds that one who pronounces the ineffable name of God will lose his or her share in the world-to-come, he is continuing an old tradition where the presence of God's name required special handling. According to Broyde, it is the Tetragrammaton that makes certain books sacred.

Understanding this still does not explain why something sacred can defile the hands. In the ritual context of the Tabernacle or the Temple, something profane could de-sanctify, that is, defile something sacred; but not the other way around. As if the rabbis knew that this idea needed explanation, the rabbis of mYad 3:5 compare the situation with Numbers 10:35 "When the Ark was set out." By this, they draw a parallel between the numinosity of the Ark and the sacred writings, both connoting God's presence. Just as the Ark was considered numinous (it killed Uzzah in 2 Sam 6), so only Jews in a state of ritual purity should handle a sacred scroll in the production process or in use.[20] The same Mishnaic tractate emphasizes that for a sacred text to defile the hands it must be written in the original language, with Assyrian letters, on parchment and with ink (mYad 4:5). For further explanation, the rabbis compare the effect of sacred writings with the sentimental value of bones from either a high priest or one's parents. I, however, would like to include an extra clarifying comparison. According to another Mishnaic tractate, the Pascal lamb defiles the hands after midnight because its status would turn into that of a rejected sacrifice (mPes 10:9). Common to both the Pascal lamb, the bones of beloved people, and sacred texts is that they all require a regulated handling: they should be handled in special ways within the boundaries of sacred time and place.

In the earliest rabbinic writings, there does not seem to be any limitations on who would have access to sacred texts within the boundaries of sacred time and place as long as they were Jewish. Archaeological material such as synagogue inscriptions testify to women's engagement in synagogue life, even as synagogue leaders.[21] This implies that women have participated in one way or another when the Torah was read and

19. Josephus 1965, 2.12,4; Philo 1935, 2.114.

20. For more on the concept of "defiling the hands," see Broyde 1995; S. Friedman 2009; Lim 2010, 502–3.

21. See Brooten 1982.

discussed. Tosefta from c. 300 CE and of Palestinian origin testifies to women being allowed to study both written and oral Torah even in states of *niddah*: "*Zabim* and *zabot*,[22] and menstruating women, and women after childbirth are permitted to read [aloud] from the Torah, the Prophets and the Writings, and to study Mishnah, midrash, halakhot and aggadot, but those who have had a seminal discharge are forbidden" (tBer 2:12; Neusner's brackets). In other words, unintentional acquisition of ritual impurity would not disqualify one from reading the Torah or the Mishnah aloud. Only men who had had seminal emission, probably on the assumption of a deliberate decision to have intercourse prior to study, would be forbidden to read the Torah.

A few decades later, men and women's equal access to Torah study becomes a matter of dispute in a passage from the Palestinian Talmud on how to guard one's daughters from sexual sin. Ben-Azzai argues that a father "is obligated to teach his daughter Torah" as a preventive means, whereas R. Eliezer holds the position that came to prevail in the later Babylonian tradition that "Anyone who teaches his daughter Torah, teaches her lasciviousness" (jSotah 3:4).[23]

Not worried about women's chastity, the Babylonian R. El'azar ben Azariah introduced not a division of labour, but a division of service to God: "Since the men come to study and the women to hear, for what do the children come? Indeed to provide reward for those that carry them" (bHag 3a).[24] Mothers serve God and thereby earn merit if they enable the Torah study of their husbands and male children. At this point, it seems that some rabbis regulate women away from direct and toward indirect access to sacred texts – which is, nevertheless, just as meritorious with regard to salvation as men's direct access. Direct Torah study would not bring them any salvific merit, and the underlying logic that explains this regulation seems to be that Torah study is in part a time-bound positive[25] commandment, from which women are exempt (cf. bKid 29a–34b).

22. *Zabim* designates men who suffer from genital flux and *zabot* designates women who experience irregular bleedings, cf. Lev 15. References to the Tosefta consist of a lower case t followed by the tractate abbreviation.

23. References to the Jerusalem Talmud consist of a lower case j followed by the tractate abbreviation.

24. Quotations are taken from *The Babylonian Talmud*, edited by William Davidson, available at sefaria.org. References consist of a lower case b followed by the tractate abbreviation.

25. In rabbinic Judaism a distinction is made between positive and negative commandments. This distinction is not normative, but designates prescriptions (dos) and proscriptions (don'ts) respectively.

The fact that women's Torah study is not meritorious does not necessarily mean that women are not allowed to study the Torah. The Babylonian Talmud renders several discussions on whether women's exemption means prohibition or not (bHag 16b; bRH 33a; bEruv 96a–b). Here, the majority of Talmudic rabbis argue that women may perform the *mitzvot* from which they are exempt.[26] With reference to the *Shema* on who should don the *tefillin*, the Babylonian R. Hamnuna presents a stricter view when he argues that women's exemption from binding the *tefillin* would disqualify her from writing a valid Torah scroll. "A Torah scroll, phylacteries, or *mezuzot* that were written by a heretic or an informer, a gentile or a slave, a woman or a minor, or a Samaritan or a Jewish apostate, are unfit" (bGit 45b).[27]

Women, like men, should hear the scroll of Esther. In fact, women are obligated to do so because the obligation can be carried out anytime during the day of Purim (mMeg 2:5). This positive commandment is not time-bound, which is why "All are valid to read the Scroll [of Esther]" (mMeg 2:4).[28] Once a woman is obligated, she not only merits from performing the commandment, she can also assist another, who is obligated to perform it, which means that she can read to others, for example, someone who is illiterate. In fact, she can even write an Esther scroll. "[If] one was writing it, explaining it, or correcting it, if he paid attention [that in doing so, he would carry out his obligation to hear the Scroll], he has fulfilled his obligation" (mMeg 2:2; Neusner's brackets). Here, any Jew, man or woman would enhance his or her religious identity by performing the commandment to read, hear, or write the scroll of Esther. In modern times, female scribes have legitimized their scribal activity as a religiously meritorious act of *imitatio* with reference to how the Book of Esther mentions that Esther wrote (Esther 9:29).[29] In late antiquity, however, and following Broyde (see above), it seems that it was the absence of the Tetragrammaton that enabled the almost all-inclusive access to the Esther scroll, which again

26. See bPes 43b; bBer 20b; bShab 44a.

27. In the eighth-century *Masekhet Soferim* (1:14), a Palestinian addendum to the Babylonian Talmud, it is not the donning of *tefillin*, but the permissibility to read from the Torah that defines who may write a Torah scroll. Accordingly, women are not mentioned as those whose writing would confer invalidity to a Torah scroll. For more, see J. T. Friedman 2007.

28. Mishnah quotations, if not translated by me, are taken from *The Mishnah*, edited by Neusner 1988. References to the Mishnah consist of a lower case m followed by the tractate abbreviation.

29. For more on modern women's scribal activity with regard to the scroll of Esther, see Homrighausen in this book.

indicates that it was not considered sacred in the technical sense of requiring a special handling within a bounded time and place. One could object that the presence of the Tetragrammaton was not important to matters of access, given the fact that some newlywed couples sometimes received copies of the Psalms, the Book of Job, and of Proverbs as wedding gifts to keep and use in their private homes (bGit 35a). These books were not part of the Torah, but they all contained the Tetragrammaton and belonged to the list of books that would defile the hands. It is, however, likely that such books for private use were written in the codex format, and not on a scroll associated with liturgical use.[30] It therefore seems that in principle women and men had equal access to all books with a potential to be sacred. Yet only the liturgically fit scrolls used for ritually regulated readings and study practices could become technically sacred. Not the textual content, but hermeneutical and artefactual uses that were regulated by positive, time-bound commandments would make these texts sacred. This processual nature of the sacredness of texts is necessary for understanding that women could study, read, and handle sacred texts, but not inside time-bound liturgical space because their performance could not assist obligated others in fulfilling their commandments due to women's exemption.

While women were exempt from the positive, time-bound commandments (bKid 29a–34b) women could "do" their religious identity by performing all other commandments of the Torah, especially those that ensured a Jewish praxis in the home. It is exactly at this point that I need to expand the notion of sacred text to sacred texture in order to capture how the embodied performance of various commandments is an indirect way of accessing and handling texts in a way that activate their sacredness, which again is so important for infusing one's religious identity. In defining sacred textures as embodied enactments of fragmentary, sequential parts from sacred texts, I would argue that sacred textures are present as a structure in the regulated acts of women's preparation of food according to *kashrut*, that is, the Jewish dietary laws. Proper preparation pertained not only to fragmentary information from the Torah on what qualifies as permitted and forbidden foods with regard to kind, age, origin, and time, but also to a texture in women's activities that reflect Torah prescriptions of the correct sequential order for slaughtering, rinsing, salting, and cooking as well as the handling of utensils.[31] Similarly, a Jewish woman

30. See Liberman 1962, appendix III, 205; Resnick 1992, 10–11.

31. Interpretations of the biblical dietary laws, cf. Lev 11, Exod 23:19 (34:26 and Deut 14:21), and Deut 12:23, are scattered all over the rabbinic corpus, especially in the tractates Taharot, Kelim, Chullin, Beitzah, and Makhshirim.

would "do" her Jewishness by conforming to the laws of *niddah*, that is, of enacting a texture of sequences where she separates herself physically from her husband during menstruation and marks the end of separation with immersion into a ritual bath, upon which she reunites with him.[32] A woman could earn respect through profane activities when she "grinds, and bakes, and washes clothes, cooks, and nurses her child, makes the bed, and processes wool" (bKet 59b). However, when she enacted fragments and sequences from the Torah on *kashrut* and *niddah* in a regulated way, she would invoke a sacred texture, which is how she could make her religious identity as Jewish intelligible and earn salvific merit.

A cluster of legends about Beruriah, the daughter of the second-century R. Hanina ben Tradyon, portrays a woman's indirect access to and handling of the Torah. Passages from the Tosefta present her as a legal expert in matters pertaining to the household. In a discussion on how to make a clay oven pure after it has become impure, a line of rabbis consults the son of R. Hananya ben Tradyon who argues that the oven has to be moved, whereas his sister, Beruriah, argues that all its parts must be disassembled. R. Yehuda ben Babba concludes that R. Hananya ben Tradyon's "daughter said better than his son" (tKBQ 4:17). Also, Beruriah knows to make a door bolt pure by removing it from one door and hanging it on another (tKBM 1:6). The Tosefta tractates Kelim Baba Qamma and Kelim Baba Metzia deal with the purity of clay and metal utensils. The mentioned utensils are often applied when cooking, which is why it is not surprising that a woman, often responsible for cooking, knows better than a man, as seen in this case where both specialists consulted are children of a renowned Jewish Torah scholar. Not only did Beruriah learn from her father, or at least her parents, according to some, she also learned from her later husband R. Meir's Torah-lessons (Leviticus R. 9:9).[33] A Talmudic passage praises Beruriah by name for having learned 300 religious laws in one day from 300 different rabbis (bPes 62b). In both passages, she seemingly learned Torah through the sense of hearing. Nothing indicates though that these passages pertained only to housekeeping. In fact, Beruriah's knowledge of the Psalms is so precise that she can admonish her husband, R. Meir, for wanting two hooligans to die as a matter of him interpreting Ps 104:36 too harshly with regard to the expression "the wicked" as wicked people. Beruriah corrects him and points to a logic in

32. The rabbinic corpus has dedicated a separate tractate to these laws, cf. tractate Niddah that builds upon Lev 15.

33. For a thorough analysis of the Beruriah narratives and women's access to Torah study, see Boyarin 1993, ch. 6.

the psalm that necessitates "the wicked" to mean "the wicked deeds". By preventing her husband from cursing and causing the hooligans to die, the legend recounts how R. Meir changed his mind, prayed for them, and the hooligans repented and became good Jews thanks to Beruriah's intervention (bBer 10a). Whether or not Beruriah had access to a material copy of the Psalms is not important. We know already that the Psalms were given to newlywed couples, most likely in a codex format, which enabled both men and women outside sacred time and place to study the content. The point here is that Beruriah facilitated some men's return to study the Torah. That Beruriah's knowledge of the Psalms is meritorious not because of her own studies, but because it facilitates men's correct Torah study becomes evident in this passage:

> Berurya came across a certain student who was whispering his studies. She kicked him and said to him: "Isn't it written as follows: 'Ordered in all things and secure' (2 Sam 23:5), which indicates that if the Torah is ordered in your 248 limbs, i.e., if you exert your entire body in studying it, it will be secure, and if not, it will not be secure" (bEruv 53b–54a).

Beruriah's admonishing of the student who hides his engagement in Torah study by whispering it activates associations to Beruriah's father, R. Hanina ben Tradyon, who insisted on public Torah study despite Roman prohibitions. As a result, the Romans forced him to be wrapped in a Torah scroll and burned to death as a martyr (bAZ 17b–18a). Beruriah's insistence on audible Torah studies does not only connote the reason for her father's martyr death, it also teaches men to "do" their male religious identity by proudly performing their Torah studies. No matter how tempting it would be to look at Beruriah as the exception to the rule of men's merit-giving Torah studies, Beruriah serves more or less the function of a rabbinic muse, because the narratives emphasize that her merit lies in facilitating and guarding men's Torah studies.

Women's Access to Sacred Texts and Textures in Medieval Ashkenaz

In the final part of this analysis, focus shall be directed at the entanglement of gender and sacred text(ure)s among *hasidei ashkenaz*; that is, the pious Jews of the German-speaking Northern areas of the Carolingian Empire, including also Northern France and Northern Italy from the ninth to the fourteenth centuries. Judaism in this context, where Jews enjoyed relative self-government and success in business, stands out with regard to biblical exegesis, halakhic innovations, and a pious worldview that spread from elite to lay Jews. The source situation is good compared to antiquity because mystical treatises, ethical guides, poetic texts, and manuals, all of a rather prescriptive or idealizing kind, are supplemented by the so-called responsa literature where specialist rabbis and Talmudic scholars reply to the inquiries of local rabbis or lay Jews with regard to disputes, problems, and questions from everyday life.

Ashkenazic rulings in matters of Jewish law had a tendency to prefer the more lenient Talmudic traditions. Women were not commanded to, but could study the Torah, even when they were in a state of *niddah* (thus following tBer 2:12).[34] The exegetical and legal expert Rabbi Solomon ben Isaac (1040–1105), known by his acronym Rashi, stated that women, while not obligated, could also blow the shofar, don *tefillin* and *tzitzit*, and act as *mohalot* (circumcisers). We know that Rashi taught his own three daughters both written and oral Torah. His youngest daughter, Rachel, was if not the producer, then co-producer of oral Torah, in that she wrote a responsum for her father when he himself was disabled by sickness. Rashi's grandson, R. Jacob ben Meir (1100–71), known as Rabbenu Tam (our straightforward teacher), mentions that women could be called to make an *aliyah* (a liturgical reading from the Torah) as long as they said the accompanying blessing.[35] In other words, some women with sufficient knowledge of Hebrew and of practices related to Torah readings, for example from Torah studies, could contribute to liturgical readings in front of the local community in cases where men could not muster a full *minyan* of ten. Rabbenu Tam even states that women's performance of a commandment, from which they are exempt, will add to their piety, if they recite the accompanying blessing,[36] which I shall argue turns women's Torah study and reading into a matter of merit.

That added piety is a matter of merit requires a brief introduction to the pious worldview that spread from elite to lay Jews in Ashkenaz. From mystical treatises as well as the ethical guide to lay Jews, known as *Sefer Hasidim*

34. Grossman 2004: 178–9.

35. We know that Rashi's granddaughter Hannah wrote a responsum in which she narrates how her mother Joheved had formulated the following blessing over the Sabbath light, when kindling it: "Blessed are You, Adonai our God, King of the World, Who sanctifies us with His mitzvot and commands us to kindle the Shabbat light." This wording is normative for practising Jewish women even today, see Anton 2005, 48–50; E. Baumgarten 2004, 65, 88–9. Hannah's responsum served other women of the Ashkenazic community, and many sources inform us that erudite women functioned as prayer leaders of other Jewish women, instructing them in what they considered the right practices. For more, see Taitz 1991; E. Baumgarten 2016.

36. The logic is that women are included in "the house of Jacob," and it was not only the "sons of Jacob" who received the commandments, but all of Israel. Accordingly, they do not produce a lie when they thank God for being obligated; see Jeselsohn 1999, 6.

(c. 200; abbreviated SH),[37] meaning "the Book of the Pious," God was conceived as incorporeal and beyond imagination. At the same time, however, God would be present everywhere and see everything, inviting strong feelings of guilt in Jews about what commandments one might have violated deliberately or unknowingly.[38] For the mystically inclined male elite, exegetical and ritual procedures could help reveal God's invisible will, but for lay Jews of both genders the proper attitude would be humility (SH §§16, 53) and atonement for past, present, and future sins. Means to atone for sins could be prayer (SH §18) or pious deeds (SH §696). To prevent future trespasses and to earn access to the world-to-come, one should live an ascetic life; that is, train oneself to live according to the Torah, or as I would call it, bodily enact sacred textures, because God would be watching. Messianic hope of an end to exile depended not only on the emergence of an extremely righteous person, but for every Jew's engagement. Accordingly, inability to study the Torah was no hindrance to work for salvation if instead one followed the advice from others on how to enact sacred textures and engage in pious deeds, charity, and neighbourly love (SH §1004). Members within the Jewish community would be responsible for each other's fate. Members should share knowledge about fragments and sequences from the Torah important for one's intelligibility as religious, and warn and chastise each other for any transgression to help avoid heavenly punishment (SH §§153, 966). Men and women's profane activities including business could become pietistic practices if conducted in just and honest ways (SH §§395, 1062). In other words, when Rabbenu Tam stated that a woman's *aliyah* accompanied by the proper blessing would add to her piety, and when lay Jews' pious enactments of sacred textures in the profane sphere would earn them salvific merit, then Rabbenu Tam reintroduces that a woman can merit from Torah study – that is, a hermeneutical use of a sacred text.

Beyond Torah readings among elite women, other elite women were also involved in Torah production. From Eleazar of Worms' (1176–1238) poetic eulogy for his wife Dolce, murdered by burglars in 1196, we learn that he admired her, among other things, for her involvement in producing sacred texts. Eleazar uses Proverbs 31:10–31 on the woman of valour as a strong intertext to explain the virtues of his wife, why he considered

37. References to *Sefer Hasidim* are made to the paragraphs of the Bologna -manuscript, available online at sefaria.org. Avraham Yaakov Finkel (1997) has translated most parts of *Sefer Hasidim*, but he has organized the content according to subject matter with new paragraph numbers. There is, however, a list, beginning on page 381 that can be used for identifying Finkel's paragraphs with those of the Bologna manuscript.

38. See e.g. the excerpt from *Sodei Razayya* by Eleazar ben Yehudah of Worms (c. 1165–1230), made available in English by Jacobs 1976, 62–70.

her pious (v. 18),[39] and why she deserves salvation to eternal life (v. 22). In the eulogy, Dolce's direct or indirect involvement in the production of sacred texts informs her piety. Eleazar mentions that she "spun threads for phylacteries, and [prepared] sinews [to bind together] scrolls and books; ... stitched together some forty Torah scrolls."[40] The eulogy also informs us that Eleazar and Dolce had his students living with them and that they ran a home-based *yeshivah* (academy) together, which included a shared effort in producing religious books and valid Torah scrolls for liturgical readings. Her investments in the *yeshivah* also included cooking for her husband's students (v. 7), mending their garments (v. 10), preparing candlewicks for the study rooms (v. 12), and "purchas[ing] milk for the students and hir[ing] teachers from her exertions" (v. 19) to enable Eleazar and his students to study the Torah. One can rightfully intervene here that Dolce is "only" facilitating men's Torah study, but my point is that her artefactual production of sacred texts, among other things, was just as meritorious according to an Ashkenazic worldview as men's hermeneutical Torah study and thus represents one kind of women's religious agency that should not be overlooked.

Once a Torah scroll was produced and inaugurated, it required a mantle to guard it and mark its sacred status when stored. *Sefer Hasidim* presents women's embroidering of Torah mantles with Torah verses as pious activities. I consider the embroidering a matter of co-producing a sacred text as an artefact. Yet the treatise stresses that women must refrain from embroidering the Tetragrammaton (SH 933), which probably would equal writing a scroll containing the Tetragrammaton, which according to one Talmudic tradition (R. Hamnuna, bGit 45b), women could not do. Here, it is the fragmentary use that makes the sacred text porous enough to enable women's access to it as texture.

In general, contributing to Ashkenazic book culture was considered a pious doing. According to the analysis above of rabbinic specifications, nothing would prohibit a woman from writing religious books in the codex format or sacred texts without the Tetragrammaton in the scroll format. Skills in book production were primarily transmitted within a family unit. Some sources inform us of women who learned the craft of scribes from

39. In the vocalized and more corrupt Heb. MS Michael 448 of the Bodleian Library, verse 1, Dolce is mentioned by name and described as pious, whereas Heb. MS Opp. 757, also of the Bodleian, only introduces whom Eleazar is eulogizing in the course of the text through a pun on the meaning of her Italian name Dolce by using the Hebrew equivalent *ne'imah* (pleasant) to describe her; cf. Marcus 1986, 44 nn. 21–2.

40. Quoted from Baskin 2001, 435.

their fathers to contribute to the family's scribal business. Pola from Rome was born into a family of scribes. She copied a codex commentary to the Prophets in 1288, a halakhic volume by R. Isaiah Di Trani in 1293, and a prayer book for her son in 1306. In the colophons of the three books, she inserts hopeful formulations that copying these works will contribute to the coming of the Messiah, an end to "the great darkness in which we find ourselves and which arose in our time," and to her son's excellence "in Torah, wisdom and fear of the Lord, with male sons who engage in the study of the Torah and observe the commandments of Israel. May he merit to study and teach, to observe, to practice and to keep."[41] Pola from Rome thus associates her scribal efforts with pious hopes of salvation from this world. A similar salvific understanding of the scribal activity is seen in Hannah from Cologne who copied *Sefer Mitzvot Katan* in 1386, hoping that her copied codex would contribute to God bringing "forth His people to freedom and sav[ing] them from trouble and distress."[42] Pola and Hannah thus understood themselves as religiously agentive, contributing to a salvific endeavour through religious book production that enabled men's Torah study.

From various responsa, one can learn that books were very expensive. One Pentateuch would be as costly as one vineyard. The costliness of sacred texts therefore led R. Gershom of Mainz (c. 960–1040) to emphasize that "it is a truly meritorious deed to lend books to one's neighbours for study purposes,"[43] instead of renting them out as a way to make money. This is repeated in *Sefer Hasidim* which explains how the sustainment of the world with Torah study depends among other things on donations and lending of religious books (SH §§404, 869, 871, 877, 927, 967, 1035, 1067). Women were considered religiously agentive in this effort. *Sefer Hasidim* mentions an incident where a man gave some money to his wife for her to buy a coat, but the woman replied, "Instead of buying a coat, allow me to buy a *sefer*, which I will lend to Torah scholars so that they may study it" (SH §874; Finkel's italics). The treatise goes on to emphasize the woman's praiseworthiness because she facilitated the access to books among Torah scholars. It interprets her later birthing of a boy of great learning as a heavenly reward. Similarly, *Sefer Hasidim* praises women for encouraging their husbands to buy religious books (SH §873).

In continuation of Talmudic ideals, women were seen to earn merit through embodied enactments of sacred textures, invoking commandments from the Torah to which they were obligated, especially the laws

41. Quoted from Riegler and Baskin 2008, 13–14.

42. Quoted from Riegler and Baskin 2008, 14.

43. Quoted from Agus 1965, 357. See also Agus 1965, 237, 395.

of *niddah* and *kashrut*. However, within the domain of childbirth that was highly feminized, Ashkenazic sources reveal that midwives were expected to enact sacred textures that invoked fragments and sequences from the prophetic and narrative parts of the Hebrew Bible. In a manual on midwifery written by the circumcisers Jacob and Gershom haGozer of Worms in the thirteenth century, the authors expect a midwife to engage in acts of *imitatio dei* and attend to the new-born child as God did in Ezekiel 16:3-6 (*Midwifery*, ll. 5–27).[44] While other women could help a birth-giving woman by holding her arms, the midwife should invoke sacred texture by reciting Genesis 3:16, thus instructing the birth-giving woman "to endure her lot" (*Midwifery*, l. 35). As a matter of hermeneutical use of sacred texts, midwives assisting at childbirth were allowed to suspend commandments pertaining to the Sabbath based on the principle of life, known as *pikuah nefesh* if the lives of mother and child were at danger (*Midwifery*, ll. 41, 49). The principle of life rests on a Talmudic interpretation (bYoma 85b) of Leviticus 18:5 that says that all commandments can be abrogated if life is endangered, because Yahweh gave the commandments to the Israelites to live by them. Here, the midwives are expected to function as rabbinic experts and estimate whether or not the birthing situation overrides the commandments, upon which they would otherwise be obligated.

The final example of how men and women, elite and lay, enacted sacred textures pertains to acts during the first crusade (1096–9). In Solomon bar Simson's crusade chronicle (SbS Chron)[45] from the twelfth century, he narrates that a Jewish woman was the first of all Ashkenazic Jews to sanctify God's name by choosing death rather than letting the crusade-inspired mobs baptize her (SbS Chron, 22). He portrays how a Mistress Rachel "spread her sleeves to receive the blood [of her slaughtered son], according to the practice in the ancient Temple sacrificial rite" (SbS Chron, 35). The chronicler interprets her bodily movements as a bodily enactment of a sequence that an officiating priest in ancient Israel would perform according to Exodus 29:16–18 and Leviticus 17:11, when they would gather blood for sprinkling and thus sanctification or atonement purposes. Women who were about to slaughter their children to prevent them from being forcefully converted to Christianity would piously enact sacred textures by reciting sequences from either the *Shema* (often beginning with Deut 6:4) or by reciting the *kiddush* for ritual slaughter before killing themselves (SbS Chron, 23, 33).

---

44. Quotations from the *Manual on Midwifery* are taken from E. Baumgarten 2019.

45. All quotations from the three crusade chronicles are taken from *The Jews and the Crusaders*, translated by Shlomo Eidelberg.

The willingness of these women to sacrifice their own children as an act of *Kiddush haShem* (sanctification of God's name) was compared with the faith of Abraham in R. Eliezer bar Nathan's crusade chronicle (EbN), also from the twelfth century. He includes four poems, eulogizing the faith of the martyred Jews in the four towns of Worms, Mainz, Cologne, and Speyer. He describes how the women's slaughtering of their children re-enacted parts of the *'Akedah* of Moriah. Yet, while God's angel stopped Abraham at Mount Moriah (Gen 22:11–12), God did not intervene in the towns of the Cologne bishopric to spare the women from killing their children. "Innocent souls withdrew to eternal life" (EbN Chron, 92). Here, R. Eliezer deems that these women, enacting sacred texture while slaughtering their children, would merit salvation to the world-to-come. Eternal life is also a motivating factor when Judah, son of Abraham, in the town of Eller explains to his daughter-in-law that she should not fear a martyr's death because "in a moment you will earn your eternal life and you will enter the precincts of the righteous and the pious" (SbS Chron, 54).

Several times, the crusade chroniclers describe an abrogation of otherwise dividing lines such as gender, age, and profession: "old and young, maidens and children, menservants and maids" (SbS Chron, 31) were all equal, all one group, while under attack.[46] Relative gender equality in martyrdom is a literary trait also known from the Books of the Maccabees, but the Ashkenazic Jews did not look to the Jews under the Maccabean Revolt (167–164 BCE) and the apocryphal literature to find inspiration for their martyrdom during the crusades. Rather, the author of the chronicle known as the Mainz Anonymous points to how the Ashkenazic martyrs, elite or lay, male or female, bodily enacted behaviours ascribed to models such as R. Akiva, the three friends of the prophet Daniel (SbS Chron, 43), or the woman of valour in Proverbs 31, which would earn them salvific merit (Mainz Anon, 105).

Conclusion

The sacredness of texts in terms of regulated use emerged as a phenomenon only in late antiquity. For most of the first millennium BCE, buildings, artefacts, and agents of the cult were set aside as sacred, but the few books that the Hebrew Bible mentions, including the scroll of Torah, do not seem to have been handled as sacred despite their presumed divine origin. Only prophetic texts indicated a requirement to be ritually pure before pronouncing the words of God.

46. See also SbS Chron, 35–7, 42.

From the second century BCE, when a dualistic worldview began to permeate large parts of Jewish religiosity, sacred texts could be considered exoteric or esoteric and with both literal and allegorical layers of meaning. Also from the second century BCE onward, Greek Jewish writings originating in the diaspora apply the term "sacred text." They reflect that purification measures were required to produce sacred texts or access their esoteric and/or allegorical content. Users or producers of sacred texts needed to be purified either by sanctification procedures associated with the sanctuary or by performing the commandments, and/or living ascetic lives. Access upon purification was seminal for preparing for salvation to the world-to-come.

Early rabbinic literature contains concrete specifications for what is required to consider a text sacred and liturgically fit. The presence of the Tetragrammaton, the scroll format (not the codex), and a ritualized handling inside sacred time and place constitute its sacredness. Since liturgical Torah readings are time-bound, women are exempt, but not barred from reading and studying the Torah within sacred time and place. Yet, because women are not commanded to study the Torah, women do not merit from Torah readings and study, but merit from facilitating men's Torah study and performing all the non-time-bound commandments from the written and oral Torah, upon which they are obligated. This leads to men and women dividing their service to God based on different kinds of affiliation with sacred texts. Women's religious activities seem to reflect mediated access to sacred texts either through men or through embodied enactments of sacred textures invoking fragments or sequences from sacred texts. Men and women's service to God are equally meritorious with regard to salvation to the world-to-come.

Ashkenazic Judaism stands in the tradition of rabbinic Judaism with a tendency to prioritize the more lenient Palestinian traditions. Rashi taught his daughters both written and oral Torah, and his grandson, Rabbenu Tam, even stated that women's liturgical Torah reading, if she said the accompanying blessing, would add to her piety, which I interpret as a matter of salvific merit given the overall pietistic worldview. Furthermore, when pietism considers every profane act meritorious, if performed piously, then religious agency extends dramatically beyond the male elite to every person. Ashkenazic sources also allow us to see how women's contributions to Jewish book culture were considered meritorious, no matter whether the contribution rested on the concrete stitching together of sheets for a scroll, the copying of religious literature in the codex format, or the distribution of scrolls and books to facilitate men's Torah and Talmud study. Women's embodied enactments of sacred textures in their performance of the commandments incumbent upon them, especially of *kashrut* and *niddah*, dominated, but were extended to other activities. In the praxis of midwifery, midwives enacted sacred textures invoking God's compassion with infants and the second creation account, just as they engaged in hermeneutical use of scripture when acting as rabbinic experts exerting judgement on when to suspend the commandments. During the first and second crusades, elite and lay, men and women, engaged in embodied enactments of sacred textures, invoking exemplary characters known from the Hebrew Bible or the early rabbinic martyr accounts, when they sanctified God's name by sacrificing themselves and/or their beloved.

In light of these findings, I conclude that in ascetic and/or pietistic contexts, some elite women did engage in hermeneutical uses of sacred texts such as Torah study and reading. Elite women also engaged in the production of sacred texts and religious books, which I consider an aspect of artefactual use. Yet most women became religiously intelligible if they facilitated men's study of the Torah by engaging in profane activities that secured a Jewish household and/or enacted sacred texture in ways that would invoke the commandments incumbent upon women, or sequences from the lives of biblical or Talmudic heroes. One crucial finding is that women's embodied enactments of sacred textures were just as meritorious as elite men's hermeneutical and artefactual uses of sacred texts. Scholarship cannot overlook women's religious agency if it is to claim representability. Thus, not only must sacred text studies include studies of texts that take their content, materiality, and uses into account, but it must also direct itself to sacred textures to capture how lay people, especially women, have made themselves religiously intelligible through embodied enactments of sacred textures, invoking fragments and sequences from sacred texts.

Acknowledgments

At an early stage of preparing this chapter, Dr Søren Holst helped me decipher the handwriting in a Dead Sea Scroll manuscript, cf. n. 12, for which I should like to extent my warm thanks. Close to finishing, I received valuable comments and suggestions from my friend and mentor, Professor Emerita Kirsten Nielsen, my doctoral student Emma Cecilie Sørlie Jørgensen, and Chief Editor of *Postscripts* Bradford A. Anderson. I owe all three my deep gratitude for engaging with me in this chapter and topic. Any shortcomings remain of course my own.

References

Primary Sources

4 Ezra, The Book of, translated by B. M. Metzger. In *The Old Testament Pseudepigrapha: Apocalyptic Literature and Testaments*, vol. 1, edited by James H. Charlesworth. New York: Doubleday, 1983.

Aristeas, Letter of, translated by R. J. H. Shutt. In *The Old Testament Pseudepigrapha: Apocalyptic Literature and Testaments*, vol. 2, edited by James H. Charlesworth. New York: Doubleday, 1985.

Josephus, *The Life; Against Apion*, translated by H. St. J. Thackeray. Loeb Classical Library. Cambridge, MA: Harvard University Press, 1926.

Josephus, *Jewish Antiquities*, translated by Louis H. Feldman. Cambridge, MA: Harvard University Press, 1965.

Philo, *On the Contemplative Life or Suppliants*. Loeb Classical Library: Philo IX, LCL 363, edited by Jeffrey Henderson; translated by F. H. Colson. Cambridge, MA: Harvard University Pres, 1954.

Philo, *On Abraham. On Joseph. On Moses*, translated by F. H. Colson. Cambridge, MA: Harvard University Press, 1935.

The Babylonian Talmud, edited by William Davidson, available at sefaria.org.

The Community Rule (1QS) (Hebrew), The Digital Dead Sea Scrolls, available at http://dss.collections.imj.org.il/community (Accessed 20 March 2023).

The Complete Dead Sea Scrolls in English, translated by Geza Vermes. London: Penguin Books, 2004.

The Jerusalem Talmud, translated and commentary by Heinrich W. Guggenheimer. Berlin: De Gruyter, 1999–2015. Available at sefaria.org.

The Jewish Study Bible. Oxford: Oxford University Press for the Jewish Publication Society, 2004.

The Jews and the Crusaders: The Hebrew Chronicles of the First and Second Crusades, translated and edited by Shlomo Eidelberg, Madison, WI: University of Wisconsin Press, 1977.

The Mishnah: A New Translation, edited by Jacob Neusner. New Haven: Yale University Press, 1988.

The Tosefta, edited by Jacob Neusner. Peabody, MA: Hendrickson, 2002.

Yehudah HeChasid. Sefer Chasidim: The Book of the Pious, condensed, translated, and annotated by Avraham Yaakov Finkel. Northvale, NJ: Jason Aronson, 1997.

Secondary Literature

Agus, Irving A. 1965. *Urban Civilization in Pre-Crusade Europe: A Study of Organized Town-Life in Northwestern Europe during the Tenth and the Eleventh Centuries Based on the Responsa Literature*. Leiden: Brill.

Anton, Maggie. 2005. "Rashi and his Daughters." *Judaism: A Quarterly Journal of Jewish Life and Thought* 54(1–2): 46–54.

Baskin, Judith. 2001. "Dolce of Worms: The Lives and Deaths of an Exemplary Medieval Jewish Woman and Her Daughters." In *Judaism in Practice: From the Middle Ages through the Early Modern Period*, edited by Lawrence Fine, 429–37. Princeton: Princeton University Press.

Baumgarten, Joseph M. 1983. "4Q502, Marriage or Golden Age Ritual?" *Journal of Jewish Studies* 34(2): 125–35. https://doi.org/10.18647/1096/jjs-1983

———. 1992: The Cave 4 Versions of the Penal Code." *Journal of Jewish Studies* 43: 268–76. https://doi.org/10.18647/1654/jjs-1992

Baumgarten, Elisheva. 2004. *Mothers and Children: Jewish Family Life in Medieval Europe*. Princeton: Princeton University Press.

———. 2016. "Praying Separately? Gender in Medieval Ashkenazi Synagogues (Thirteenth–Fourteenth Centuries)." *Clio. Women, Gender, History* 44(2): 43–62. https://doi.org/10.4000/clio.13213

———. 2019. "Ask the Midwives: A Hebrew Manual on Midwifery from Medieval Germany." *Social History of Medicine* 32(4): 712–33. https://doi.org/10.1093/shm/hkz024

Boyarin, Daniel. 1993. *Carnal Israel: Reading Sex in Talmudic Culture*. Berkeley, CA: University of California Press.

Broyde, Michael J. 1995. "Defilement of the Hands, Canonization of the Bible, and the Special Status of Esther, Ecclesiastes, and Song of Songs." *Judaism* 44(1): 65–79.

Brooten, Bernadette. 1982. *Women Leaders in the Ancient Synagogue: Inscriptural Evidence and Background Issues*. Chico, CA: Scholars Press.

Butler, Judith. 1990. *Gender Trouble: Feminism and the Subversion of Identity*. New York: Routledge.

Crawford, Sidnie White. 2003. "Mothers, Sisters, and Elders: Titles for Women in Second Temple Jewish and Early Christian Communities". In *The Dead Sea Scrolls as Background to Postbiblical Judaism and Early Christianity*, edited by James R. Davila, 177–91. Brill: Leiden.

Deleuze, Gilles, and Guattari, Félix. 1987. *A Thousand Plateaus: Capitalism and Schizophrenia*, translated by Brian Massumi. London: Bloomsbury.

Durkheim, Émile. 2001. *The Elementary Forms of Religious Life*, translated by Carol Cosman. Oxford: Oxford University Press.

Engberg-Pedersen, Troels. 1999. "Philo's 'De Vita Contemplativa' as a Philosopher's Dream." *Journal for the Study of Judaism* 30(1): 40–64. https://doi.org/10.1163/157006399x00136

Friedman, Jen Taylor. 2007. "Women's Eligibility to Write Sifrei Torah." *Meorot - A Forum of Modern Orthodox Discourse* 6(2): 1–28.

Friedman, Shamma. 2009. "The Holy Scriptures Defile the Hands: The Transformation of a Biblical Concept in Rabbinic Theology." In *Minhah le-Nahum: Biblical and Other Studies Presented to Nahum M. Sarna in Honour of his 70th Birthday*, edited by Michael A. Fishbane, 117–32. London: Bloomsbury.

Grossman, Avraham. 2004. *Pious and Rebellious: Jewish Women in Medieval Europe*. Waltham, mA: Brandeis University Press.

Halliday, Michael Alexander Kirkwood, and Hasan, Ruqaiya. 1976. *Cohesion in English*. London: Routledge.

Harrison, Verna E. F. 1994. "The Feminine Man in Late Antique Ascetic Piety." *Union Seminary Quarterly Review* 48(3–4): 49–71.

——— 1995. "The Allegorization of Gender: Plato and Philo on Spiritual Childbearing." In *Asceticism*, edited by Vincent L. Wimbush and Richard Valantasis, 520–34. Oxford: Oxford University Press.

Hezser, Catherine. 2001. *Jewish Literacy in Roman Palestine*. Tübingen: Mohr Siebeck.

Holdrege, Barbara. 1989. "The Bride of Israel: The Ontological Status of Scripture in the Rabbinic and Kabbalistic Traditions." In *Rethinking Scripture*, edited Miriam Levering, 180–261. Albany, NY: State University of New York Press.

Jacobs, Louis. 1976. *Jewish Mystical Testimonies*. New York: Schocken Books.

Jeselsohn, Noa. 1999. "Women and the Fulfillment of Positive Time-Bound Commandments." *JOFA Journal* 1(4). 4–6.

Leiman, Sid Z. 1989. "Josephus and the Canon of the Bible". In *Josephus, the Bible, and History*, edited by Louis H. Feldman and Gohei Hata, 50–8. Detroit, MI: Wayne State University Press.

Liberman. Saul. 1962. *Hellenism in Jewish Palestine. Studies in the Literary Transmission, Beliefs, and Manners of Palestine in the 1 Century B.C.E.-IV Century C.E.* New York: Jewish Theological Seminary of America.

Lim, Timothy H. 2010. "The Defilement of the Hands as a Principle Determining the Holiness of Scriptures." *Journal of Theological Studies* 61(2): 501–15. https://doi.org/10.1093/jts/flq079

Malley, Brian. 2004. *How the Bible Works: An Anthropological Study of Evangelical Biblicism*. Oxford: AltaMira Press.

Marcus, Ivan G. 1986. "Mothers, Martyrs, and Moneymakers: Some Jewish Women in Medieval Europe." *Conservative Judaism* 38(3): 34–45.

Resnick, Irven M. 1992. "The Codex in Early Jewish and Christian Communities." *Journal of Religious History* 17(1): 1–17. https://doi.org/10.1111/j.1467-9809.1992.tb00699.x

Ricoeur, Paul. 1976. *Interpretation Theory: Discourse and the Surplus of Meaning*. Fort Worth, TX: Texas Christian University Press.

Riegler, Michael, and Baskin, Judith R. 2008. "'May the Writer Be Strong': Medieval Hebrew Manuscripts Copied by and for Women." *Nashim: A Journal of Jewish Women's Studies and Gender Issues* 16(2): 9–28. https://doi.org/10.2979/nas.2008.-.16.9

Schleicher, Marianne. 2009. "Artifactual and Hermeneutical Use of Scripture in Jewish Tradition." In *Jewish and Christian Scripture as Artifact and Canon*, edited by Craig A. Evans and H. Daniel Zacharias, 48–65. London: T&T Clark.

———. 2010. "Accounts of a Dying Scroll: On Jewish Handling of Sacred Texts in Need of Restoration or Disposal." In *The Death of Sacred Texts: Ritual Disposal and Renovation of Texts in World Religions*, edited by Kristina Myrvold, 11–29. London: Ashgate.

———. 2017 [2012]. "Engaging All the Senses: On Multi-sensory Stimulation in the Process of Making and Inaugurating a Torah Scroll." *Postscripts* 8(1–2): 39–65. https://doi.org/10.1558/post.32694

Scholem, Gershom. 1974. *Major Trends in Jewish Mysticism*. New York: Schocken Books.

Schuller, Eileen M. 1994: "Women in the Dead Sea Scrolls." *Annals New York Academy of Sciences* 116–31. https://doi.org/10.1111/j.1749-6632.1994.tb30466.x

Stern, David. 1987. "Midrash." In *Contemporary Jewish Religious Thought*, edited by Arthur A. Cohen and Paul Mendes-Flohr, 613–20. New York: Charles Scribner's Sons.

Taitz, Emily. 1991. "Women's Voices, Women's Prayers: Women in the European Synagogues of the Middle Ages." In *Daughters of the King: Women and the Synagogue: A Survey of History, Halakhah, and Contemporary Realities*, edited by Susan Grossman and Riva Haut, 59–71. Philadelphia, PA: Jewish Publication Society.

Watts, James W. 2008 [2006]. "The Three Dimensions of Scriptures." *Postscripts* 2: 135–59.

———. 2015. "Iconic Scriptures from Decalogue to Bible." *Mémoires du livre / Studies in Book Culture* 6(2): §§1–23. https://doi.org/10.7202/1032712ar

About the Author

Marianne Schleicher is Associate Professor of Jewish Studies at Aarhus University, Denmark where she works on individual and collective uses of sacred texts, its materiality and intra-action with bodies, gender, and sexuality in both mainstream and mystical traditions. Her publications include the monograph *Intertextuality in the Tales of Rabbi Nahman of Bratslav* (Brill 2007), "Constructions of Sex and Gender: Attending to Androgynes and Tumtumim through Jewish Scriptural Use" (2011), "Attitudes to Deviation from Gender Norms in Israelite and Early Jewish Religion" (2018), and the co-edited volume *Entanglements and Weavings: Diffractive Approaches to Gender and Love* (2021). (ms@cas.au.dk)

4

The Gender of Purple Manuscripts and the Makeup of Sacred Scriptures

Thomas Rainer

Abstract

In his letters to Roman aristocratic women about the proper use of scripture, Jerome dismissed purple makeup and any adornment of books with luxurious materials as wasteful distraction from the content of the text. He contrasts makeup and precious clothing with the textual correctness of his scholarly emended manuscripts and with corporal mortification and ascetic practices. Jerome's dismissal of the materiality and sensuality of books goes hand in hand with a binary gender model that associates the philological work upon the text and the renunciation of its adornment with male scholarship. In order for women to become equal to men through the study of scripture, Jerome extols the performance of a textual asceticism that suppresses the makeup of books and of female bodies alike. His makeup criticism is part of a larger discourse that expresses a persistent fear of a sensual engagement with the materiality of scripture in binary gender stereotypes. A close reading of the purple metaphors employed by Jerome reveals their roots in the rhetorical appraisal of eloquence and poetic language precisely through the materiality of the text.

Keywords: Jerome, materiality, purple manuscripts, book ornament, asceticism, gender stereotypes

In an essay on the French actress Brigitte Bardot published in the August 1959 issue of the "magazine for men" *Esquire*, the figurehead of French feminism Simone de Beauvoir spelled out one of her long-standing arguments against the trappings and constraints of female adornment. Beauvoir contrasts the natural and unornamented eroticism of Bardot with makeup that turns women into dolls for men. Bardot, "man's fellow and equal," instead "goes about barefooted, she turns her nose at elegant clothes, jewels, girdles, perfumes, make-up, at all artifice" (Beauvoir 1959, 34. 36). The historical baggage that came with this critique of female adornment and artifice was huge and heavy. Its topical denunciation, which Simone de Beauvoir here placed in the service of women's sexual liberation, had been formulated in strikingly similar enumerations in a decidedly different context by patristic authors such as Jerome. In a letter sent to Principia in 412 or early 413 CE, Jerome praised the Christian widow Marcella by contrasting her renunciation of all adornments to the comportment of non-Christian widows:

> She put the Gentiles to confusion by showing to all what sort of thing that Christian widowhood is which she revealed in every thought and look. Gentile widows are wont to paint their faces with purple rouge and white lead [*purpurisso et cerussa*], to flaunt in silk dresses, to deck themselves in gleaming jewels, to wear gold necklaces, to hang from their pierced ears the costliest Red Sea pearls, and to reek of musk. Rejoicing that they have at length escaped from a husband's dominion, they look about for a new mate, intending not to yield him obedience, as God ordained, but to be his lord and master [by manipulating the new partner with their luxurious adornment and their inherited wealth]. With this object they choose poor men, husbands only in name, who must patiently put up with rivals, and if they murmur can be kicked out on the spot. (Jerome 1933, Ep. 127.3, 445)[1]

In this quote, Jerome alludes to men's fear of economically independent, sexually dominant women and associates female dominance with luxurious makeup and dress (cf. Kuefler 2001, 72–4; Kuefler 2007, 354–5 for the social and legal context).

The equally wealthy Christian widow Marcella, on the other hand, won praise for her sexual abstinence, her renunciation of all adornment, the distribution of her wealth to the poor, and, above all for her inquisitive and tireless study of scripture. In this, according to Jerome, she attained equality, if not superiority over men, although she feigned dependence on male teachers so as not to appear superior, especially in those instances when in fact she was not a student of men but their teacher (Jerome 1933,

1 Jerome, Ep. 127.3 (CSEL 56, ed. Hilberg, 147.15–23). For an alternative translation see White 2010, 62.

Ep. 127,7, 455; see Munkholt Christensen and Gemeinhardt 2019, 313–17; Stenger 2022, 130–7; Cain 2009a, 52–6).

In the following essay, I will reflect on the contrast between makeup and the study of scripture that Jerome uses as a crucial argument in several key letters to Roman aristocratic women when he sets forth his vision of female education. I do so by taking into account the fundamental shifts in feminist and queer scholarship that have addressed the issue of adornment formulated by Simone de Beauvoir since Judith Butler's theory of performativity in gender constructions (Butler 1986, 1990; C. Evans 2012). How fruitful such a perspective can be for historic studies of patristic literature has been shown, among others, by Kate Wilkinson in her dissertation on *Women and Modesty in Late Antiquity* (Wilkinson 2015) and by a host of critical studies on gender and asceticism (Castelli 1991, Cooper 2013, Betancourt 2020, 89–106). What is largely missing from these studies, however, is an extension of perspective to the material makeup of the written text itself and its iconic dimension (Watts 2006). A good starting point to illuminate this relationship of corporal and textual makeup and texture is the August 1959 cover of *Esquire*. Who would expect the men's magazine to have a stack of books on its cover with the erotic photographs of supposedly "unadorned" Brigitte Bardot by Richard Avedon accompanying Simone de Beauvoir's text inside (Figure 4.1).

The books on the cover are shown with their similarly decorated encyclopedia-like spines, with only one book open. The piled-up books virtually support the sub-title of the publication "The Magazine for Men." The cover image presents a literary canon: it shows on the spines of the books in combination with Paul Rand's *Esquire* logo the names of all Nobel Prize winners who have ever published a text in *Esquire* magazine, a canon that is exclusively male, with the latest addition, François Mauriac, represented by the open book.[2] What is missing in *Esquire's* rhetorical book ornament is any female contribution. How would Simone de Beauvoir fit into or infiltrate this stack? Should her spine avoid any ornament and artifice that differs from the male spines and what would that mean for the gendering of the entire stack? Or should her spine stand out with particular artifice and makeup underlining the performativity of the rhetorical gender ascriptions generated by this cover image?

I will address these questions not by further analysing the iconic construction of a literary canon by a men's magazine but by examining the iconic construction of scriptural canon through Jerome's writing. What

2 Maurice Maeterlinck, Knut Hamsun, George Bernard Shaw, Thomas Mann, Sinclair Lewis, Iwan Bunin, Luigi Pirandello, William Faulkner, Bertrand Russell, François Mauriac, Ernest Hemingway, Albert Camus, Boris Pasternak.

Figure 4.1 Spread (Brigitte Bardot photographed by Richard Avedon above an article by Simone de Beauvoir) and cover (stack of books of Nobel Prize winners) from the August 1959 issue of Esquire, screenshot from the website of Esquire magazine (consulted 6 Jan. 2023). https://classic.esquire.com/article/1959/8/1/brigitte-bardot-and-the-lolita-syndrome

role did this male author ascribe to the materiality and dress of scripture owned, used, and studied by women? Would he assign it a different make-up than his own books? And what would be the implications if women modelled their books after his? To answer these questions, we will take a close look at three important quotes from Jerome's writings that have long been cornerstones in the scholarly discussions about the materiality of sacred scriptures in Christianity. In these quotes, Jerome condemns the use of books made of purple-coloured parchment with gilt lettering and precious covers for the study of scripture, and compares the adornment of such books to female clothing and makeup. While aspects of clothing in these passages have recently been explored in pioneering studies on book ornament and its critique in an interreligious context (Ganz 2019; Flood 2019; see also Ganz 2015, 57–8), the implied gender dichotomies and their consequences for the materiality and sensuality of sacred books have not been sufficiently explored.

Jerome's Letters on the Materiality of Scripture

In 384, Jerome sends a long letter to a young woman, named Eustochium, on the virtues of virginity. Following her ascetic mother Paula, Eustochium – aged 14 or 15 years – was convinced to lead the life of a virgin and later joined Jerome along with her mother in a newly founded nunnery in Bethlehem (Feichtinger 1995, 209–12; Adkin 2003, 8-10; Cooper 2013, 533–8; Cain 2009b, 100–2). To Eustochium, Jerome writes:

> But today you see many women packing their wardrobes (*amaria*) with dresses, putting on a fresh frock every day, and even so unable to get the better of the moth. The more scrupulous sort wear one dress till it is threadbare, but though they go about in rags their boxes (*arcis*) are full of clothes. Parchments are dyed purple (*inficitur membrana colore purpureo*), gold is melted for lettering (*aurum liquescit in litteras*), manuscripts are decked with jewels (*gemmis codices vestiuntur*): and Christ lies at their door naked and dying. (Jerome 1933, Ep. 22.32, 130–3)[3]

Jerome formulates an interesting variant of the same theme eighteen years later in a letter to Laeta on the education of her daughter Paula, who later joined her aunt Eustochium as a virgin in the nunnery of Bethlehem (Feichtinger 1995, 220–2):

> Instead of jewels or silk let her love the manuscripts of the Holy Scriptures, and in them let her prefer correctness and accurate punctuation to gilding and Babylonian parchment with elaborate decorations (*auri et pellis Babyloniae vermiculata pictura*). Let her learn the Psalter first, with these songs let her

3 Jerome, *Epistula* 22,32 (CSEL 54, ed. Hilberg, 193). For alternative translations see Jerome 2011, 100, commentary 254–6; White 2010, 138; and the commentary by Adkin 2003, 306–8.

> distract herself, and then let her learn lessons of life in the Proverbs of Solomon. (Jerome 1933, Ep. 107.12, 364–5)[4]

This echoes a passage written in 391 in the preface to Jerome's translation of Job:

> Let those who will keep the old books with their gold and silver letters on purple skins (*in membranis purpureis auro argentoque descriptos*), or to follow the ordinary phrase, in "uncial characters", loads of writing rather than manuscripts, if only they will leave for me and mine, our poor pages and copies which are less remarkable for beauty than for accuracy (*non tam pulchros codices quam emendatos*). (Jerome 1890, 492)[5]

Comparing these three quotes about book ornament, two basic arguments can be discerned. First, the purple colouring, gilded script, and jewelled ornament of the books are intimately linked to questions of dress. Jerome follows a logic of stripping the silken, gilded, and jewelled ornaments from the female body, an argument of ascetic nakedness, which is contrasted to useless storage of clothes – abundance and wealth not made fruitful as alms, but serving as fodder for moths (Kearney 2009, 11–12; Ganz 2015, 57–8; cf. Flood 2019, 65–6). In a second line of reasoning, the embellishment of body and books is set against the philological correctness of the written text, whose material beauty is deemed unfit to judge worthiness in the eyes of those who actually learn from and work upon the text. Jerome applies this ascetic ideal, which places the accuracy of the text above its material beauty, to his own books, that is, to the books containing the fruits of his philological labour in translating the biblical canon with the help of the Hebrew text, as well as to the books he recommends for study to his female correspondents. The women should use such ascetic books in their quest of an ascetic and celibate lifestyle in order to become superior according to the ideal of a male scholar: masculine in study and asceticism rather than attractive to the common gaze.

This sexually tinged argument was by no means entirely new. Actually, it stands in a long tradition of ancient criticism of luxurious books (Williams 2006, 181–4). From the first century on, it was a well-known theme in Roman literature to criticise the *nouveaux riches* who owned an abundance of beautifully adorned books. They treated them with the utmost care and

4 Jerome, *Epistula* 107,12 (CSEL 55, ed. Hilberg, 302,16–19). For an alternative translation see White 2010, 160. For the expression *pellis Babyloniae vermiculata pictura* see Booker 1995, who translates *vermiculata pictura* as "painted scarlet". Expensive purple coloured Babylonian leather (or parchment?) was mentioned in the edict of Emperor Diocletian on maximum prices. See Herz 1985.

5 Bruyne 2015, 38–41. For a discussion of the translation of the term *litterae unciales* cf. Mayvaert 1983.

stored them away in exquisite *amaria* – book cases, the same word Jerome used for the storage of the beautiful female clothes – without ever making use of their contents by reading or studying the texts within. I cite as one example Seneca, who in his moral essay *De tranquillitate animi* states, "many who lack even a child's knowledge of letters use books, not as the tools of learning, but as decorations for the dining-room." And he continues:

> But excess in anything becomes a fault. What excuse have you to offer for a man who seeks to have bookcases (*armaria*) of citrus-wood and ivory, who collects the works of unknown or discredited authors and sits yawning in the midst of so many thousand books, who gets most of his pleasure from the outsides of volumes and their titles? Consequently it is in the houses of the laziest men that you will see a full collection of orations and history with the boxes piled right up to the ceiling; for by now among cold baths and hot baths a library also is equipped as a necessary ornament of a great house. (Seneca 1932, 248–9)

In a similar vein, the ostentatious display of wealth, intellectual laziness, bathing pleasures, and book ornament are criticized in a second-century satirical text by Lucian, which further emphasizes in a more explicit way the negative parallelism of body care in a bathing environment and book care in the nearby library. The target of Lucian's scorn is, to quote the Greek title of the satire, a man "who lacks *paideia* – proper education – and buys a lot of books" (Johnson 2010, 158). In his shopping sprees, he values the outward appearance of the books and their prestige based on hearsay more than their textual accuracy, prompting Lucian to make a curious comparison: "Yet even if I grant that you have selected out those very books that Callinus or the celebrated Atticus [famous editors of classical works] copied out calligraphically with every care [i.e. with attention to textual accuracy], what benefit does the possession afford you, o amazing one – you who neither perceive the beauty nor make good use of it, any more than a blind man gets anything from the beauty of young boys" (Lucian, *Adv. Ind.* 2, cited after Johnson 2010, 159–60). Lucian deliberately calculates the sexual innuendo here. Throughout his text, he pursues an agenda of viciously attacking the sexual habits of his satirical adversary. In doing so, he draws an implicit parallel between the care of books and the body care of his opponent. The excessive buyer is always trying to make the surface of his papyrus scrolls as smooth as possible by unrolling and rolling them up, gluing them, trimming them, rubbing them with saffron and cedar oil, and clothing them with precious purple slipcovers (Lucian, *Adv. Ind.* 16, 1921, 194–5; see Lambert 2022, 188–90). This echoes the skin care he bestows on himself and, as Lucian implies, on his slave boys. He cites the regulations written for our booklover by the *cinaedus* – a derogatory term for a homosexual man – Hemitheon of Sybaris. The regulations state, "that you must use cosmetics and depilatories..." Lucian then describes the appearance of the book collector who covers his face with lead white, mastic, and purple rouge (Lucian, *Adv. Ind.* 23, 1921, 202–3; see Johnson 2010, 161–3).

What appears as a personal attack had in fact literary antecedents. In the literary debates of the first and second century, especially in the sophistic milieu of *literati* like Lucian, contrasting the smooth and the rough style of rhetoric and poetry was often linked to cosmetic metaphors emphasizing gender and sexual distinctions. One example among many is Quintilian, who in his widely read handbook on rhetoric, the *Institutio Oratoria*, comments: "[rhetorical ornament] must not favor effeminate smoothness or the false coloring of cosmetics, it must shine with health and vigor" (Quintilian, *Inst. Or.* 8.3.6; Johnson 178, n. 13; cf. Copeland 1994, 146). The innuendo of smooth and ornate papyrus scrolls, polished with pumice stones, oiled with saffron and dressed in purple was a literary topos already used by Augustan poets such as Catullus, Martial, and Ovid (Dupont and Parker 2011, 148–56; Booker 1997, 449). Depending on the context, these polished scrolls associated with "beautiful boys" could either be praised or condemned. For proponents of an elitist Greek classicism, overly pleasing, polished, and smooth language without any ruptures was considered a sign of an effeminate character expressed in ostentatiously ornate dress and cosmetics (Gleason 1995; Bartsch 2015, 149–60). Cosmetic polish stood in contrast to the virtues of ascetic, virile scholarship, which came along rough, hairy, unkempt, and without external embellishment. Lucian himself presents those two alternatives in a text titled *Rhetorum praeceptor* - Teacher of Rhetoric. Therein the disciple can choose between two different paths, one steep and narrow; the other pleasant and brief. The guide to the first is "a strong, rather tough-looking fellow, who has a manly step, a deep tan, and a masculine, vigilant look" (Lucian, *Rhetorum praeceptor* 9; translation after Gleason 1995, 127). He recommends - to cite Maud Gleason's fundamental study of this gendering of rhetorical teaching - a training programme whose ascetic elements would appeal to Jerome: "hard work, scant sleep, abstention from wine, and untidiness" (Lucian, *Rhetorum praeceptor* 10, 1925, 146–7) whereas "the guide of the easy road to rhetoric is all effeminate charm," the total opposite of the "hairy specimen of excessive virility" (Gleason 1995, 127). These gendered topoi of rhetorical ornament were played with extensively in ancient rhetoric schooling and they were still present in the rhetoric classroom in late antiquity. The repercussions of these literary tropes for the discussion of precious book ornament by Jerome, who in his teens had a thorough rhetoric schooling in Rome (Rebenich 1992, 21–31), can be seen in the reception of a famous quote by the poet Ovid about the missing purple dress of one of his books.

In the opening verses of Ovid's poem *Tristia*, which he sent from exile to imperial Rome, the rough and unkempt appearance of the book comments on the dire conditions of its author:

> Little book ... you shall have no cover dyed with the juice of purple berries [*nec te purpureo velent vaccinia fuco*] – no fit colour is that for mourning; your title shall not be tinged with vermilion nor your papyrus sheets with oil of cedar ... Let no brittle pumice polish your two edges; I would have you appear with locks all rough and disordered. Be not ashamed of blots; he who sees them will feel that they were caused by tears. (Ovid, *Tristia* 1.1.3–14, 1924, 2–3; cf. Williams 1992)

As has been suggested by Jan R. Stenger, the verses of *Tristia* could resonate with Jerome at the time when he wrote his letter to Eustochium (Stenger 2021, 225). We know that he was acutely aware what important part cosmetic book ornament played in determining literary status in the elite circles of power in Rome. In his *Chronicon* written around the year 380, four years before the letter to Eustochium, he reports that Emperor Constantine pardoned the poet Optatianus Porfyrius and allowed him to return from exile in the year 328/329, after Optatianus Porfyrius had dedicated an unsurpassed book (*insigni volumine*) to the emperor (Jerome, *Chronicon*, ed. Helm 1956, 232; see Körfer 2020, 104–5). The first verses of this book reframe Ovid's purple topos by addressing the poetic muse Thalia:

> You, who once, adorned by a pretty little book, Thalia, were accustomed
> to carry my poem to the hands of Augustus; you, who shining all in
> purple, written in flashing letters of silver and gold, traced my words
> with a painted line; you who, carefully adorned by the author's hand, as
> befits the sacred eyes of (your) master, pleasantly smiled as you deserved;
> now, you are pale, your pages bathed in sombre colour, barely highlighting
> the verses with poor red ink, you seek with trembling step the roof
> of the venerable palace, fearful that your present face is too repulsive.
> (Optatian, *Carm*. 1.1–10; translated by Bruhat 2017, 261)

Here the evocation of cosmetic purple hopes to reintroduce the author of a jewelled and refined style to the spheres of imperial power. For Optatian, the optics and material embellishment of his verses were intrinsically interwoven with their panegyric content. Purple, which was an unsurpassed status symbol of power in the dress code of the imperial court, was meant to match the splendour of his poetic language and secure the poet a place in the "venerable palace of Augustus" (Bruhat 2017; Squire 2017a, 57–61; Körfer 2020, 94–107). Jerome took an opposite path – not the road of rhetorical power play in the imperial sphere, but that of ascetic self-mortification in exile. Shortly after he wrote his letter to Eustochium, he broke with his former life as a powerful, rhetorically schooled cleric in Rome, in order to live as an ascetic literary scholar in Bethlehem. This break was explicitly styled as turn away from purple. In the autobiographic preface of Jerome's translation of the Greek treatise *De spiritu sancto,* which he wrote during his transition from Rome to Bethlehem between 384 and 387, Jerome describes himself as a former inhabitant of Babylon that he calls the purple-clad whore (*meretrix purpurata*) (Jerome, *Didym. spir. praef*, PL 23, 107–8; see Stenger 2021, 218–19 and Grig 2012, 140–2). From there, from purple, the senate of the Roman clerical elite chases him away, driving him into exile in Bethlehem.

The underlying conflict involved both gender and language. Jerome coupled ascetic mortification of the body with his philological work as translator and commentator of the sacred text. He rejected the poetic persuasion, which could be achieved through colourful language and precious style, and espoused instead the prose of biblical commentary. In a letter to Pope Damasus, written in 384, he stated: "I know that these things are burdensome for the reader, but when discussing Hebrew literature, it is not fitting to look for the arguments of Aristotle. Likewise, one's stylistic stream should not be drawn from the river of Cicero's eloquence, nor should the ears be soothed by declamation of the schools or by the rhetorical refinements of Quintilian." Flowery word arrangement is denied. "Let others be grandiloquent, let them receive praise as they wish, and let them balance their frothy words in swollen cheeks. As for me, it suffices to speak so that I may be understood and so that when I discuss the Scriptures, I may imitate their simplicity" (Jerome, Ep. 36.14; translated by Cain 2009b, 83).[6]

The riches of classical language were explicitly coupled with adultery (*adulterum ... linguae*; see Jerome Ep. 22.29; Stenger 2021, 221). In his letter to Eustochium, a dream vision of the author takes centre stage. In this dream, Jerome is dragged naked before God, who punishes him with severe beatings. The punishment stops only when Jerome swears never again to read a sentence by a pagan author (Jerome Ep. 22.30, 3–5; Stenger 2021, 222–3; see Adkin 2003, 283–97 and the commentary in Jerome 2011, 244–51). Years later, when confronted by his former friend and new arch-enemy Rufinus with numerous examples in which he refers to classical authors such as Cicero and Plautus, Jerome again defends himself with a purple metaphor. What you learn as a child, he says, is imbued in your memory and cannot be extinguished easily. After his classical rhetorical schooling, quotes from many pagan authors still fill his memories. These quotes are "like purple colouring wool, impossible to wash away by water" (Jerome, *Adv. Rufin.* 1.30; Stenger 2021, 233–5).

6 Cf. Jerome, Ep. 125.12; Cain 2009b, 153. For the dating see Cain 2009b, 55–8.

Purple washed away not by water but by tears was the cosmetic alternative that Jerome offered to his female companions whom he invited to follow his path of ascetic penance and biblical study. In praise of the widow Paula, the mother of Eustochium, from one of the noblest senatorial families in Rome, who joined Jerome in founding the nunnery in Bethlehem, Jerome writes:

> When I frequently admonished her to take it easy on her (weeping) eyes and preserve them for readings of the Gospels she said: "The face which in disobedience to God's precept has often been decorated with purple rouge (*purpurissum*), lead white (*cerussum*) and black eyeliner, must be soiled. The body which has given free reign to numerous pleasures must be punished." (Jerome, *Epitaphium Sanctae Paulae* 15.4; edited and translated by Cain 2013, 64–67, commentary 323–324)

After Paula's death in 404, Jerome strikingly contrasts the soiled face of a widow intently reading and studying the Gospels with her former makeup, which combines white lead and purple superficiality (on this pairing see Cain 2013, 323–324; Olson 2009, 294–297). This eulogy follows the ancient critique of makeup that equates ornament and embellishment with distraction from the content of the text. In the context of the sophistic debate the gender ambiguities of male subjects exemplified this critique. Here it is a female reader, whose former makeup symbolizes the dangerous distraction from the content of the text. In his letters to Eustochium and Laeta, Jerome creates a new category of literary study. By means of a strict pedagogical programme of Psalter and Gospel readings from the earliest age, the thus supervised virgins should become free from the dichotomies of pagan rhetoric ornament. I think it is not by chance that women were the prime addressees of this programme. As Jerome makes clear on his own example, the extinction of real purple makeup was far easier than its rhetoric equivalent. Classical literature as ornament of speech was deeply ingrained in the education of every young man of elite upbringing in late antiquity. A polished speech and a polished language were ideals that trumped the makeup critique. Only by internalizing them in his programme of biblical philological study and commentary could Jerome create – as Mark Vessey has shown – an alternative to the shunned art of pagan poetry (Vessey 2007).

The advice that Jerome gives to Laeta on behalf of the education of her daughter Paula exemplifies how this internalizing worked:

> So you must take care not to let your daughter get into the habit of speaking in a clipped manner in imitation of women's silly baby talk (*ineptis blanditiis feminarum*; alt. translation: women's silly allurements) or of wearing clothes of gold and purple while she plays, for the former harms her speech and the latter

> her character. We certainly do not want her to learn something as a child that she will have to unlearn ... It is difficult to erase what has seared itself into a child's mind. Who can restore the wool to its original whiteness once it has been dyed purple? (White 2010, 154; cf. Jerome 1933, Ep. 107.12, 348–349; Reitzenstein 1916, 617–618; Denecker 2015, 408–409; more generally Katz 2007)

Paula's mind here becomes the blank, undyed sheet, which Jerome longed to fill exclusively with biblical content. The girl formed in the image of ascetic scripture ought to extinguish the staining colour of purple language, with which Jerome himself struggled throughout his life.

What does this mean for the gender of purple manuscripts? My analysis has made clear that the relegation of such coloured manuscripts to the sphere of women's dress and makeup is a rhetorical performance that serves a male author to distance himself from his peers. Jerome's letters ascribe to female bodies masculine qualities he himself is eager to achieve: the rough versus the smooth. The same is true for the body of scripture. Its austerity is a mirror image of Jerome's "men making" asceticism (Gleason 1995). How could women position themselves in this masculine rhetoric of scripture? Can we find out anything about their strategies of gender performance in reading scripture? The question whether women's voices and their struggles with male gender ascriptions can be heard from behind the rhetorical scene that Jerome creates in his letters is a contentious one in recent literature on gender and asceticism (Clark 1998; Clark 2004; Wilkinson 2015, 9–14). In her study *The Gendered Palimpsest: On Women, Writing and Representation in Early Christianity*, Kim Haines-Eitzen warned not to "concede that we have nothing more than male representations of 'reality' – a claim that relegates any attempts at historical reconstruction to an outdated positivism and simultaneously reifies an assumed essentialising difference between men and women" (Haines-Eitzen 2012, 38). Not without reason she points to various shreds of evidence that "demonstrate that women were (occasionally? rarely? sometimes?) involved in the many and various stages of the production, reproduction, and dissemination of early Christian literature" (Haines-Eitzen 2012, 37).

According to the *Historia Ecclesiastica* of Eusebius, Origen who served as the scholarly role model for Jerome had at his disposal "seven shorthand writers, who relieved each other at fixed times and as many copyists, as well as girls for the purpose of beautiful writing" (Eusebius, *Historia Ecclesiastica* 6.23; Haines-Eitzen 2012, 31). Gerontius, who wrote a biography on the ascetic aristocrat Melania the Younger (383–439), reports in the fifth century that Melania "read the Old and New Testament three or four times a year. She copied them herself and furnished copies to the saints by her own hands" (Gerontius, *Life of Melania* 26; Haines-Eitzen 2012, 31).

In the sixth-century biography on Caesarius of Arles (470–542), one can read that his sister Caesaria along with her female companions – all virgins in a newly founded convent – "beautifully copy out the holy books" (*Life of Caesarius* 1.58; Haines-Eitzen 2012, 31); and in the Coptic version of Palladius's *Lausiac History* (written in Greek 419–420), Litia of Thessalonica is praised as "a scribe writing books and living in great asceticism in the manner of men" (Butler 1898, 150). Haines-Eitzen observes with regard to ascetic women, whose praise in hagiographic literature and patristic letters regularly combines sleepless fasting, reading scripture, especially the Psalms, and weeping:

> We are caught here by the problem of our evidence, which is almost entirely meditated through the lens of male representations. On the one hand, we might be tempted to argue that women's reading here becomes yet one more strategy for men to control the female body, to keep women silent, and to circumscribe their activities ... Yet, on the other hand, we might read against the grain of our literary remains and argue – compellingly, to my mind – that one of the reasons that our patristic writers take such pains to construct a program of reading is because women (at least elite women within ascetic circles) were not reading what [and I would add "how"] they should read ... (Haines-Eitzen 2012, 51–2)

Haines-Eitzen invites the question: is there any material evidence of such improper books that would fit Jerome's rhetorical damnation of luxury codices for women's "superficial" reading? If so, one should not "read" these books per se as evidence for women's books – trying to assign to them a female gender. To do so would affirm the rhetorical trap set up by Jerome. Rather than reaffirming the contrast between superficial reading, which Jerome associates with women's clipped talk and makeup, and a close philological reading of text, we should seek to give the material evidence of the colour purple a voice of its own by closely reading the material surfaces of books not as superficialities but as essential qualities for the construction of gender identities that transcend a strictly binary model (cf. Kay 2017, 17–20).

Reading Purple Surfaces: The Author Portraits in the *Vergilius romanus*

For such a surface reading, which takes account of the sensory effects of a book's materiality, I shall turn to a manuscript that represents all the dangerous temptations by pagan literature evoked in Jerome's letters. The *Vergilius romanus* (Vatican, Biblioteca Apostolica Vaticana, Cod. Vat. lat. 3867) is one of the rare surviving examples of a late antique luxury codex that contains an illustrated copy of some of the most revered classical Latin texts, the verses of Virgil's iconic works of poetry, the *Eclogues*, the *Georgics*, and the *Aeneid*. The text of the manuscript is written in black/

brown display script (a *Capitalis rustica*, a noble script used for deluxe copies of ancient literature) on fine uncoloured parchment with titles, incipits, and excipits in purple as well as an extensive image cycle. The manuscript was most probably produced in an elite senatorial milieu of the late fifth century that may have been very similar to Jerome's Roman connections (Eggenberger 1977; Wright 2001; Bernabò 2014/2015 suggesting Gaul). Looking at the three author portraits placed in framed miniatures at the openings of *Eclogue* 2, 4, and 6 (on fols. 3v, 9r, and 14r), shades of purple play an important role in representing poetic language.

In each of these similarly styled portraits of a poet enthroned frontally beside a closed *capsa* (bookcase) and a writing desk, he wears a glaring white dress adorned with flashing purple coloured vertical stripes (*clavi*) on the tunic (the garment worn beneath the mantle) and in two images, additional purple ornaments called *gammadiae* (fols. 3v and 9r) – here H-shaped decorations on the *pallium*, which is the mantle worn above the tunic (Figure 4.2). Such purple stripes and signs signalled senatorial honour that distinguished ancient Roman nobility (Reinhold 1970; Bessone 1998; Pausch 2003, 104–22; Scholz 2005, 419). A purple slipcover of exactly the same colour envelops the scroll that the poet holds in his hands. Covered like this, the scroll perfectly embodies the purple of the poet's noble speech, touched by elegant fingers with brightly polished white nails. The main colours of the dress are also echoed in the face of the poet, who appears in each of the three portraits as a pubescent boy. He has a waxy skin, a makeup mask of lead white (*cerussa*, cf. Olson 2009, 295–6) with a touch of rouge (particularly visible on fol. 14r; for rouge Olson 2009, 296) and dark purple-coloured lips (Cain 2013, 323; but cf. Olson 2009, 299).

The fifth-century poet and Christian writer Sidonius Apollinaris comments on polished and smooth skin like that seen here. Sidonius tells how the barber of the barbarian king Theoderic II trims back his sprouting hair – no doubt a metaphor for the Latinization of the foreign elite: "his barber is assiduous in eradicating the growth on the lower part of the face on a regular basis like you do with adolescent boys. Chin, throat, and neck are tight not fat, and of a milky-white skin tone; seen close, their colour is red as that of youth; they often flush, but from modesty, and not from anger" (Sidonius, Ep. 1.2, translated after Dalton 1915, 3 with slight changes; cf. Sidonius 1936, edited by Anderson, 336–7; Berschin 1994, 187–8). It is easy to see in this adolescent poet-boy an echo of the old equation of the beautiful boy's well-groomed skin and the polished writing surface of scrolls (Dupont and Parker 2011, 148–56) and later codices containing the smooth verses of purple speech. Indeed, if we look at the ground surface of this painting on the extremely thin and finely polished parchment

Figure 4.2 Author portrait of a poet depicted as a purple-clad pubescent boy holding a purple covered scroll, late fifth/early sixth century, various colorants on sheep parchment, Vergilius romanus, Biblioteca Apostolica Vaticana, Cod. Vat. lat. 3867, fol. 3v. © Biblioteca Apostolica Vaticana https://digi.vatlib.it/view/MSS_Vat.lat.3867

skin (Eggenberger 1977, 62), we find the same mixture of white and red in shades of purple, a pinkish colour that resembles skin, although it has deteriorated through the ageing process (Figure 4.3). Comparing this painting surface of the author portraits on fol. 3v and 9r to the naked skin of the Olympian gods on fol. 234r/235v in the same manuscript, the artist's original intentions become clear. The surface here is pinkish skin, a mixture of milky white and red, the perfect makeup for Latin poetry.

How can these surfaces be "read"? Are they vestiges of a bygone era to be washed away by ascetic tears? Are they to be found only in books for

Figure 4.3 Makeup with cerussa (lead white) and purpurissum (purple), shades of purple colorants on sheep parchment, detail of Figure 4.2, Vergilius romanus, Biblioteca Apostolica Vaticana, Cod. Vat. lat. 3867, fol. 3v. © Biblioteca Apostolica Vaticana https://digi.vatlib.it/view/MSS_Vat.lat.3867

women not yet sufficiently trained in exclusive biblical reading? The *Vergilius romanus* presents no evidence to support such an interpretation. The surface of the manuscript shows us instead that beneath the ornament critique of Jerome lies a more fluid gender than his moralistic admonition of female dress and adornment makes us believe. At the heart of the debate is the persuasive, sensual quality of poetic and rhetoric speech that could materialize in purple images. Jerome gives us a glimpse of how this debate made its way from Augustan and imperial poetry to biblical scholarship and exegesis. This development was by no means driven exclusively by women or pagans, but rather by the new senatorial Christian elite and the imperial circles of power with their highly prized rhetorical training. In the Constantinian milieu of poets such as Optatianus Porfyrius, the purple colour, previously associated with slipcovers of scrolls, was combined with the gilded and silver script and the skins of parchment codices (Ernst 1993, 353–5; Squire 2017b, 30–6). In this transition from scrolls to codices, the continuing use of purple colour found imperial favour and may have been used by imperial order in copying the biblical texts for the churches of the new Christian empire. (cf. Grafton and Williams 2006, 215–21; Wallraff 2013, 37–48)

The Development of the Christian Purple Codex

In the fourth century and the lifetime of Jerome, this development of the purple codex is only documented by our written sources. The few materially preserved purple coloured parchment codices from late antiquity that contain writings with silver and gold lettering are all dated after the death of Jerome in the later fifth century and the first half of the sixth century. They are six Latin Gospel manuscripts containing the *Vetus Latina* text of the pre-Jeromian translation of the New Testament (Motteran 2012),[7] a manuscript with the Gothic translation of the Gospels by Wulfila (*Codex argenteus*, Uppsala University Library, DG 1; Bigus 2011), and four Greek gospel manuscripts (Hixson 2019).[8] Then there is one Greek manuscript of the Book of Genesis (Vienna Genesis, Vienna, ÖNB, Cod. Theol. gr. 31; Hofmann 2020) and two Psalters, one Greek (Zürich Purple Psalter, Zürich, Zentralbibliothek, RP 1; Crisci and Eggenberger 2007; see Figure 4.4), one Latin (Paris, BnF, lat. 11947; Huglo 1982, 54–9), palaeographically dated to the sixth century.

All these purple codices are written by professional scribes in silver display scripts on entirely purple coloured parchment folia (Motteran 2012; Crisci and Eggenberger 2007; Hixson 2019). In addition to the silver script, in most of these manuscripts *nomina sacra*, initials, titles, incipit and excipit texts are written in gold. Three manuscripts – two Greek Gospels (*Codex Rossanensis* and *Codex Sinopensis*) and the Book of Genesis – feature extensive pictorial cycles with magnificent illuminations (Cavallo 1987; Speciale 2019; Grabar 1948; Lowden 1999; Zimmermann 2003). The Gothic Gospel manuscript (*Codex argenteus*) and a related Latin Gospel (*Codex Brixianus*)

7 Codex Palatinus (Dublin, Trinity College 1709; London, British Library, Add MS 40107; Trento, Museo Castello del Buonconsiglio, cod. 1589); Codex Vindobonensis (Napoli, Biblioteca Nazionale, Lat. 3 [olim codex Vindobonensis Lat. 1235]); Codex Veronensis (Verona, Biblioteca Capitolare 6 (6)); Codex Sarzanensis A and B (Sarezzano, Biblioteca Parrocchiale, s.n.); Codex Brixianus (Brescia, Biblioteca Queriniana, s.n.); Codex Perusinus (Perugia, Biblioteca Capitolare Ms. 1; Perugia, Biblioteca Capitolare Ms. 3 (fragm.)).

8 Codex Purpureus Petropolitanus (Gregory-Aland N 022); Codex Sinopensis (Gregory-Aland O 023); Codex Purpureus Rossanensis (Gregory-Aland Σ 042); Codex Beratinus 1 (Gregory-Aland Φ 043).

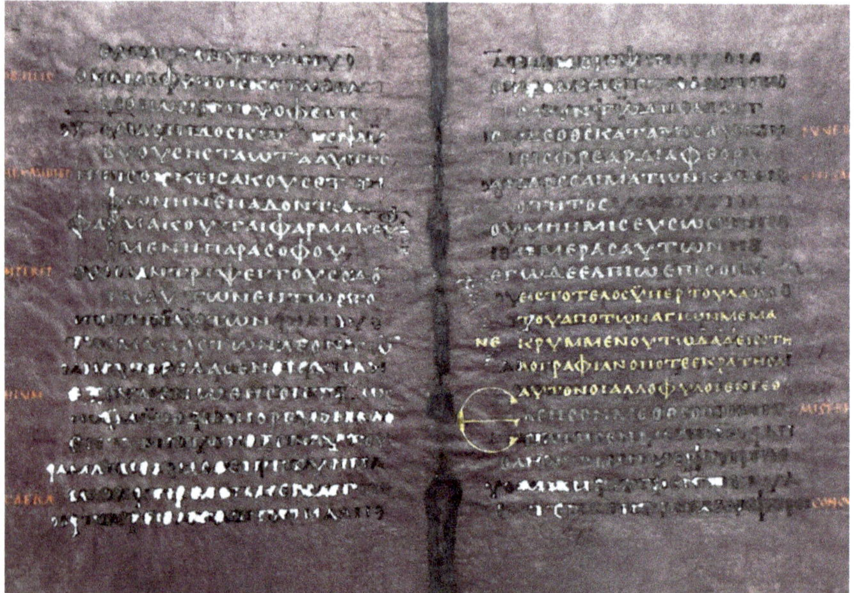

Figure 4.4 Bifolio of the Zürich Purple Psalter with the initial and beginning of Psalm 55 (56) in gold script, sixth and eighth centuries, 22.0 × 15.5 cm (folio), gold, silver and minium on purple dyed parchment with orchil (Rocella tinctoria L.) as colorant; Psalter with Cantica, Zürich, Zentralbibliothek, RP1, fols. 35v (94) and 30r (87). Public Domain Mark: Photo by the author.

also have additional pictorial elements, namely silver arcades at the bottom of their pages referring to the Eusebian canon tables (Brown 2006, 206 Kat.-Nr. 60 (Kessler); Reudenbach 2009, 64).

For these purple-coloured, late antique manuscripts, no textual evidence – inscriptions or documents – are preserved that would allow us exactly to pinpoint their places of origin or to name the donors or first owners of the manuscripts, let alone the gender of their patrons. For the Gospel books and at least the Latin Psalter (Huglo 1982, 54–9) most scholars assume that they were books for liturgical use (Cavallo 1987, 15). In the scholarly debate over their origins, imperial patronage has been claimed for many of them (McKitterick 1989, 143; Kessler 1994; Booker 1997; Furlan 1998; Bigus 2011; Brown 2006; H. Evans 2012), often citing the imperial privileges that granted the late antique emperor special rights to own and display clothes, regalia, and imperial signed documents coloured by this most expensive dye (Avery 1940; Steigerwald 1990; Booker 1997, 468–71). Although the association of purple with power was ancient and fuelled the assumption of imperial or royal donations of certain purple manuscripts already in medieval times,[9] this relation was, however, by no means straightforward. The imperial allusions did not preclude other possibilities of ownership or donation. Purple gifts were embedded in a web of poetic and rhetorical associations, often transgressing the boundaries between real and imaginary; between the material persuasiveness of the object and its rhetorical performance.

The recent spectroscopic analysis of most of the late antique purple manuscripts has shown that in none of the documented cases was the colorant of their parchment surfaces genuine sea snail purple – the costliest product used to dye imperial clothing. The colorant was plant substitutes; e.g. lichen dyes that could reproduce the effect of the purple lustre in a less expensive and probably technically simpler way (Fuchs and Oltrogge 2007; Baroni 2012; Bicchieri 2014; Porter 2018; Aceto et al. 2019; Hofmann 2020; cf. Denoël et al. 2018 for the Carolingian era). This does not mean that these manuscripts were purple "fakes" precluding imperial ownership, but rather shows that they had to be performed in a certain way for their material persuasiveness to work. The material gifts came with panegyric rhetoric – with the performance of purple poetry in spoken and written language, by gestures and by body language. It is this "application" of verbal and corporal polish that was necessary to make the purple shine. A good example is the use of such manuscripts in the liturgy. In the staging of holiness, the metaphor of purple skin could develop new tints and colours. The purple Gospel book placed on the altar could become an image of the Word made flesh, symbolizing a central dogma of the Christian faith (Booker 1997; Carmassi 2011; Motteran 2012; Ganz 2015; Bücheler 2018; Denoël et al. 2018). Another example is the Psalter and its liturgical and contemplative performance, combining eloquence and song with prayer. I think it is not by chance that along with the Gospels it was this utmost poetic book of the Bible which was coloured purple. It was the combination of poetic language with royal authorship that made its purple shine, a rhetorical strategy that was well established as a panegyric metaphor for classical texts.

Purple Eloquence and the Gendered Book Stack

In the *Historia Augusta*, written around 400 by an anonymous author, probably with ties to the Roman senate, the following is reported. Among the good omens enumerated to promote the son of Maximinus Thrax (172–238) as a future emperor, the legendary story reports that, when the boy was

9 The Latin purple Psalter was believed to be a gift from the Merovingian king Childebert II (cf. Denoël 2015, 160).

sent to a grammarian to polish his language skills, a certain female relative "gave him the works of Homer all written in letters of gold on purple" (*Historia Augusta*, The Two Maximini 30.4–6, ed. Magie 1924, 374–5, cf. Booker 1997, 453–5). We do not know what role the author, in explaining this gift, assigned to this female relative. Was she a commissioner, former owner, teaching reader, or simply sponsor of the precious book? It is an example that closely connects imperial status, language, eloquence, and education, in this case explicitly promulgated by a woman with purple books. If we think of the doubtful family roots of Maximinus Thrax, who was rumoured to be of "barbarian" origin (Booker 1997, 455) and whose literary refinement and proper Latin and Greek pronunciation could be doubted, another aspect comes to the fore. The purple books of the classic epics underline the thorough language skills essential for senatorial approval of a foreign-born military man who was wed into old Roman nobility and whose rusty cuirass was supposed to have a purple shine – another prestigious omen stated in his biography (*Historia Augusta*, The Two Maximini 30.3, ed. Magie 1924, 374–5).

Later in the fifth century this purple ennobling by language skills was thematized by the aforementioned Sidonius Apollinaris in a letter to his friend Hesperius. Sidonius admonishes his friend that he should not neglect his literary studies. This would help him defend the pure and correct Latin language from the "rust of everyday barbarisms" and save it from extinction. Otherwise, "all the purple[s] of this noble language will lose its colour because of the people's negligence" (Sidonius, Ep. 2.10, ed. Hindermann 2022, 37). Tim Denecker has pointed out interesting similarities in the language attitudes of Sidonius and Jerome in this argument (Denecker 2015, 412–13; cf. Banniard 1992). They both set the hard work of language training in contrast to negligence and rust that they both associated with the dangerous influences of foreign accent and female distraction.

But while Jerome volunteered to style himself as fugitive from purple, giving his language training a distinctly ascetic touch, the politically influential aristocrat and later bishop of Clermont, Sidonius, embraced a purple home in Latin language (as opposed to the "barbarian" street) and could imagine therein a literary collaboration between married men and women. To this end, Sidonius cites a list of married and also non-married couples such as Terentia and Cicero, Corinna and Ovid, or Lesbia and Catullus, where women either assisted men in their literary studies or composed poetry together with them (Sidonius 2022, ed. Hindermann, 292–3; Hindermann 2022). How the differing rhetorical strategies of men like Jerome or Sidonius affected women behind the male perspectives can only be guessed at.

In a letter to his friend Donidius, Sidonius recounts his visit to the exquisitely furnished villa of Tonatius Ferreolus, where he especially admired the library. In it, stacks of books were placed in various bookshelves and bookcases according to a specifically gendered arrangement: "The books were arranged in such a way that around the armchairs of the ladies (*inter matronarum cathedras*) were the *codices* of religious literature (in a religious style – *stilus religiosus*), while those near the benches of the [male] heads of the family (*subsellia paterfamilias*) were distinguished by the high style of Latin eloquence" (Sidonius, Ep. 2.9, ed. Hindermann 2022, 32–3) The latter books of similarly elevated style, which were placed near the men's benches, included volumes by Christian and non-Christian authors. Sidonius mentions and correlates the books of Augustine and Varro, as well as those of Horace and Prudentius. He also notices Rufinus's translation of Origen, which Jerome had attacked as unreliable. Sidonius, on the contrary, praises this book and compares it to Cicero's sublime translation of the famous Greek orator Demosthenes (Sidonius, ed. Hindermann 2022, 263–71; cf. Haines-Eitzen 2012, 44–5; Eigler 2015, 13–16). In this enumeration of Christian and non-Christian authors, Sidonius tells us nothing about the colouring and ornament he saw or envisioned for these books. Were there purple-coloured books? And which stack would they fit into?

We could easily imagine a purple ornament for the classics, for Horace or Virgil – the last, though not mentioned, certainly present in such a library. What about the Christian authors whose style is praised as elevated and equal to the ancient classics? Could a book of the Christian poet Prudentius have had an author portrait on purple similar to Virgil's author portraits? Such a portrait might have resembled the miniature of Prudentius framed by a purple-coloured ground in a Carolingian manuscript from the Lake Constance region that copies a late antique model (Bern, Burgerbibliothek, Cod. 264, p. 67. https://www.e-codices.unifr.ch/de/bbb/0264/67; Eggenberger 1986). If there were such purple-coloured books in the book stack near the men's benches, could there also have been purple books in the book stack near the ladies' seats? Could we imagine that among their works of "stilus religiosus" was the Psalter and if so, could this codex have been written on purple-coloured parchment? Or would such an ornament assign the thus coloured book to the men's high style stack? What would this mean for the women's stack as well as for the men's stack? We are at the heart of the problem of the gendered book stack, with which we introduced this essay. If we assign women agency and not only read them through the lenses of the male authors, their colouring could transgress and subvert the male gender designations, inherent in the description of the combined pagan and Christian library by Sidonius as well as in the vision of the exclusion of pagan literature in women's ascetic literary education promulgated by Jerome. His model of decolouring and seclusion as the only way for women to gain equality with men in the study of scripture cast a long shadow on the efforts of women to free themselves from male dominance in their reading choices. On the other hand, it opened possibilities for alternative models of literary education controlled by women, which became fruitful in the context of women's monasticism. It is in this milieu that asceticism and a "religious style" of writing could be praised with the same purple metaphors that once distinguished the eloquence of classical poets.

The best example of this development is the author portrait of the nun Baudonivia in a late eleventh-century illuminated copy of the biography of St Radegund (Poitiers, Bibliothèque municipale de Poitiers, MS. 250, fol. 43v; Carrasco 1990). The manuscript was produced for the women's convent dedicated to this sixth-century female ascetic, who combined literary study, nightly scripture reading, letter writing, and the renunciation of a worldly life in favour of monastic seclusion. Between 599 and 614, Baudonivia, one of Radegund's successors in the convent, described the saint's life in detail. In her portrait, Baudonivia holds a gilded *stilus* (a pen that one uses to write on a wax tablet but also associated with style) and a writing diptych coloured with purple ground (Figure 4.5).

The purple writing surface here subverts gender stereotypes. It sets a female literary composition of "religious style" on equal ground with a male literary composition. We know that Baudonivia wrote her biography of St Radegund shortly after the completion of another version of the saint's biography by the highly educated and classically trained poet Venantius Fortunatus. Both versions were later joined in the same illuminated manuscript and both were introduced with author portraits. But whereas Venantius is shown in the process of writing on undyed parchment, it is Baudonivia who writes on purple. It is her portrayal that most closely resembles the poet boy thus distinguished in the *Vergilius romanus*. She holds in her hand the embodiment of her literary excellence, the purple tablets of her perfect composition and sublime style in religious, monastic writing (cf. Graf 2002, 83–91).

This subversion of Jerome's gender ascription to purple makeup could also work the other way round. The pairing of literary study and religious writing that is epitomized and embodied by Baudonivia's purple diptych could set Jerome himself on polished purple ground. His philological care in translating the biblical books – especially the Psalter – was regularly praised as perfection and polishing of the text, equal to the highest standards of classical poetry and eloquence (cf. as one example the poem in

Figure 4.5 Author portrait of the nun Baudonivia holding a gilded stilus and purple-coloured writing diptych, last quarter of the eleventh century, various colorants, detail, Illustrated Life of Saint Radegund of Poitiers, Poitiers, Bibliothèque municipale de Poitiers, MS. 250, fol. 43v, detail. Document du domaine public: https://www.mediatheques-grandpoitiers.fr/Default/digital-viewer/c-1117076

the Carolingian Lothar Psalter, London, British Library, Add MS 37768, fol. 5v). This praise could manifest itself once again in purple images in the Carolingian era. In the late ninth-century Golden Psalter from St. Gallen, Jerome introduces his translation of the biblical text, standing upright, framed by purple, blessing and holding with delicately elongated gilded fingers a golden book with purple ornament on its jewelled cover (St. Gallen, Stiftsbibliothek, Cod. 22, p. 14; Euw 2008, 400–8; see Figure 4.6).

This purple queering of the ascetic role-model of male roughness was made possible by liturgical performance, royal praise, and the equation of philological study with poetic eloquence.[10] If we take a close look at the

10 For another pictorial tradition of "queering" Jerome, see the late medieval images of the "cross-dressing" saint: Mills 2015, 1–24; Griffiths 2018, 77–109; Amy Richlin, The

Figure 4.6 Jerome standing on purple ground holding a gilded book with purple ornament, detail, orchil (for colouring the purple ground), gold and various other colorants, c.880/890, Golden Psalter (*Psalterium aureum*), St. Gallen, Stiftsbibliothek, Cod. Sang. 22, p. 14, detail. Public domain: https://www.e-codices.unifr.ch/de/csg/0022/14

only surviving late antique Greek purple Psalter, a book that shows all earmarks of Jerome's condemnation of purple makeup for biblical books, this equation becomes visible in the traces of its continuous usage. Roughly a quarter of a millennium after its production, it had been transferred from Rome to a new location, reaching the Reichenau monastery at Lake Constance in the late eighth century (Bogaert 1983, 205–7). In this monastery, a monk studying the Greek text added with orange minium the Latin beginnings of the psalm verses quoted after Jerome's "Gallican" translation in the margins of the purple-coloured pages: Instead of traces of blots caused by women's tears we find notes adapting Jerome's own philological study

Thomas Spencer Jerome lecture series, Fall 2022, https://www.aarome.org/events/calendar/amy-richlin-jerome-captive-slave-woman-latin-canon.

on the purple makeup of the text (Zürich, Zentralbibliothek, RP1, Crisci and Eggenberge 2007, 64–5, 69; see Figure 4.4).

Conclusion

In his letters to Roman aristocratic women about the proper use[11] of scripture in the pursuit of an ascetic Christian lifestyle, Jerome dismissed purple makeup and any ornamentation of books with luxurious materials as wasteful distraction from the content of the text. Following the ancient sophistic tradition Jerome's dismissal of the materiality and sensuality of books goes hand in hand with a binary gender model that associates the philological work upon the text and the renunciation of its adornment with male scholarship. In order for women to become equal to men through the study of scripture, Jerome extols the performance of a textual asceticism that suppresses the makeup of books and of female bodies alike. His makeup criticism is part of a larger discourse that expresses a persistent fear of a sensual engagement with the materiality of scripture in binary gender stereotypes. It reduces the complex relationships between the body, the material book, and the performance of language in the practice of reading and contemplating scripture to a strict opposition of, on the one hand, a correct semantic understanding of the text associated with male scholarship and, on other hand, material distraction linked to female adornment. However, a close reading of the purple metaphors employed by Jerome reveals their roots in the rhetorical appraisal of eloquence and poetic language precisely through the materiality of the text. In the development of the purple-coloured parchment codex adornment and linguistic sensibility are not opposites but join forces in the panegyrics of scripture. Only by reading the purple surfaces of these codices with utmost care can we rediscover the traces of this verbal and material polishing of the sacred text open to male and female performances of reading, studying and contemplating scripture.

References

Aceto, Maurizio et al. 2019. "Mythic Dyes or Mythic Colour? New Insight into the Use of Purple Dyes on Codices." *Spectrochimica Acta: Part A, Molecular and Biomolecular Spectroscopy* 215: 133–41. https://doi.org/10.1016/j.saa.2019.01.091

Adkin, Neil. 2003. *Jerome on Virginity: A Commentary on the "Libellus De Virginitate Servanda" (Letter 22)*. Cambridge: Francis Cairns.

Ahmed, Sara. 2019. *What's the Use? On the Uses of Use*. Durham, NC: Duke University Press.

11 For this expression cf. Ahmed 2019, 206–7.

Avery, W. T. 1940. "The Adoratio Purpurae and the Importance of the Imperial Purple in the Fourth Century." *Memoires of the American Academy in Rome* 17: 66–80. https://doi.org/10.2307/4238611

Banniard, Michel. 1992. "La rouille et la lime: Sidoine Apollinaire et la langue du classique en Gaule au Ve siècle." In *De Tertullien aux Mozarabes: Mélanges offerts à J. Fontaine*, edited by Louis Holtz. vol. 1, 413–27. Paris: Institut d'Etudes augustiniennes.

Baroni, Sandro. 2012. "Pergamene purpuree e scritture metalliche nella letteratura tecnico artistica: Un quadro introduttivo." In *Oro, argento e porpora: Prescrizioni e procedimenti nella letteratura tecnica medievale*, edited by Sandro Baroni. Trento: Tangram Edizioni Scientifiche.

Bartsch, Shadi. 2015. *Persius: A Study in Food, Philosophy and the Figural.* Chicago: University of Chicago Press.

Beauvoir, Simone de. 1959. "Brigitte Bardot and the Lolita Syndrome." *Esquire Magazine* 8: 32–8. https://doi.org/10.5406/illinois/9780252039003.003.0017

Bernabò, Massimo. 2014/2015. "Virgil Illustrated in Gaul: A Reassessment." *Bizantinistica* 16: 239–57.

Berschin, Walter. 1994. "Personenbeschreibung in der Biographie des frühen Mittelalters" In *Historiographie im frühen Mittelalter*, edited by Anton Scharer and Georg Scheibelreiter, 186–93. Vienna/Munich: Böhlau.

Bessone, L. 1998. "La porpora a Roma." In *La porpora. Realtà e immaginario di un colore simbolico. Atti del Convegno di Studio, Venezia, 24 e 25 ottobre 1996*, edited by O. Longo, 149–202. Venice: Istituto veneto di scienze lettere ed arti.

Betancourt, Roland. 2020. *Byzantine Intersectionality. Sexuality, Gender and Race in the Middle Ages.* Princeton, NJ: Princeton University Press.

Bicchieri, M. 2014. "The Purple Codex Rossanensis: Spectroscopic Characterisation and First Evidence of the Use of the Elderberry Lake in a Sixth Century Manuscript." *Environmental Science and Pollution Research* 21: 14146–57. https://doi.org/10.1007/s11356-014-3341-6

Bigus, Marta. 2011. "*Codex Argenteus* and Political Ideology in Ostrogothic Kingdom." *Lychnos* 7–27.

Bogaert, P.-M. 1983. "Précisions sur l'histoire de deux manuscrits en onciale de la Septante (T et G)." *Le Muséon* 96: 205–16.

Booker, Courtney M. 1995. "Vermiculatus as Scarlet in Jerome." *Orpheus: Rivista di umanità classica e cristiana* 16: 124–6.

Booker, Courtney M. 1997. "The Codex Purpureus and its Role as an Imago Regis in Late Antiquity." In *Studies in Latin Literature and Roman History VIII*, edited by Carl Deroux. 441–77. CollLatomus 239. Brussels: Éditions Latomus.

Brown, Michelle P. ed. 2006. *In the Beginning: Bibles Before the Year 1000.* Exh.Cat. Washington, DC: Smithsonian Institution.

Bruhat, Marie Odile. 2017. "The Treatment of Space in Optatian's Poetry." In *Morphogrammata/The Lettered Art of Optatian: Figuring Cultural Transformations in the Age of Constantine*, edited by Michael Squire and Johannes Wienand, 257–81. Paderborn: Wilhelm Fink.

Bruyne, Donatien de. 2015. *Prefaces to the Latin Bible.* Turnhout: Brepols.

Bücheler, Anna. 2018. *Ornament as Argument: Textile Pages and Textile Metaphors in Medieval Manuscripts.* Berlin/Boston: De Gruyter.

Butler, Dom Cuthbert, ed. 1898. *The Lausiac History of Palladius.* 2 vols. Texts and Studies 6. Cambridge: Cambridge University Press.

Butler, Judith. 1986. "Sex and Gender in Simone de Beauvoir's Second Sex." *Yale French Studies* 72: 35–49. https://doi.org/10.2307/2930225

Butler, Judith. 1990. *Gender Trouble: Feminism and the Subversion of Identity*. New York and London: Routledge.

Cain, Andrew. 2009a. "Rethinking Jerome's Portraits of Holy Women." In *Jerome of Stridon: His Life, Writings and Legacy*, edited by Andrew Cain and Josef Lössl, 47–57. Farnham: Ashgate.

Cain, Andrew. 2009b. *The Letters of Jerome: Asceticism, Biblical Exegesis, and the Construction of Christian Authority in Late Antiquity*. Oxford: Oxford University Press.

Cain, Andrew, ed. 2013. *Jerome's Epitaph on Paula: A Commentary on the "Epitaphium Sanctae Paulae"*, Oxford: Oxford University Press.

Carmassi, Patrizia. 2011. "Purpurismum in martyrio. Die Farbe des Blutes in mittelalterlichen Handschriften." In *Farbe im Mittelalter: Materialität - Medialität - Semantik*, edited by Ingrid Bennewitz and Andrea Schindler, 251–73. Berlin: Akademie-Verlag.

Carrasco, Magdalena Elizabeth. 1990. "Spirituality in Context: The Romanesque Illustrated Life of St. Radegund of Poitiers (Poitiers, Bibl. Mun., MS 250)." *The Art Bulletin* 72: 414–35. https://doi.org/10.2307/3045749

Castelli, Elizabeth. 1991. "'I Will Make Mary Male': Pieties of the Body and Gender Transformation of Christian Women in Late Antiquity." In *Body Guards: The Cultural Politics of Gender Ambiguity*, edited by Julia Epstein and Kristina Straub, 29–49. New York: Routledge.

Cavallo, Guglielmo. 1987. "Il codice purpureo di Rossano: Libro, oggetto, simbolo." In *Codex Purpureus Rossanensis: Commentarium*, edited by Guglielmo Cavallo, 1–21. Rome: Salerno Editrice.

Clark, E. A. 1998. "The Lady Vanishes: Dilemmas of a Feminist Historian After the'Linguistic Turn.'" *Church History* 67: 1–31. https://doi.org/10.2307/3170769

Clark, E. A. 2004. *History, Theory, Text. Historians and the Linguistic Turn*. Cambridge, MA: Harvard University Press.

Cooper, Kate. 2013. "The Bride of Christ, the 'Male Woman', and the Female Reader in Late Antiquity." In *The Oxford Handbook of Women and Gender in Medieval Europe*, edited by Judith Bennett and Ruth Mazo Karas, 529–44. Oxford: Oxford University Press.

Copeland, Rita. 1994. "The Pardoner's Body and the Disciplining of Rhetoric." In *Framing Medieval Bodies*, edited by Sarah Kay and Miri Rubin, 138–59. Manchester: Manchester University Press.

Crisci, Edoardo, and Eggenberger, Christoph. 2007. *Il Salterio Purpureo Zentralbibliothek Zürich, RP 1 Il salterio purpureo Zentralbibliothek Zürich, RP 1*. Cassino: Università degli Studi (Segno e testo 5).

Dalton, Omonde Maddock, ed. 1915. *The Letters of Sidonius*. 2 vols. Oxford: Clarendon Press.

Denecker, Tim. 2015. "Language Attitudes and Social Connotations in Jerome and Sidonius Apollinaris." *Vigiliae Christianae* 69: 393–421. https://doi.org/10.1163/15700720-12341228

Denoël, Charlotte. 2015. "Le scriptorium de Saint-Germain-des-Prés au temps de l'abbé Adelard (v. 1030–1060): Les manuscrits enluminés par Ingelard, scriptor honestus." In *Saint-Germain-des-Prés Mille ans d'une abbaye à Paris*, edited by Roland Recht and Michel Zink, 159–212. Paris: Académie des Inscriptions et Belles-Lettres.

Denoël, Charlotte, et al. 2018. "Illuminating the Carolingian Era: New Discoveries as a Result of Scientific Analyses." *Heritage Science* 6(28): 28. https://doi.org/10.1186/s40494-018-0194-1

Dupont, Florence, and Parker, Holt N. 2011. "The Corrupted Boy and the Crowned Poet or, The Material Reality and Symbolic Status of the Literary Book at Rome." In *Ancient Literacies: The Culture of Reading in Greece and Rome*, edited by William A. Johnson and Holt N. Parker, 143–63. Oxford: Oxford University Press.

Eggenberger, Christoph. 1977. "Die Miniaturen des Vergilius Romanus, Codex Vat. Lat. 3867." *Byzantinische Zeitschrift* 70: 58–90. https://doi.org/10.1515/byzs.1977.70.1.58

Eggenberger, Christoph. 1986. "Zur Farbe im Berner Prudentius: Ein Versuch im Gedenken an Heinz Roosen-Runge." *Zeitschrift für schweizerische Archäologie und Kunstgeschichte* 43: 3–8.

Eigler, Ulrich. 2015. "Überlieferung durch die Hintertür? Die Tradition klassischer lateinischer Autoren als Rekonstruktion des Wissenshintergrunds der Kirchenväter." In *Karolingische Klöster: Wissenstransfer und kulturelle Innovation*, edited by Julia Becker, Tino Licht, and Stefan Weinfurter, 7–22. Berlin: De Gruyter.

Ernst, Ulrich. 1993. "Farbe und Schrift im Mittelalter unter Berücksichtigung antiker Grundlagen und neuzeitlicher Rezeptionsformen." *Settimane di studio del Centro Italiano di Studi sull'Alto Medioevo* 41: 344–415.

Euw, Anton von. 2008. *Die St. Galler Buchkunst vom 8. bis zum Ende des 11. Jahrhunderts*. St. Gallen: Verlag am Klosterhof.

Evans, Caroline. 2012. "On Rereading Simone de Beauvoir's 'The Second Sex' After Thirty-Five Years." *Women's Studies Quarterly* 41: 194–6. https://doi.org/10.1353/wsq.2013.0061

Evans, Helen C. 2012. "Leaves from the Purple Vellum Gospels." In *Byzantium and Islam: Age of Transition 7th–9th Century*, edited by Helen C. Evans and Brandie Ratliff, 41. New Haven, CT: Yale University Press.

Feichtinger, Barbara. 1995. *Apostolae apostolorum. Frauenaskese als Befreiung und Zwang bei Hieronymus*. Frankfurt am Main: Peter Lang

Flood, Finbarr Barry. 2019. "Bodies, Books, and Buildings: Economies of Ornament in Juridical Islam." In *Clothing Sacred Scriptures. Book Art and Book Religion in Christian, Islamic, and Jewish Cultures*, edited by David Ganz and Barbara Schellewald, 49–68. Berlin/Boston: Walter de Gruyter.

Fuchs, Robert, and Oltrogge, Doris. 2007. "Gold und Purpur. Zwischen Ideal und Werkstattpraxis." In *Il Salterio Purpureo Zentralbibliothek Zürich, RP 1 Il salterio purpureo Zentralbibliothek Zürich, RP 1*, edited by Edoardo Crisci and Robert Fuchs, 82–98. Cassino: Università degli Studi.

Furlan, Italo. 1998. "Introduzione ai Codici Purpurei." In *La Porpora: Realtà e Immaginario di un colore simbolico. Atti del Convegno di Studio, Venezia, 24 e 25 ottobre 1996*, edited by Oddone Longo, 317–33. Venice: Istituto veneto di scienze, lettere ed arti.

Ganz, David. 2015. *Buch-Gewänder: Prachteinbände im Mittelalter*. Berlin: Reimer.

Ganz, David. 2019. "Clothing Sacred Scriptures: Materiality and Aesthetics in Medieval Book Religions." In *Clothing Sacred Scriptures. Book Art and Book Religion in Christian, Islamic, and Jewish Cultures*, edited by David Ganz and Barbara Schellewald, 1–46. Berlin/Boston: Walter de Gruyter.

Gleason, Maud W. 1995. *Making Men: Sophists and Self-Presentation in Ancient Rome*. Princeton, NJ: Princeton University Press.

Grabar, André. 1948. *Les peintures de l'Évangéliaire de Sinope (Bibliothèque Nationale, Suppl. Gr.1286): Réproduites en facsimilé*. [Paris]: Bibliothèque nationale.

Graf, Katrin. 2002. *Bildnisse schreibender Frauen im Mittelalter. 9. bis Anfang 13. Jh.* Basel: Schwabe Verlag.

Grafton, A., and Williams, M. 2006. *Christianity and the Transformation of the Book: Origen, Eusebius and the Library of Caesarea*. Cambridge, MA: Harvard University Press.

Griffiths, Fiona J. 2018. *Nuns' Priests' Tales: Men and Salvation in Medieval Women's Monastic Life*. Philadelphia: University of Pennsylvania Press.

Grig, Lucy. 2012. "Deconstructing the Symbolic City: Jerome as Guide to Late Antique Rome." *Papers of the British School at Rome* 80: 125–43. https://doi.org/10.1017/s0068246212000074

Haines-Eitzen, Kim. 2012. *The Gendered Palimpsest: Women, Writing, and Representation in Early Christianity*. Oxford: Oxford University Press.

Herz, P. 1985. "Parthicarius und Babyloniarius: Produktion und Handel feiner orientalischer Lederwaren." *Münstersche Beiträge zur antiken Handelsgeschichte* 4: 89–106.

Hindermann, Judith. 2022. "Lucubratio (Night Work) and the Candelabra as a Symbol of Marriage and Inspiration in Sidonius Apollinaris (ep. 2,10,5)." In *Women and Objects in Antiquity*, edited by H. Harich-Schwarzbauer and C. Scheidegger Lämmle. 205–22. Trier: Wissenschaftlicher Verlag Trier.

Historia Augusta. 1924. *Volume II: Caracalla. Geta. Opellius Macrinus. Diadumenianus. Elagabalus. Severus Alexander. The Two Maximini. The Three Gordians. Maximus and Balbinus*, translated by David Magie. Loeb Classical Library 140. Cambridge, MA: Harvard University Press.

Hixson, Elijah. 2019. *Scribal Habits in 6th Century Greek Purple Codices*. Leiden/Boston: Brill.

Hofmann, Christa, ed. 2020. *The Vienna Genesis: Material Analysis and Conservation of a Late Antique Illuminated Manuscript on Purple Parchment*. Vienna: Böhlau.

Huglo, Michel. 1982. "Le répons-Graduel de la Messe : Evolution de la forme. Permanence de la fonction." *Annales suisses de musicologie* 2: 53–73. https://doi.org/10.2307/928345

Jerome. 1890. *Letters and Select Works*, edited by Henry Wace and Philip Schaff, translated by W. H. Freemantle. A Select Library of Nicene and Post-Nicene Fathers of the Christian Church. 2nd ser. 6. New York: The Christian Literature Co.

Jerome. 1933. *Epistolae. Select Letters*, translated by F. A. Wright. Loeb Classical Library 262. Cambridge, MA: Harvard University Press.

Jerome. 1956. *Die Chronik des Hieronymus. Hieronymi Chronicon*, edited by Rudolf Helm. Berlin: Akademie-Verlag.

Jerome. 2011. *La letter 22 à Eustochium: De virginitate seruanda*, translated and commentary by Yves Marie Duval and Patrick Laurence. Bégrolles en Mauges: Abbaye de Bellefontaine.

Johnson, William A. 2010. *Readers and Reading Culture in the High Roman Empire: A Study of Elite Communities*. Oxford: Oxford University Press.

Katz, Phyllis B. 2007. "Educating Paula: A Proposed Curriculum for Raising a 4th-Century Christian Infant." In *Constructions of Childhood in Ancient Greece and Italy*, edited by Ada Cohen and Jeremy B. Rutter, 115–27. Princeton, NJ: American School of Classical Studies at Athens (Hesperia Supplements 41).

Kay, Sarah. 2017. *Animal Skins and the Reading Self in Medieval Latin and French Bestiaries*. Chicago: University of Chicago Press.

Kearney, James. 2009. *The Incarnate Text: Imagining the Book in Reformation England*. Philadelphia: University of Pennsylvania Press.

Kessler, Herbert L. 1994. "Codici purpurei." In *Enciclopedia dell'arte medievale*, vol. 5, 140–5. Rome: Istituto della Enciclopedia Italiana.

Körfer, Anna-Lena. 2020. *Kaiser Konstantin als Leser: Panegyrik, performance und Poetologie in den "carmina" Optatians*. Berlin/Boston: De Gruyter.

Kuefler, Mathew. 2001. *The Manly Eunuch: Masculinity, Gender Ambiguity, and Christian Ideology in Late Antiquity*. Chicago: University of Chicago Press.

Kuefler, Mathew. 2007. "The Marriage Revolution in Late Antiquity: The Theodosian Code and Later Roman Marriage Law." *Journal of Family History* 32: 343–70. https://doi.org/10.1177/0363199007304424

Lambert, Cat. 2022. "Bad Readers in Ancient Rome." Ph.D. dissertation, Columbia University.

Lowden, John. 1999. "The Beginnings of Biblical Illustration." In *Imaging the Early Medieval Bible*, edited by John Williams. 5–59. University Park, PA: Pennsylvania University Press.

Lucian. 1921. *The Dead Come to Life or The Fisherman. The Double Indictment or Trials by Jury. On Sacrifices. The Ignorant Book Collector. The Dream or Lucian's Career. The Parasite. The Lover of Lies. The Judgement of the Goddesses. On Salaried Posts in Great Houses*, translated by A. M. Harmon. Loeb Classical Library 130. Cambridge, MA: Harvard University Press.

Mayvaert, Paul. 1983. "'Uncial Letters': Jerome's Meaning of the Term." *Journal of Theological Studies* 34: 185–8. https://doi.org/10.1093/jts/34.1.185

McKitterick, Rosamond. 1989. *The Carolingians and the Written Word*. Cambridge: Cambridge University Press.

Mills, Robert. 2015. *Seeing Sodomy in the Middle Ages*. Chicago: University of Chicago Press.

Motteran, Giulia. 2012. *Le Sang des Evangiles : Etude systématique des manuscrits tardo-antiques pourprés contenant les Evangiles*. Master's thesis dir. by Filippo Ronconi. Paris: EHESS.

Munkholt Christensen, Maria, and Gemeinhardt, Peter. 2019. "Holy Women and Men as Teachers in Late Antique Christianity." *Zeitschrift für Antikes Christentum/Journal of Ancient Christianity* 23: 288–328. https://doi.org/10.1515/zac-2019-0015

Olson, K. 2009. "Cosmetics in Roman Antiquity: Substance, Remedy, Poison." *Classical World* 102: 291–310. https://doi.org/10.1353/clw.0.0098

Ovid. 1924. *Tristia. Ex Ponto*, translated by A. L. Wheeler, revised by G. P. Goold. Loeb Classical Library 151. Cambridge, MA: Harvard University Press.

Pausch, Matthias. 2003. *Die römische Tunika: Ein Beitrag zur Peregrinisierung der antiken Kleidung*. Augsburg: Wissner.

Porter, Cheryl, et al. 2018. "Looking for Lichen, Fooled by Folium and Tricked by Tyrian: A Brief Tour and New Research on Purple in Manuscripts." In *Manuscripts in the Making. Art and Science*. Vol. 2, edited by Stella Panayotova and Paola Ricciardi, 67–79. London/Turnhout: Brepols Publishers.

Rebenich, Stefan. 1992. *Hieronymus und sein Kreis. Prosopographische und sozialgeschichtliche Untersuchungen*. Stuttgart: Steiner.

Reinhold, Meyer. 1970. *History of Purple as a Status Symbol in Antiquity*. Brussels: Latomus.

Reitzenstein, R. 1916. "Philologische Kleinigkeiten. 4. Zu Minucius Felix." *Hermes* 51: 609–23.

Reudenbach, Bruno. 2009. "Der Codex als heiliger Raum. Überlegungen zur Bildausstattung früher Evangelienbücher." In *Codex und Raum*, edited by Stephan Müller, Lieselotte E. Saurma-Jeltsch, and Peter Strohschneider, 59–84. Wiesbaden: Harrassowitz.

Scholz, Peter. 2005. "Zur öffentlichen Repräsentation römischer Senatoren und Magistrate: Einige Überlegungen zur (verlorenen) materiellen Kultur der republikanischen Senatsaristokratie." In *Die Dinge als Zeichen: Kulturelles Wissen und materielle Kultur*, edited by Tobias L. Kienlin, 409–31. Bonn: Habelt.

Seneca. 1932. *Moral Essays, Volume II: De Consolatione ad Marciam. De Vita Beata. De Otio. De Tranquillitate Animi. De Brevitate Vitae. De Consolatione ad Polybium. De Consolatione ad Helviam*, translated by John W. Basore. Loeb Classical Library 254. Cambridge, MA: Harvard University Press.

Sidonius. 1936–65. *Poems and Letters*, with an English translation by William B. Anderson, finished by W. H. Semple and E. H. Warmington. 2 vols. Loeb Library. Cambridge, MA: Harvard University Press.

Sidonius. 2022. *Sidonius Apollinaris' Letters, Book 2: Text, Translation and Commentary*, by Judith Hindermann. Edinburgh: Edinburgh University Press.

Speciale, Lucinia. 2019. "ΤΗΣ ΤΩΝ ΕΥΑΓΓΕΛΙΣΤΩΝ ΣΥΜΦΩΝΙΑΣ: Il programma decorativo originale del Tetravangelo di Rossano: Osservazioni e ipotesi." In *Codex purpureus Rossanensis*, edited by Maria Letizia Sebastiani and Patrizia Cavalieri, 181–91. Rome: Gangemi editore.

Squire, Michael. 2017a. "Optatian and his Lettered Art: A Kaleidoscopic Lens on Late Antiquity." In *Morphogrammata/The Lettered Art of Optatian: Figuring Cultural Transformations in the Age of Constantine*, edited by Michael Squire and Johannes Wienand, 55–120. Paderborn: Wilhelm Fink.

Squire, Michael. 2017b. "POP Art: The Optical Poetics of Publilius Optatianus Porfyrius." In *Towards a Poetics of Late Latin Literature*, edited by J. Elsner and J. Hernández Lobato, 25–99. New York: Oxford University Press.

Steigerwald, Gerhard. 1990. "Das kaiserliche Purpurprivileg in spätantiker und byzantinischer Zeit." *Jahrbuch für Antike und Christentum* 33: 209–39.

Stenger, Jan R. 2021. "'Eines der ärgerlichsten Musterstücke verlogener Rhetorik': Hieronymus Traum und die Begründung seiner Autorschaft." In *Auf der Suche nach Autofiktion in der antiken Literatur*, edited by Gregor Bitto and Bardo Maria Gauly, 213–40. Berlin/Boston: De Gruyter.

Stenger, Jan R. 2022. *Education in Late Antiquity: Challenges, Dynamism, and Reinterpretation, 300–550 CE*. Oxford: Oxford University Press.

Vessey, Mark, 2007. "*Quid facit cum Horatio Hieronymus?* Christian Latin Poetry and Scriptural Politics." In *Poetry and Exegesis in Premodern Latin Christianity: The Encounter between Classical and Christian Strategies of Interpretation*, edited by Willemien Otten and Karla Pollmann, 29–48. Leiden: Brill.

Wallraff, Martin. 2013. *Kodex und Kanon. Das Buch im frühen Christentum*. Berlin/Boston: De Gruyter.

Watts, James W. 2006 "The Three Dimensions of Scriptures." *Postscripts* 2: 135–59.

White, Carolinne, ed. 2010. *Lives of Roman Christian Women*, translated and edited with an introduction and notes. London: Penguin Books.

Wilkinson, Kate. 2015. *Women and Modesty in Late Antiquity*. Cambridge: Cambridge University Press.

Williams, G. D. 1992. "Representations of the Book-Roll in Latin Poetry: Ovid, Tr. 1, 1,3–14 and Related Texts." *Mnemosyne* 45, 178–89. https://doi.org/10.1163/1568525x-90000029

Williams, Megan Hale. 2006. *The Monk and the Book: Jerome and the Making of Christian Scholarship*. Chicago/London: University of Chicago Press.

Wright, David H. 2001. *The Roman Vergil and the Origins of Medieval Book Design*. London: British Library.

Zimmermann, Barbara. 2003. *Die Wiener Genesis im Rahmen der antiken Buchmalerei. Ikonographie, Darstellung, Illustrationsverfahren und Aussageintention*. Wiesbaden: Reichert.

About the Author

Thomas Rainer studied art history and ancient history at the University of Innsbruck and Freiburg im Breisgau and received his PhD from the University of Innsbruck in 2008. From 2008 to 2018, he was a curator at the Bavarian Administration of Palaces, Gardens and Lakes in Munich and from 2020 to 2024, he was a research fellow at the SNSF research project Textures of Sacred Scripture at the University of Zurich, in which capacity he coordinated the material analytical studies on dyes, pigments, and metal inks in Carolingian and Ottonian manuscripts of various libraries. Since 2024, he has been Managing Director and Program Coordinator of eikones, the research Center for the Theory and History of the Image at the University of Basel. (thomas.rainer@uzh.ch)

5

"Then Queen Esther Daughter of Abihail Wrote": Gendered Agency and Ritualized Writing in Jewish Scriptural Practice

Joanna Homrighausen

Abstract

*This article focuses on how the material form of the Esther scroll and the ritualized practices of copying it reflect changes in how Jews remember the events of Purim. I demonstrate how Purim and writing intersect with contemporary changes in women's roles in Jewish ritual, as well as new interpretations of the Book of Esther informed by feminist readings and heightened awareness of the relationship between gender and agency. I examine Esther scrolls made by contemporary female ritual scribes (*soferot*) who add their own creative marks to the scrolls they copy: Nava Levine-Coren, Avielah Barclay, Jen Taylor Friedman, and Rachel Jackson. These creative touches convey their readings of the biblical text, which magnify women's perspective and agency.*

Keywords: scribes; gender; Esther; scroll; Book of Esther; Jewish art; sofrut; feminist biblical criticism; biblical reception history

> Esther has been written out, or written over. But if we pay attention to the book of Esther, we should not be overly dismayed by this. Write more. Write again. (Jobling and Roughley 2009, 333)
>
> We save ourselves as best we can, we use whatever we have. Beauty, friends in high places, a rifle in the woods with the partisans, a fountain pen, whatever works. (Ostriker 1997, 228)

If many Jewish festivals are festivals of memory, then Purim is a festival of memory enabled by acts of writing. Purim retells the story of the biblical Book of Esther, a brief diasporic tale in which a young Jewish woman becomes queen of the Persian empire and, using her royal power and feminine charm, thwarts an attempted genocide on her people. Like the festival of Hanukkah, Purim serves as a generative ritual and textual site for Jews to make sense of perennial issues of life in diaspora in Gentile-majority cultures. Though not one of the major Jewish festivals such as Yom Kippur or Passover, Purim is unique in its propensity toward excess, humour, parody, and drunkenness, which has led some observers to deem it the Jewish carnival (Fisch 1994; Polish 2018).

Purim is also, however, a festival of writing, a "celebration of textuality" (Fisch 1994). In the Book of Esther from which it derives, acts of writing feature heavily in the plot: we find the king's edicts, royal chronicles, written Persian law, and letters written by Esther and Mordecai to institute the Purim festival. The book both lampoons the ineffectiveness of the Persian written bureaucracy and underscores the power of writing for Jewish deliverance (Polaski 2018; Blondheim and Katz 2015). Further, Esther is the only Jewish woman in the Hebrew Bible whom the narrator explicitly reports writing (Esth 9:29), a point of interest for feminist readers (Howard 2015; Wood 2021). This depiction of Esther writing appears in a concluding section narrating Esther and Mordecai's writing Purim letters (Esth 9:20–32), a section which some Jewish interpreters see as describing the authoring of the Book of Esther itself.[1] Jewish tradition puts writing at the centre of Purim as well. At Purim, Jews must read or hear Esther read from a handwritten scroll – a *megillah* – a practice attested as early as the Mishnah in tractate Megillah 1:1–4 (c. 200 CE).[2]

Purim thus provides a useful case study in how Jewish tradition, from the Mishnah to the present, understands concepts of writing, textuality, and imagined authorship. This article considers these concepts by examining how contemporary female scribes writing *megillot* Esther for ritual use engage issues of gender and agency in the Book of Esther and in Jewish ritual life today. Like Esther herself, they enact their gendered agency in a

1 See e.g. Greek Esther (F:11), TgRishon 9:26 and 9:29; b. Meg. 19a; Leqakh Tov on 9:29 (Buber 1886, 111); Saadiah Gaon (Wechsler 2015, 111); Rashi on Esther 9:20; Ibn Ezra, in his introduction to his first commentary on Esther (Ibn Ezra 2019, 57–8).

2 In this essay I employ the Hebrew terms. The *megillat Esther*, or the "Scroll of Esther," refers to the handwritten scroll. It is often called "the megillah" for short. The plural is *megillot* or *megillot Esther*. Jewish law holds that Esther must be read from a scroll, not a codex. I use the term "The Book of Esther" to refer to the text of the story regardless of its physical format.

way that loyally subverts Jewish life even as it preserves Jewish texts. And like Esther, their agency is hidden, not immediately apparent.

Methodological Reflections on Purim: Memory, Ritual, and Manuscripts

Five methodological presuppositions help us connect the dots between Purim observance, the iconic scroll as a material object, and the ritual significance of copying the scroll.

First: Purim is a festival of communal memory – specifically, a commemorative ceremony which is enabled by the technology of writing (Connerton 1989). Many of the observances of Purim, as recorded in late antique Jewish writings, repeat the actions of the Jews in the Book of Esther itself (Esth 9:22–8): giving gifts to friends and to the poor, feasting, and (in some communities) getting drunk (Fishbane 2018).[3] Purim does not merely recollect the past, but ritually re-enacts it, transforming its participants into the Jewish protagonists of the ancient book via "a ritualization of the myth in sacred time" (Langer 1998; 2013, 121–2). In this re-enactment, Jews on Purim reshape their communal memory of Purim to better fit their present realities – memory is, after all, malleable – and map those memories of the ancient past onto their present and future to make sense of current social, religious, and political challenges (O'Donnell 2015; Rubenstein 1992). This can already be seen in the large quantity of interpretive literature on Purim in late antique Judaism, such as Esther Rabbah and the full midrash to Esther in the Babylonian Talmud (b. Meg. 10b-17a) (Lerner 2006, 176–229; Koller 2014, 161–225). Some of these interpretive traditions made their way into Purim liturgy via hymns, expanded Aramaic translations, and choices of lections (Stern 2012). We can see how Purim reshapes the memory of Esther by studying Purim rituals throughout history, which respond to issues including empire, Zionism, race, Nazism, and gender (H. Shoham 2014; Ben-Ur 2013; Horowitz 2006; Freedman 2011). These Purim rituals reflect Jewish communal identity and imagine possible Jewish futures.

Second: the megillat Esther, as one of Purim's central symbols and its key liturgical prop, plays the role of an iconic text in Jewish life. By "iconic text" I mean a sacred text which a religious community deems important qua its very material and visual form, above or separate from its semantic contents (Watts 2019, 13–54). Iconic texts are manipulated and displayed in ritual, and often become symbols themselves. Iconic texts exist across religious traditions and can be seen in the Hebrew Bible, as in the standing

3 For sources, see m. Meg. 1:4, t. Meg. 1:5, b. Bab. Metz. 78b; b. Avod. Zar. 17b; b. Meg. 4b, y. Meg. 1:5.

stones in Joshua (8:35–6) or Ezra reading the Law (Neh 8:1–12) (Frevel 2018). For Watts, iconic texts serve rhetorical functions: they authenticate scriptures, religions, and religious authorities.

Third: beyond Watts's rhetorical function, the Esther scroll as visual symbol and material object mediates networks of agents and meanings: between humans and divine presence (Parmenter 2013); between Jews past and present; between "individual memories, cultural representations, and the immediate environment" (Schleicher 2018, 39). In other words, the scroll functions as an enchanting object, a hub connecting agents, agencies, representations, and meanings (Morgan 2021). Other scholars refer to this aspect as "transitivity" (Schleicher 2011; Malley 2004, 83–5). If rituals may be defined as "embodied, condensed, and prescribed enactment[s]" which "make meaning by deploying symbols to communicate networks of embodied knowledge" (Grimes 2013, 195–6, 328), then the scroll is one of those central symbols for Purim. Iconic texts, like other symbols, change meaning over time. People invest new affective relations and meaningful associations into them (Parmenter 2018; Larson 2013). These parallel changes in communal memory.

Fourth: changes in communal Purim memories appear in the visual and material medium of the Esther scroll. While the Hebrew text of Esther has stayed largely stable since at least the tenth century, Jewish scribes over the centuries have found ways to invest the material scroll with new meanings by adding colophons, blessings, illustrations, and decorations (Budzioch 2019, 45–66). These paratexts reveal facets of biblical reception and use (Lied and Lundhaug 2017; Krauss et al. 2020). Scribes also generate new interpretations through word-image interplays in the scroll, modifying individual letters or layouts of longer sections of text in ways that reflect or spark new readings of the story (Diamond 2019). Scholars of Jewish ritual have indeed noted that changes in ritual objects often reflect or create changes in ritual practices (Ochs 2007), including manuscripts used as ritual objects (Kogman-Appel 2018). However, these insights from ritual studies and material religion have not yet been applied to Purim and the Esther scroll.

Fifth: copying the megillah is a ritual – a form of "ritualized writing" which enacts more meanings in and performs more functions for the religious community than merely copying textual information (Lowe 2017, 2–3; Watts 2019, 38–43). For example, in Jewish law and custom, norms for the writing of *sifrei kodesh* (holy books) reflect broader practices of ritual purity: the scribe's intention must be correct for the scroll to be kosher, and materials used for the making of holy books must be kept ritually separate from those same materials when used for non-holy books (Martini 2017, 2019).

Since many Jewish interpreters understand the Book of Esther's authoring to be narrated in the book itself (Esth 9:20–32), the act of copying a megillah is also a ritual which re-enacts the original authoring of the book as understood in later Jewish textual traditions. Those traditions variously credit authorship to Mordecai, to Esther, or to both. In the case of Esther, then, the gender of the scribe is part of the ritualized writing of the scroll: a woman copying Esther foregrounds Esther as author of the megillah.

This article focuses on the final two points: how the material form of the megillah and the ritualized practices of copying the megillah reflect changes in how Jews remember the events of Purim. I demonstrate how Purim and writing intersect with contemporary changes in women's ritual roles in Jewish life, and new interpretations of the Book of Esther informed by feminist readings and their heightened awareness of the relationship between gender and agency. Each section of this article engages one or more Esther scrolls made by contemporary female ritual scribes (*soferot*) who add their own creative marks to the scrolls they copy: Nava Levine-Coren, Avielah Barclay, Jen Taylor Friedman, and Rachel Jackson. These creative touches convey their readings of the biblical text, which magnify women's perspective and agency.[4]

Visualizing Esther as Author and Agent

The question of Esther's agency in the book is intimately tied with the way readers imagine Esther involved in the writing of the book itself. Here I speak of authorship not in the historical sense, in which biblical scholars seek to reconstruct or hypothesize the setting of a biblical text's authorial voice(s). Rather, I speak of authorship in the sense of the author function and cultural discourses of authorship (Foucault 1979; Beecroft 2020). The illustrated megillot of Nava Levine-Coren, a soferet who has created several Esther scrolls with "author portraits," visually speak to the discourse of authorship around Esther. They emphasize the authorial agency of Esther herself, an agency which Levine-Coren re-enacts in her own copying.

Levine-Coren grew up in an Orthodox community in New York where women did not do scribal work. Yet her earliest stirrings of desire to scribe came from an encounter with a megillat Esther – specifically, in her words:

4 Hebrew is a highly gendered language, with no grammatical neuter. *Sofer* is the masculine singular "scribe"; *soferim* the masculine/mixed-gender plural; *soferet* the feminine singular; and *soferot* the feminine plural. Much of the information about these contemporary works derives from conversations with these scribes over Zoom and email between April and September 2022. I also shared a draft of this essay with each of them to ensure I represented their words and ideas accurately.

> from my experience learning to chant megillat esther and layning (reading from the scroll) at Midreshet Lindebaum, Purim 1999. That was my first time layning anything, ever. It was amazing. I got to do what for my entire life I had only seen and heard done by men. It was so empowering and vital to my connection with Judaism. I had never seen it done in [New York], and I did not want to "go back" to hearing the megillah read by men, so the following year (I was living in NY and attending my freshman year of art school) I returned to Israel for Purim 2000. I took a photo of women with the scroll at Migdal Oz in Purim 2000. I think I still did not know at the time that I wanted to scribe. I think I just wanted a more active role in Jewish ritual life especially around communal prayer and megillah/torah reading.

Her print of the scene at Migdal Oz (Figure 5.1) depicts these women lovingly handling a scroll which joyfully bundles out onto the table. Levine-Coren recalled that before the 1999 Purim, she had never seen women publicly reading in synagogue, and the way they took ownership of Jewish practice inspired her. Her own desire to write came a few years later, in 2002:

> My own desire to write surfaced in the years that followed, as I studied illustration at SVA [The School of Visual Arts in New York City]. As graduation approached and we all talked about what area of the illustration world we wanted to work in, I realized that what I truly wanted to be was a scribe (not a children's book illustrator). I made both of these prints in 2002, my senior year of art school. My desire to scribe emerged gradually and I think what came first was a desire to engage with the scroll / the sacred object - to touch it, hold it, read from it, roll it ... and then finally, to create one myself.

In particular, a print she made in her senior year (Figure 5.2) helped encapsulate this desire. In this print, she depicts herself as a scribe. As she related to me, making this print helped her realize her desire to do *sofrut* (Jewish ritual scribing):

> I think it started as an "illustration" of the verse in Esther 9:29. but I was drawing in my studio and didn't have a model, so I propped up a mirror and just drew myself. Only after printing it did I realize – hey, this is also a self portrait that expresses a hidden dream.

In 2005, Levine-Coren began studying with Dov Laimon, who taught (and still teaches) a *sofrut* course at the Pardes Institute in Jerusalem, open to men and women. Since then, she has completed eleven megillot Esther, four of which have illustrations. At this point, unlike the other women profiled here, Levine-Coren does not write Torah scrolls, which many rabbinic authorities consider more prohibited to female scribes than Esther scrolls.

Levine-Coren's third illustrated megillah (Figure 5.3) employs one of her sisters as the model. Levine-Coren chose to depict this Esther-scribe as a modern woman in today's garb – a "message of female empowerment," in

Figure 5.1 Nava Levine-Coren, Women reading the Megillah at Migdal Oz, Purim 2000. 2002. Woodblock. Image supplied by artist.

Figure 5.2 Nava Levine-Coren, Esther 9:29 self-portrait. 2002. Woodblock. Image supplied by artist.

Figure 5.3 Nava Levine-Coren, Esther 9:29 scribal portrait in Megillat Esther. Ink on parchment. Image supplied by artist.

her words, from the ancient text to her own time. The myrtle branches at the start of the scroll – around the Esther portrait, and atop Esther's head – suggest Esther's Hebrew name, *hadassah*, which means myrtle (Esth 2:7). Levine-Coren quips that the hadassim berries remind her of the *tagin* (lit. "crowns") on the tops of the Hebrew letters, small decorative elements used in the writing of Jewish sacred texts.

Levine-Coren's work explicitly responds to the long history of Jewish engagements with the Book of Esther through the lens of gender. The biblical text itself is ambiguous regarding Esther's level of agency. While scholars generally agree that the book portrays Esther moving from passivity to agency, it is possible to read Esther as mostly acting under the influence of her cousin Mordecai (Fox 2001, 196–204). Indeed, long before the twentieth-century advent of explicitly feminist or gender-focused biblical readings, the Book of Esther served as a site at which Jews and Christians constructed gender and agency. In reading Esther and the other women in the story, these interpreters both read their own gender norms into the text, and used the text to shape gender norms in their present (e.g. b. Meg 13a). For example, much classical Jewish interpretation of Esther praises the protagonist as active in the plot to save her people, but confines this praise largely to the way she conforms to feminine ideals such as self-sacrifice, piety, or loyalty to her people (e.g. b. Meg. 14a–b) (Bronner 1995; Cordoni 2020). These readings which praise "feminine virtue" often express discomfort with elements of Esther which do not fit their ideals of womanhood, such as her marriage to a Gentile (Walfish 2002; Baskin 2007, 231–6). These interpretations often reflect men fashioning gendered ideals for women, not women's own voices. Some interpreters made clear that Mordecai was the more active agent of the Jews' deliverance; one of the earliest extrabiblical references to Purim calls it "the day of Mordecai" (2 Macc 15:36).[5] Levine-Coren's portrayals of Esther engage both the biblical text itself and Jewish interpretations of it.

The question of Esther's level of agency in the story as a whole directly relates to the way one reads Esther's agency in the acts of writing described in Esther 9:20–32. As mentioned above, Jewish interpreters vary on how much credit they assign to Esther. One tradition ascribes the Book of Esther to the men of the Great Assembly (b. Bab. Bat. 15a). Many ascribe it to Mordecai alone, including medieval commentators such as Rashi and Abraham ibn Ezra.[6] However, a strand of classical Jewish interpretation reads this section as narrating the writing of the Book of Esther itself. The crucial verse here is Esth 9:29: "Then Queen Esther daughter of Abihail wrote, with Mordecai, with full authority to confirm this second letter of Purim" (Esth 9:29, my translation). The grammar of this verse suggests that Esther and Mordecai both wrote, but that Esther was the main agent. This is the only time in the Hebrew Bible an Israelite woman is the subject of the verb כתב, "to write." Most commentators suggest that this is a startling and powerful description of female agency in the Bible. Yet in the same section, Mordecai also writes to the Jews of Persia charging them to observe Purim (Esth 9:20–6). The text is ambiguous on whose act of writing matters most, and whose act (if any) describes the authoring of the Book of Esther. In short, Esther's agency and Esther's act of writing are intertwined in how one interprets the megillah.

Levine-Coren draws on the trajectory of interpretation which foregrounds Esther's agency as an author of Purim letters, if not the possibility

5 The title of the book, which suggests Esther as the main character, is unattested before fifth-century codices of the Greek Bible (Fox 2001, 196; Goswell 2021, 200–3).

6 Rashi on Esther 9:20; ibn Ezra, in his introduction to his first commentary on Esther (Ibn Ezra 2019, 57–8). See also Aggadat Esther on 9:23 (Buber 1897, 76).

of her authoring the Book of Esther as it stands in the Hebrew Bible.[7] She refers to a comment in the *Lishkat HaSofer* ("Treasury of the Scribe") of Rabbi Shlomo Ganzfried (1804–86), which itself is a commentary on Ganzfried's *Qeset HaSofer* ("Inkpot of the Scribe"), a concise halakhic guide for scribes still used in sofrut training. While the *Qeset* concisely explains the rules of scribing, the *Lishkat* supplies the thought process behind Ganzfried's rulings and the sources on which he draws. The *Qeset* states: "If a Megillah was written with the left hand, or by a woman or child, some say it is invalid and some say it is valid" (28:9). On this, the *Lishkat* comments: "And there is some support, in my humble opinion, that because we learn from the verse 'And Esther wrote' (Esth 9:29) that we are required to write 'in a book and with ink' (b. Meg. 19a), so likewise we learn that a woman is kosher to write [a megillah]."[8] The halakhic argument suggests that these women are themselves re-enacting Esther 9:29 as they copy the megillah.

The halakhic argument echoes other types of Jewish sources. *Seder Olam Rabbah*, a second-century CE rabbinic chronicle of Jewish history, employs Esther 9:29 to describe the writing of the biblical book.[9] More recently, feminist Jewish scholars read Esther as the author: "She moves from silence to *author*-ity, not only as author of the *Megillah*, but also as a maker of laws and customs incumbent upon her people ever after" (Adelman 2017, 227; see also O. Shoham 2022). In the Jewish art of decorated and illustrated Esther scrolls, a tradition which begins in the sixteenth century and continues to this day, many megillot depict Esther as a scribe: Esther writing at a table;[10] writing with Mordecai;[11] or just holding a pen as if it is her central

---

7 This is separate from the question of whether or not a female voice really does lie behind the composition of the Book of Esther. While historical evidence suggests the presence of some literate women in the eastern Mediterranean, it is not possible to isolate "authentic" female voices in the Bible (cf. Kraemer 1991; Tamber-Rosenau 2020).

8 This passage from the *Qeset* can be found in https://www.sefaria.org/Keset_HaSofer.28.9?lang=en&with=all&lang2=en; for the *Lishkat*, see https://www.sefaria.org/Lishkat_HaSofer.28.7?lang=bi&with=all&lang2=en. The *Qeset* translation, by Taylor Friedman, can be found at https://www.hasoferet.com/halakha-for-scribes/keset-ha-sofer/chapter-28/; the *Lishkat* translation is mine. Rabbi Ross Singer likewise cites 9:29 in his halakhic argument for a megillah scribed by a woman being kosher for public reading (Singer 2004, 9). A special thanks to Levine-Coren for showing me this source and walking me through its halakhic terminology.

9 *Seder Olam Rabbah* 21 (translated by Guggenheimer 1998, 184).

10 France, mid-eighteenth century, Paris, Musée d'art et d'histoire du Judaïsme Paris, D.98.04.077.CL. Image at https://cja.huji.ac.il/esther/browser.php?mode=set&id=34758.

11 Aryeh Leib ben Daniel of Goray (scribe and painter), Italy, 1740s. Paris, Musée d'art et d'histoire du Judaïsme Paris, D.98.04.073.CL. Image at https://cja.huji.ac.il/esther/browser.php?mode=set&id=34761.

attribute.[12] Though these do not depict her writing something that looks like an Esther scroll, they do highlight her agency as writer and author. Such scrolls may well have been displayed in Purim liturgy.

Levine-Coren highlights Esther's status as agentive figure by employing visual language of authorship and authority known mainly from medieval Christian art, but resonant with Jewish interpretation. Levine-Coren drew inspiration for her Esther portraits from a portrait of St Matthew writing his gospel in the ninth-century Ebbo Gospels.[13] Such "evangelist portraits" are a constant feature in Gospels books and lectionaries from early medieval times onwards. The power of these evangelist portraits, often accompanied by symbols associated with each evangelist and an angel dictating to the evangelist, lies partly in how they represent textual authority. These images conflate apostle, evangelist, and copyist to collapse the layers of history, copying, and meditation which separate the reader from the eyewitnesses to Christ who (in the medieval Christian reader's mind) wrote the Gospels. This collapsing suggests that the text which the readers have in front of them is indeed the true record of Christ (Karkov 2016, 33–41, 205–12; Betancourt 2021). At times, as in the Anglo-Norman Eadwine Psalter (c.1150), the scribe (Eadwine) is given a full-page portrait in the style of an evangelist portrait (Karkov 2015). Visually, these portraits remove the layers of mediation between the ancient author (Esther) and the present-day reader – reflected in Levine-Coren's third megillah in which Esther is dressed as a modern woman.

These author portraits also authorize and authenticate the scripture at hand by tying it to the memory of these revered figures. They are the visual parallels to what Hindy Najman has described as the "Mosaic discourse" at work in Hellenistic Jewish texts such as Jubilees (Najman 2003, 2004). Whereas Exodus describes Moses receiving the Torah, Deuteronomy emphasizes that Moses not only orally transmitted this Torah, but wrote it down (e.g. 4:13, 5:19, 9:10, 10:4, 27:3, 31:24). In this shift, writing is not only a technology, but an authoritative vessel for transmitting authoritative teaching. The association of Moses's physical hand (an extension of God's finger on the tablets) as the authoritative scribe persists in later Second Temple literature – as in Jubilees, a text claiming not only to be *from* Sinai, but claiming to have been written *at* Sinai by Moses himself (Najman 2003,

12 Nehemiah Leib Cohen of Pressburg (printer), Bratislava, 1791. Prague, Jewish Museum in Prague (JMP), JMP 178.265. Image at https://cja.huji.ac.il/esther/browser.php?mode=set&id=36305.

13 Épernay, Bibliothèque Municipale, MS 1, fol. 18v. See image at https://en.wikipedia.org/wiki/Ebbo_Gospels#/media/File:Saint_Matthew2.jpg.

50). In Watts's terms, the physical manuscript is an index to the scribal author's presence (Watts 2018, 174). Levine-Coren's author portraits, then, connect the material megillah to the memory of Esther, a Jewish cultural heroine. By creating author portraits for Esther scrolls, portraits which feature Esther alone and not Mordecai, Levine-Coren suggests Esther's authorship in Esther 9:29 and foregrounds her agency in the story as a whole.

Esther Writing to the Sages

Levine-Coren's author portraits also stand for another act of Esther's writing, one found not in the Bible but in the aggadah; that is, Jewish homiletic expansions of biblical texts. In one aggadic addition, Esther is remembered not only for her acts of writing in the Book of Esther, but for writing to rabbinic authorities so that the Book of Esther and/or the observance of Purim would become part of the Jewish Bible and Jewish tradition. Levine-Coren inserts this act of writing into one of her Esther scribal portraits.

This story is found in different versions in two different sources, each of which emphasizes Esther's agency in different ways. First, the Babylonian Talmud (Bavli):

> Rav Shmuel bar Yehuda said: "Esther sent a letter to the Sages: 'Establish me for all time [קבעוני לדורות].' They sent a letter to her: 'You will arouse jealousy against us from the nations.' She sent a letter to them: 'I am already written about in the Annals of the Kings of Media and Persia [דברי הימים למלכי מדי ופרס].'" (b. Meg. 7a)

The Sages' reply about jealousy "from the nations" refers to the Gentile nations. Here Esther says: "The Gentile nations already know about us, since we are in their annals." She quotes from the end of the Book of Esther: "All his mighty and powerful acts, and a full account of the greatness to which the king advanced Mordecai, are recorded in the Annals of the Kings of Media and Persia" (Esth 10:2, NJPS). The text continues with another story of Esther and the Sages:

> Rav and Rabbi Ḥanina and Rabbi Yoḥanan and Rav Ḥaviva taught ... : "Esther sent to the Sages: 'Write about me for future generations [כתבוני לדורות].' They sent a letter to her: 'It is written "Have I not written for you three times?" (Prov 22:20), "three" and not four.'" (b. Meg. 7a)

Later interpreters often take this passage to refer to the canonization of the Book of Esther in the Jewish Bible itself (Soloveitchik 2017, 182–6). The Jerusalem Talmud (Yerushalmi) retells the story, but subtly shifts the credit given to Esther:

> Rabbi Jeremiah said in the name of Rabbi Samuel bar Isaac: "What did Mordecai and Esther do? They wrote a letter and sent it to our Rabbis. Thus they said

> to them: 'Do you accept these two days [of Purim] every year as an obligation upon yourselves?' They [the Rabbis] said to them [Mordecai and Esther]: 'Do we have not have enough troubles upon us, and you want to add the trouble of Haman as well?' [Mordecai and Esther] replied and wrote a second letter to them, as it is written: 'to confirm this second letter of Purim' (Esth 9:29). What was written in it? [Mordecai and Esther] told them, 'If this is the thing you fear, look, it is written and accounted for in the archives: "Are they not written in the book of the Annals of the Kings of Media and Persia?"' (Esth 10:2)." (y. Meg. 1:5)

This version downplays Esther's agency: Mordecai and Esther both write this letter to the sages of the Great Assembly. The text correlates this with 9:29 – but while 9:29 lists Esther as the primary agent of the action, the Jerusalem Talmud puts Mordecai before Esther and changes the verbs to plural. Further, while the Bavli leaves it ambiguous whether Esther is writing to establish her fame, her book, or her festival of Purim for all time, the Yerushalmi narrows the request to Purim itself. Both the Bavli and the Yerushalmi go on to enumerate how the Great Assembly changed their mind about the authority of the Book of Esther by finding it already discussed, implicitly, in the Torah: "Then the Lord said to Moses, 'Inscribe this in a document (*sefer*) as a reminder, and read it aloud to Joshua: I will utterly blot out the memory of Amalek from under heaven!'" (Exod 17:14). This "document" in Exodus 17:4 is, conveniently, the Book of Esther. As one reader puts it: "I want to become a book, Esther pleaded to the Jewish leaders of her time. She wasn't satisfied with her story being preserved as a letter that would likely become discarded, her story lost in the crumpled trash bin of history" (Bashevkin 2022).

Levine-Cohen's first illuminated megillah, commissioned by a rabbi as a gift for his wife, also depicts Esther writing the scroll (Figure 5.4). In typical midrashic fashion, Levine-Coren intended this image of Esther to allude to other key biblical women. Her headdress suggests the matriarch Sarah, while the mandrake in front of her on the table alludes to Rachel, who used mandrakes to enhance her fertility (Gen 30:15–16). Levine-Coren explains that this image illustrates Esther writing the megillah (9:29). The rolled-up scrolls in front of her represent the aggadic tradition of Esther writing to the rabbis to confirm the canonicity of the Book of Esther and the obligation to celebrate Purim. Like the Jerusalem Talmud, she sees Esther 9:29 as narrating Esther's act of writing to the Sages. But like the Babylonian Talmud, Levine-Coren ascribes Esther more credit: she writes to the Sages alone, and she writes to get her book canonized. By alluding to this

ויהי בימי אחשורוש הוא אחשורוש המלך
ההדו ועד כוש שבע ועשרים ומאה מדינה
בימים ההם כשבת המלך אחשורוש על כסא
מלכותו אשר בשושן הבירה בשנת שלוש
למלכו עשה משתה לכל שריו ועבדיו חיל פרס
ומדי הפרתמים ושרי המדינות לפניו בהראתו
את עשר כבוד מלכותו ואת יקר תפארת גדולתו
ימים רבים שמונים ומאת יום ובמלואת הימים
האלה עשה המלך לכל העם הנמצאים בשושן
הבירה למגדול ועד קטן משתה שבעת ימים
בחצר גנת ביתן המלך חור כרפס ותכלת אחוז
בחבלי בוץ וארגמן על גלילי כסף ועמודי שש
מטות זהב וכסף על רצפת בהט ושש ודר וסחרת
והשקות בכלי זהב וכלים מכלים שונים ויין
מלכות רב כיד המלך והשתיה כדת אין אנס
כי כן יסד המלך על כל רב ביתו לעשות כרצון
איש ואיש גם ושתי המלכה
עשתה משתה נשים בית המלכות אשר למלך
אחשורוש ביום השביעי כטוב לב המלך ביין
אמר למהומן בזתא חרבונא בגתא ואבגתא זתר
וכרכס שבעת הסריסים המשרתים את פני המלך

Figure 5.4 Nava Levine-Coren, Esther 9:29 scribal portrait in Megillat Esther. Woodblock on parchment. Image supplied by artist.

tradition of Esther writing to the Sages, Levine-Coren again highlights the agency of Esther as expressed in acts of writing. She explains:

> I do imagine both Esther and Mordecai composing the text together. I imagine Mordecai sitting across the table from Esther as she writes; I picture them as a pair. However, I have not been interested in portraying Mordecai visually or featuring him in my illustrations. (I've seen enough images of Jewish men, and not nearly enough images of Jewish women.)

For Levine-Coren, there is no ambiguity: Esther writes. Mordecai may write too. But he does not appear in this image.

However, to avoid becoming part of the "crumpled trash bin of history," Esther needs many acts of writing. She needs the copying of centuries of scribes to keep her alive. Some of those scribes were women.

Female Scribes, Past and Present, and Colophons

As we have discussed, the ritualized writing (copying) of the megillah re-enacts the authoring of the scroll as imagined in Esther 9:20–32. Some soferot heighten the female agency in the story by adding another dimension: colophons in which the scribe inscribes herself as the copyist, some of which allude to female Jewish scribes of centuries past. Colophons are a manuscript convention in which a scribe writes a personal message at the end of a work they have copied. Colophons often tell us the name of a scribe, the time and place when they completed the manuscript, and often a brief personal reflection, complaint, or prayer about the labour they have completed (Sirat 2002, 50, 204–11; Beit-Arié 2021, 123–217). According to Jewish law, a Torah scroll may not have a colophon; but Esther scrolls have more leniency in this and other areas of halakhah. Nava Levine-Coren, Rachel Jackson, and Jen Taylor Friedman, in their Esther scroll colophons, engage communal memory of female scribes present and past.

Levine-Coren's fourth illustrated megillah concludes with another scribal self-portrait (she served as the model for this) and a colophon (Figure 5.5). The colophon begins: "I, soferet Nava Miriam daughter of Shabbetai Moshe and Rena Bracha, wrote and illuminated this Megillat Esther ..." The colophon to this scroll, which was commissioned by a husband as a gift to his wife on the occasion of her having a baby, underscores the fact that a woman copied the text. The colophon reminds the readers that a female scribe copied the text.

At times, soferot colophons allude to the work of Jewish female scribes of the past. In 2022, soferet Rachel Jackson completed a scroll in English, a practice which is not the norm in Jewish communities but is within the

Figure 5.5 Nava Levine-Coren, Esther 9:29 scribal portrait in Megillat Esther. Ink on parchment. Image supplied by artist.

bounds of halakhah as she understands it. The scroll was commissioned as a gift, and the client wanted a colophon dedicating the scroll to its recipient. Jackson insisted on adding her own name to the colophon, though the client did not like the idea at first: "Written by Rachel Binah Marbach Jackson / 5782." The Esther scroll's openness to a colophon, Jackson told me, allows women to be present in the scribal tradition in a way that Torah scrolls, mezuzot, and tefillin do not. In an essay about her work as a scribe and her identity as a woman, Jackson explains that "women have always been at the very center of what Purim is all about" – an interpretation perfectly in line with contemporary Jewish readings of Esther informed by feminist thought (Jackson 2016). Citing Esther 9:29, Jackson surmises that "the megillah itself reports that Esther was an active agent in the creation of written history." She continues:

> I am not the first soferet and will definitely not be the last. The production of sofrut, scribal work, is a humbling experience. The goal is for my handwriting to look identical to the writing of thousands of anonymous scribes throughout the ages. For some this may sound claustrophobic. But for me it is a chance to show that I am as educated, committed and skillful as any other scribe. We don't have to look much further than Purim for inspiration: from Esther to Estellina women have always taken active roles in the continuation of our intellectual history and now I can be a part of that too.

Jackson delineates her heritage as a Jewish scribe in the "thousands of anonymous scribes throughout the ages" whose work is valuable not because of their personal identity, but because of their skill and commitment. When Jackson cites Estellina as her role model, she is referring to a famous decorated Esther scroll written by a young Italian woman named Estellina (Budzioch 2019, 83–6). This manuscript is the earliest dated decorated Esther scroll, by a scribe of any gender. We have the date, 1564 CE, because Estellina left a colophon with both date and name.[14] Jackson reaches back to Esther and Estellina to delineate her heritage as a *female* scribe. Here she is not making a strictly halakhic argument for her scroll's validity for public chanting in synagogue ritual. Rather, she is importing Jewish history into Jewish communal memory, by inscribing that history into a ritual object.

A third scribe, Jen Taylor Friedman, not only adds her name to a colophon, but quotes from the colophon of a previous female scribe. Taylor Friedman wrote this scroll under commission by Jewish art historian Marc

14 Braginsky Collection Megillah 102. Venice, 1564. See images at https://braginskycollection.com/phpviewer/index.php?path=BCS/BCS_102.

Michael Epstein (Somekh 2019; Epstein 2021). The scroll is being decorated by Epstein and his students in a style reminiscent of the Bird's Head Haggadah, about which Epstein has written extensively. The colophon reads:

> I, Yonah Esther the soferet, wrote this megillah and completed it ... [formulaic language for the date and place of the colophon's completion follows]. Do not lay blame upon me if you find errors in it, for a nursing woman am I.

Taylor Friedman explained that she wrote this scroll while nursing her newborn. She felt it meaningful to mark the occasion – especially since, as she told me, that baby would be her only child and she did not know if she would have the chance to use this colophon again, since most of her work lies in writing, correcting, and repairing Torah scrolls. However, the line "Do not lay blame upon me if you find errors in it, for a nursing woman am I" is in fact quoted from the colophon of a *taj* (a Yemenite Pentateuch codex) copied by the Yemenite scribe Miriam bat Benayah (fifteenth–sixteenth centuries) (Riegler and Baskin 2008, 15). In quoting it, Taylor Friedman, like Jackson, brings to the reader's attention multiple layers of female agency in the writing of the megillah: Esther herself, soferot in centuries past such as Estellina and Miriam, and women scribes present.

While much discourse around Jewish iconic texts – especially Torah scrolls – focuses on how these scrolls mediate or even represent the presence of God, these Esther scrolls suggest another mode of transitivity. They have not only the vertical mediation between human and divine, but a horizontal meditation of humans past to humans present. As David Morgan writes, this is a form of enchantment, in which focal objects act upon viewers and beholders to enchant them into a relationship with a broader collective (Morgan 2018). This enchantment is most obvious in the realm of more mundane manuscripts, as in the excitement generated when writings from the hand of Maimonides were found in the Cairo Genizah. The Czech Memorial Scrolls project, which restores Torah scrolls from Jewish communities murdered in the Shoah and sends them around the world for use in synagogues, likewise connects Jews past and present, ensuring a kind of "afterlife" for communities with few or no survivors (Bernard 2005). The broader collective which Morgan speaks of may be, at times, the divine; it may also be the weight and depth of historical tradition.

Levine-Coren, Jackson, and Taylor Friedman create such networks of transitivity between past and present. Their colophoned scrolls insert their own bodily labour into the handwritten heritage of Jewish sacred texts. They also evoke a broader history of women scribing Jewish texts, both holy books and more mundane documents. Interest in this history continues: in 2021–2, the Israel Museum's acquisition of an Esther scroll at auction written in 1767 by one Luna, daughter of Yehudah Ambron, elicited headlines in *The Jerusalem Post* and *The Times of Israel* (Sudilovsky 2022; *Times of Israel* 2021). In her trailblazing 1990 book *Standing Again at Sinai*, Jewish feminist Judith Plaskow notes that, because Judaism is such a past-oriented tradition, a past relived and re-enacted in rituals such as the Passover seder, "we too cannot redefine Judaism in the present without redefining our past, because our present grows out of our history" (Plaskow 1990, 31). She calls for studies in Jewish women's history to impact not just academic historiography, but part of the "collective memory" of the Jewish people (Plaskow 1990, 36). Putting these memories into ritual objects is one effective way to do so.

Voicing Vashti

For Esther to be written into the book which bears her name, another woman has to be written out: Vashti (Beal 1997, 29–39). The scribal midrash of one contemporary soferet, Avielah Barclay, parallels the reclamation of Vashti among contemporary feminist readers. Barclay earned her certification to write megillot Esther in 1998, and has written several megillot over the past nineteen years. She has also added her own creative touches within halakhic bounds. Specifically, she adds ornamentation to the name of Vashti, and thus honours her as a heroine.

Barclay shared a sketch of the design, which she has inscribed in multiple megillot (Figure 5.6). On Vashti's name, she adds extra *tagin*: decorations on the letters in the form of small lines with dots at the end. Though the origins of these scribal features are unclear, over time they have come to be associated with the scripts used for writing sacred books such as the Torah scroll (Segal 2007; Yardeni 2002, 268–71). Typically these dots are in black ink; Barclay describes these ones as "golden orbs." She explains what she calls her "visual midrash," interpretations of the text in visual form:

> I always ensure Vashti's name and title are beautiful and fancy with visual midrash because she deserves better in the story, considering she stood up for herself and expected an ounce of respect and dignity. ... I see a very typical – and archetypical – women's story here. Vashti doesn't get the credit she [should]. She's like the big sister Esther has to grow into.

Barclay intends her *tagin* to honour Vashti, aligning her with many other contemporary feminist readers, both Jewish and non-Jewish, who see Vashti not as a villain but as a heroine parallel to Esther. She describes this visual design as "restor[ing] Vashti's crown," since the word *tagin* literally means "crowns."

Figure 5.6 Avielah Barclay, sketch for taggin design for Vashti in the Megillah Esther. Image supplied by artist.

The biblical text, contrary to later Jewish interpretation, provides no sense that Vashti did anything wrong in the narrator's eyes. The king commands his attendants to bring her, not to request her presence (Esth 1:11); the narrator already conditions the reader to discern Ahasuerus's evil intent by divulging that he was "glad of heart with wine." We are given no reason for her refusal. The narrator does not comment on her action directly, only revealing through dialogue that she has offended the king and, in his courtier's eyes, all the men of Persia (Esth 1:16). However, this charge is so ludicrous that we might question whether the narrator intends the reader to accept it at face value. Though the narrator is not interested in fleshing out Vashti's character or explaining her motives, he does indirectly characterize her through comparison with characters that are more explicitly characterized: the drunken king, the corrupt courtiers (Fox 2001, 164–9). At worst, Vashti is a stubborn and impolitic woman who did not play court politics well. At best, some argue, she might be called "prophetic" (Day 2005, 43).

By contrast, the dominant Jewish traditional interpretation has shamed Vashti as a wicked queen whose punishment by Ahasuerus (and indirectly, by God) was right and just (Shemesh 2002). These traditions narrate, for example, that she degraded her Jewish maidservants by forcing them to work nude on Shabbat. Others state that she was just as licentious as her husband – and just as vain! – and only said no to appearing before his banquet nude because she spontaneously grew a tail and developed leprosy (b. Meg. 12b). Barclay responds: "I don't like the visual midrash practice of putting a tail on Vashti, I find that quite misogynistic." While Vashti's tail is not such a prominent theme in Jewish art, another possibly misogynistic Jewish reading of Vashti does appear in many illustrated Esther scrolls: the execution of Vashti, often shamefully nude, via bloody beheading or cruel strangulation (Budzioch 2017, 410–15).

In modern times, many feminist readers rehabilitated Vashti's reputation and claimed her as a hero in her own right. This reading was made famous by Elizabeth Cady Stanton's *The Woman's Bible* (Stanton and Chandler 1895). In this view, Vashti stood up for herself against the king who degraded her – indeed, Jewish traditions hold that Ahasuerus asked Vashti not only to show her beauty to his friends, but to do so nude. In 1976, Jewish feminist Mary Gendler penned an essay rejecting the model of Esther she was taught in childhood Purim plays: "except for her momentary lapse when Mordecai asks her to petition the king, she is 'perfect,' a kind of ultimate Jewish Mother who risks her life in order to save her children (the People Israel)" (Gendler 1976, 245). She proposes that "Vashti be reinstated on the throne along with her sister Esther," seeing the former as a source of "dignity, pride and independence" (Gendler 1976, 247). For Gendler, the Esther as presented by much Jewish tradition is a flawed figure, a woman who chooses luxury over female empowerment – whereas Vashti is the woman who claimed her bodily autonomy and said no to the king. Barclay's visual design inscribes such a Vashti-empowering interpretation into the scroll's very letters.

In *Standing Again at Sinai*, Plaskow calls on women to incorporate women's perspectives not only in scholarship, but in creative expression, especially midrash and liturgy (Plaskow 1990, 53–9). By incorporating her take on Vashti in visual expression, Barclay joins the ranks of other Jewish feminists who have penned "feminist midrash" on Vashti (Reimer 1998; Shemesh 2002, 370–2). These may depict her as a curious and intelligent woman who willingly steps aside for Esther (Hammer 2001, 213–28) and secretly aids Esther after she is deposed (Rosen 1996, 173–81), a friendly figure who just wanted to wear pyjamas and enjoy her friends at her banquet (Berkowitz 2021), or a modern woman whose husband, a young senator, demands that she strip nude to advance his career (Solomon 2020).

Such creative reinterpretations of Esther make the feminist readings more vivid and increase their impact on the Jewish community.

By incorporating contemporary feminist reading of Vashti into a ritual object for Purim – realistically, the only time most Jews really think about Esther at all – Barclay also follows Plaskow's dictum to incorporate women's perspectives into Jewish liturgy as well. She does so by literally re-forming the text. She does not change the words of the Bible. This would make the megillah unfit for ritual use. Rather, by incorporating her own scribal midrash through the *tagin*, she enacts the kind of "rewriting" which Jewish rhetorician Susan Zaeske describes happening in the Book of Esther itself:

> There is no portrayal of rewriting, only writing over – creating a new text to cover over the old rather than altering an existing text. ... In the megillah as in the midrash, new contexts, new interpretations, new authors lead to the composition of new texts. Rather than replacing the preexisting text, the new texts are piled one atop the other, creating a layered, ever-changing, living text that resists fixity or containment. (Zaeske 2014, 184)

Here the "new text" is not a change in the words or letters, but a change in the visual forms of the letters which communicates a new meaning. Barclay, in Zaeske's language, writes over sexist interpretations of the text, interpretations which degrade a woman who – at least in the biblical text alone – was punished merely for saying no to a request which most women would refuse. Her writing over sexist interpretations of the megillah as a scribe also parallels the Jewish women who have claimed the ritual privilege of chanting the megillah in community – the women who inspired Nava Levine-Coren. These women scribes and cantors are not changing the text itself. But by voicing that text through a woman's vocal cords, through writing the text with a woman's interpretation of the words, the message changes. Likewise, by writing the letters themselves slightly differently, the message changes.

Concluding Reflections: Gender and Agency in the Megillah

In this article, I have examined the works of contemporary soferot who insert their own creative voice and agency into the Esther scrolls which they copy. I have drawn parallels between their scribal copying and Esther's acts of scribal authoring in the Book of Esther itself. In both cases, the physical act of writing claims agency – whether that writing is Esther's authoring or a soferet's copying.

These parallels suggest my own reading of gender and agency in the Book of Esther and its scribal copying in Jewish life. Interpreters of the biblical text differ in how they construe Esther's level of agency in the story. Some view Esther as a virtuous woman who does not buck the system, and perhaps even see Mordecai as the real agent in the anti-genocidal plot. Another sees Vashti as a feminist hero, and at times puts down Esther for working within the system. Both readings, I suggest, lack nuance. Both fail to take the Persian palace's power dynamics and Esther's overlapping identities into account.

A third approach holds that Esther is both victim and victor. This mediates the extremes of the earlier positions, and better captures the nuance of the biblical text.

Esther is a victim. Some interpreters describe her being taken to Ahasuerus's palace as a form of sex trafficking, comparing her to African women taken into the trans-Atlantic slave trade (Dunbar 2019) or Japan's "comfort women" during World War II (Smith-Christopher 2018). Further, she lives as an ethnic minority under the control of a foreign empire. Esther symbolizes Israel in diaspora as a whole (White 1989). The Jews are feminized in relation to the masculine might of Persian kings, both in the book's narrative world and in the historical reality of Persian-era Yehud. Like Israel, Esther faces a world of limited options. Viewing her in this light, I find it difficult to morally evaluate her against the standards of certain modern feminists (e.g. Fuchs 1982), let alone judge her.

Yet she is also a victor. She exerts agency on behalf of her people within the limited options presented by Persian colonial rule and its legally enforced oppression of women and Jews. She displays the "pragmatism of the powerless" in using the limited tools at her disposal (including sex appeal and deceit) to save her family and people (Song 2010). Far from being a mute pawn of Mordecai, she is strategic and tactical in persuading the king to do her bidding by throwing banquets (Cho 2021). In this reading, Esther and Vashti are not enemies, but complementary models of gendered agency (Kondemo 2021). One rejects the system of patriarchy *en toto*, while the other uses it for her own ends in a display of strategy and tactic. Narratively, Esther and Vashti mirror one another; for example, Ahasuerus de-crowns Vashti for fear that her words will influence his kingdom, but by the book's end, Esther's words go out to the whole kingdom via her letters. Further, even if Esther seems passive at the start of the book, over the course of the story she claims more agency: she speaks for herself (4:15–16), she calls a fast and the Jews obey, she risks her life by going to the king's throne by herself (5:1), and she writes letters (Esth 9:29).

Contrary to the views of some feminist readers, then, Esther did employ agency. But her agency is relatively hidden, behind the scenes – at least within the narrative world. She strategically hides her agency, just as she hides her Jewishness, because that form of agency was the most effective way to transform her situation. This form of agency also fits the work of the soferot discussed here. Just as Esther discerns the type of agency that best fits the system in which she finds herself, these soferot engage in the form of agency which best benefits their personal goals – in this case, to take on the mitzvah of writing sacred scrolls, and to contribute to Torah and Jewish life in a way that acknowledges their own gendered existence, within the bounds of halakhah.

At this point, a reader may object to the tale I am spinning. Sure, these soferot are incorporating their voices via minor dots on letters, oft-unread colophons at the end of the scrolls, and author portraits which may or may not be visible to a Purim congregation. But is any of this effective in changing the tradition? As Rachel Jackson aspires, "The goal is for my handwriting to look identical to the writing of thousands of anonymous scribes throughout the ages." In biblical scholarship, this view is paralleled in Wood's argument that Esther's act of writing is not a heightening of her voice, but a diminishing of it. Wood argues that Esther's voice and body are in fact replaced by the written word; she sacrifices herself for the phallic symbol of the pen (Wood 2021). At the end of the book, Esther still lives in a world in which sexual exploitation of women goes unpunished. Patriarchy still wins the day. Similarly, traditional halakhah remains a system by and large crafted by male authorities of the past. So, my dissenting reader may declare: the real feminist Jew should reject traditional halakhah as a normative structure in Jewish life, join a Jewish movement which understands halakhah as egalitarian and non-binding, or turn secular.

My counter-argument to this objection comes from a comparison to another feminist scribal project: the Toratah project, a project to rewrite the Torah with reversed genders (Kanarek 2021). This project has already written the Book of Mordekhai, in which a young Jewish man goes before the Persian queen Akhashveroshni to save her people.[15] Though they have not had a scribe write this Book of Mordekhai in a scroll, they have hired soferot to scribe a mezuzah scroll, and hope to have a complete Toratah scroll in the future.[16] We can imagine they plan a scribed Book of Mordekhai too. Without denying the importance of these womens' voices and the effectiveness of their subversive textual editing, these regendered

15 See discussion at https://www.beittoratah.org/mordekhai-scroll. Biala and Kanarek read and discussed this scroll on Zoom for Purim in April 2022 (Biala and Kanarek 2022).

16 https://www.beittoratah.org/tudaica/toratah-mezuzah-scroll; https://www.beittoratah.org/toratah-scroll.

scrolls are not likely to replace the traditional Torah scroll or Esther scroll. In one sense, a Megillat Mordekhai and the megillot Esther discussed here fall into the same category: they all foreground the presence of women and their gendered agency in building and transmitting Judaism past and present. But while the Megillat Mordekhai does so more explicitly, it does so by sacrificing halakhic norms, making it more of a niche artistic and exegetical project than a transformation of mainstream Jewish life. It will not replace the Megillat Esther in any mainstream Purim service. To be clear, I am not saying one is better than the other. I am merely noting that they exert different kinds of agency. The subtle agency of scrolls which change the tradition within halakhic boundaries can impact mainstream Jewish life in ways which Toratah cannot.

By choosing to work within the recognized halakhic frameworks of scribal practice, these women choose a different form of agency. They work from within the system, holding to the halakhic framework while claiming a woman's place in it. In Judith Butler's terms, they perform gender (here, the performance of ritual craft in the context of halakhah) in ways which are "culturally intelligible" within their religious context (Butler 1990, xxiii–xxv, 175–203, esp. 198). In this case, cultural intelligibility means that any cultural critique must fit within known modes of discourse (here, halakhah) of their community. Rather than rejecting halakhah, these women use its mode of argument to argue for the validity of their ritual writing. By doing so, they subvert those modes of argument, enacting what some scholars of Orthodox Jewish feminism refer to as "devoted resistance."[17]

As Taylor Friedman in particular made clear to me, her goal in becoming a soferet was not to put on a feminist stunt. Indeed, she expressed frustration that the public discourse and media coverage around her work was often framed mainly, if not solely, through the lens of her gender. Barclay echoes Taylor Friedman's experience, recalling that "people were obsessed with my body doing the writing and not my brain or spirit offering Avodat She-Ba-Lev [worship/service of the heart]." Rather, Taylor Friedman emphasized, her primary interest was in Torah and the ritual craft of sofrut – the devotion. Only once her dedication to Torah (and the specific *mitzvah* of writing a Torah scroll) became cemented did she set about carving out a halakhic space for a woman to perform that ritual.

17 See Zion-Waldoks 2015; Sperber 2020. These views echo Saba Mahmood's influential critique of Western feminist thought as too often discounting the agency of women in traditional religious settings which secular feminists might discount as wholly patriarchal (Mahmood 2005), a critique which Butler has agreed with (Butler 2006, 286).

These scribes insist that their work be seen first and foremost as the same kind of sacred ritual craft that the male scribes produce. And in all essential components, the work is the same. In the context of any Jewish community which accepts *sifrei qodesh* written by women as liturgically fit for communal reading, the megillot made by Avielah Barclay, Nava Levine-Coren, Rachel Jackson, and Jen Taylor Friedman are all kosher for ritual chanting at Purim. As Butler says: "there is no subverting of a norm without inhabiting that norm" (Butler 2006, 285). These soferot inhabit the norms of halakhic Torah scribing, as well as the "worship of the heart" required for such holy craft. Yet precisely by inhabiting those norms, they change them. Without a colophon, the viewer cannot tell the difference between a scroll copied by a man and one copied by a woman. The agency is hidden.

Like these soferot, Esther enacts hidden agency for the sake of her people and her tradition. She hides her Jewishness in the palace until the strategic time to reveal it. Certainly, her activity is largely confined to the feminized spaces of the royal palace, rather than the public and visible courtyard and city, in which Haman and Mordecai enact their agency. In this sense she is hidden, spatially, perhaps in the "house of women" in the palace. But given the way in which the Book of Esther reveals that the private life of the king, his sexual desires and personal vendettas serving as the real site of imperial policy, this public–private dichotomy is not so clear (Hancock 2013). Esther's agency, exerted within the confined space of the palace, is hidden agency which still impacts the public sphere. The same goes for the soferot profiled here.

Though her Persian name, Esther, likely comes from the goddess Ishtar, rabbinic tradition commonly re-etymologizes it from the Hebrew root *satar* (סתר), "to hide" (b. Hull. 139b). From that standpoint of hiddenness, Esther is able to enact her agency through writing. But her agency in writing is not hidden from the reader: the narrator tells us of it (Esth 9:29) and rabbinic tradition expounds on it (b. Meg. 7a; y. Meg. 1:5). It is this agency which, ultimately, saves her people.

Acknowledgments

I would like to thank Marianne Schleicher for her generosity and warmth in every stage of the writing process – not least her hospitality in organizing a workshop in Rebild Bakker which enabled my husband and I to explore Denmark. Her suggestions in terms of gender theory, and her prod to incorporate Judith Butler's concepts, enriched my thoughts considerably. I would also like to thank the other participants in the workshop, as well as Laura Lieber and Deborah Thompson, for their comments. Finally, a special thanks to Jen Taylor Friedman, Nava Levine-Coren, and Avielah Barclay for sharing their work and ideas with me. This article is one chapter of a forthcoming book project, tentatively titled *Writing Esther*, on how Jewish traditions have conceived of the writing of the megillah from the Second Temple era to the present, and how such conceptions are reflected in the form, liturgical use, and ritualized writing of the megillah.

References

Adelman, Rachel E. 2017. *Female Ruse: Women's Deception and Divine Sanction in the Hebrew Bible*. HBM 74. Sheffield: Sheffield Phoenix Press.

Bashevkin, Dovid. 2022. "Letter Perfect." *Tablet Magazine*, 10 January. https://www.tabletmag.com/sections/belief/articles/letter-perfect-tractate-megillah

Baskin, Judith R. 2007. "Erotic Subversion: Undermining Female Agency in BMegillah 10b–17a." In *A Feminist Commentary on the Babylonian Talmud: Introduction and Studies*, edited by Tal Ilan, 227–44. Tübingen: Mohr Siebeck.

Beal, Timothy K. 1997. *The Book of Hiding: Gender, Ethnicity, Annihilation, and Esther*. Biblical Limits. New York: Routledge.

Beecroft, Alexander. 2020. "Beginnings: A World History of Authorship." In *World Authorship*, edited by Tobias Boes, Rebecca Braun, and Emily Spiers, 18–29. Oxford: Oxford University Press.

Beit-Arié, Malachi. 2021. *Hebrew Codicology: Historical and Comparative Typology of Medieval Hebrew Codices Based on the Documentation of the Extant Dated Manuscripts until 1540 Using a Quantitative Approach*, edited by Nurik Pasternak, translated by Ilana Goldberg. Jerusalem: Israel Academy of Sciences and Humanities. https://doi.org/10.25592/uhhfdm.9349

Ben-Ur, Aviva. 2013. "Purim in the Public Eye: Leisure, Violence, and Cultural Convergence in the Dutch Atlantic." *Jewish Social Studies* 20(1): 32–76. https://doi.org/10.2979/jewisocistud.20.1.32

Berkowitz, Leah Rachel. 2021. *Queen Vashti's Comfy Pants*. Millburn, NJ: Apples & Honey Press.

Bernard, Philippa. 2005. *Out of the Midst of the Fire*. London: Westminster Synagogue.

Betancourt, Roland. 2021. *Performing the Gospels in Byzantium: Sight, Sound, and Space in the Divine Liturgy*. Cambridge: Cambridge University Press.

Biala, Tamar, and Kanarek, Yael. 2022. "The Scroll of Mordekhai: Everything Upside Down." 12 April. https://youtu.be/_yobmsuJuq4

Blondheim, Menahem, and Katz, Elihu. 2015. "Communications in an Ancient Empire: An Innisian Reading of the Book of Esther." In *Traffic: Media as Infrastructures and Cultural Practices*, edited by Marion Näser-Lather and Christoph Neubert, 181–204. Leiden: Brill.

Bronner, Leila Leah. 1995. "Esther Revisited: An Aggadic Approach." In *A Feminist Companion to Esther, Judith and Susanna*, edited by Athalya Brenner, 176–97. FCB 7. Sheffield: Sheffield Academic Press.

Buber, Salomon, ed. 1886. ספרי דאגדתא על מגלת אסתר [Books of Aggadah on Megillat Esther]. Vilna: Romm. https://hebrewbooks.org/39237

———, ed. 1897. אגדת אסתר. Krakow: Yosef Fisher. https://hebrewbooks.org/26867

Budzioch, Dagmara. 2017. "Midrashic Tales in the Seventeenth and Eighteenth Century Illustrated Esther Scrolls." *Kwartalnik Historii Żydów* [Jewish History Quarterly] 263(3): 405–22.

———. 2019. *Zdobione zwoje Estery ze zbiorów Żydowskiego Instytutu Historycznego na tle tradycji dekorowania "megilot Ester" w XVII i XVIII wieku* [The Decorated Esther Scrolls from the Jewish Historical Institute in Warsaw and the Tradition of Megillot Esther Decoration in the Seventeenth and Eighteenth Centuries]. Warsaw: Jewish Historical Institute.

Butler, Judith. 1990. *Gender Trouble: Feminism and the Subversion of Identity*. New York: Routledge.

———. 2006. "Afterword." In *Bodily Citations: Religion and Judith Butler*, edited by Ellen T. Armour and Susan M. St. Ville, 276–92. New York: Columbia University Press.

Cho, Paul K.-K. 2021. "A House of her Own: The Tactical Deployment of Strategy in Esther." *Journal of Biblical Literature* 140(4): 663–82. https://doi.org/10.1353/jbl.2021.0031

Connerton, Paul. 1989. *How Societies Remember*. Cambridge: Cambridge University Press.

Cordoni, Constanza. 2020. "'Wenn du in diesen Tagen schweigst' (Est 4,14): Zum mittelalterlichen Nachleben der biblischen Heldin Ester." In *Das jüdische Mittelalter*, edited by Carol Bakhos and Gerhard Langer, 37–56. Die Bibel und die Frauen, 4.2. Stuttgart: Kohlhammer.

Day, Linda. 2005. *Esther*. AOTC. Nashville, TN: Abingdon.

Diamond, James S. 2019. *Scribal Secrets: Extraordinary Texts in the Torah and their Implications*, edited by Robert Goldenberg and Gary A. Rendsburg. Eugene, OR: Pickwick.

Dunbar, Ericka S. 2019. "For Such a Time as This? #UsToo: Representations of Sexual Trafficking, Collective Trauma, and Horror in the Book of Esther." *Bible and Critical Theory* 15: 20–48. https://bibleandcriticaltheory.com/issues/vol-15-no-2-2019-bible-and-critical-theory/for-such-a-time-as-this-ustoo-representations-of-sexual-trafficking-collective-trauma-and-horror-in-the-book-of-esther/

Epstein, Marc Michael. 2021. "A New View of the Purim Story." Presented at the Community Scholar Program, 26 February. https://youtu.be/PaVTomJGCUY

Fisch, Harold. 1994. "Reading and Carnival: On the Semiotics of Purim." *Poetics Today* 15(1): 55–71. https://doi.org/10.2307/1773203

Fishbane, Simcha. 2018. *The Meaning of the Jewish Festival of Purim: What its Rituals and Customs Symbolize*. Lewiston, NY: Edwin Mellen.

Foucault, Michel. 1979. "What is an Author?" In *Language, Counter-Memory, Practice: Selected Essays and Interviews by Michel Foucault*, edited by Donald Bouchard, translated by Donald Bouchard and Sherry Simon, 113–38. Ithaca, NY: Cornell University Press.

Fox, Michael V. 2001. *Character and Ideology in the Book of Esther*. 2nd ed. Grand Rapids, MI: Eerdmans.

Freedman, Jean R. 2011. "The Masquerade of Ideas: The Purimshpil as Theatre of Conflict." In *Revisioning Ritual: Jewish Traditions in Transition*, edited by Simon J Bronner, 94–132. Oxford: Littman Library of Jewish Civilization.

Frevel, Christian. 2018. "On Instant Scripture and Proximal Texts: Some Insights into the Sensual Materiality of Texts and their Ritual Roles in the Hebrew Bible and Beyond." In *Sensing Sacred Texts*, edited by James W. Watts, 57–79. Comparative Research on Iconic and Performative Texts. Bristol: Equinox.

Fuchs, Esther. 1982. "Status and Role of Female Heroines in the Biblical Narrative." *Mankind Quarterly* 23(2): 149–60.

Gendler, Mary. 1976. "The Restoration of Vashti." In *The Jewish Woman: New Perspectives*, edited by Elizabeth Koltun, 241–7. New York: Schocken.

Goswell, Gregory R. 2021. "The Main Character of the Book of Esther: The Contribution of the Textual Divisions and the Assigned Titles of the Book of Esther to Uncovering its Protagonist." *Journal for the Study of the Old Testament* 46: 193–205. https://doi.org/10.1177/03090892211032243

Grimes, Ronald L. 2013. *The Craft of Ritual Studies*. Oxford: Oxford University Press.

Guggenheimer, Heinrich W., ed. 1998. *Seder Olam: The Rabbinic View of Biblical Chronology*. Lanham, MD: Rowman & Littlefield.

Hammer, Jill. 2001. *Sisters at Sinai: New Tales of Biblical Women*. Philadelphia, PA: Jewish Publication Society.

Hancock, Rebecca S. 2013. *Esther and the Politics of Negotiation: Public and Private Spaces and the Figure of the Female Royal Counselor*. Emerging Scholars. Minneapolis: Fortress.

Horowitz, Elliott. 2006. *Reckless Rites: Purim and the Legacy of Jewish Violence*. Jews, Christians, and Muslims from the Ancient to the Modern World. Princeton, NJ: Princeton University Press.

Howard, Cameron B. R. 2015. "When Esther and Jezebel Write: A Feminist Biblical Theology of Authority." In *After Exegesis: Feminist Biblical Theology*, edited by Patricia K. Tull and Jacqueline E. Lapsley, 109–22. Waco, TX: Baylor University Press.

Ibn Ezra, Abraham ben Meïr. 2019. שני פירושי ר' אברהם אבן עזרא על מגילת אסתר [Abraham Ibn Ezra's Two Commentaries on Megillat Esther: An Annotated Critical Edition], edited by Ayala Mishaly, Moshe A. Zipor, and Uriel Simon. Ramat Gan: Bar-Ilan University Press.

Jackson, Rachel. 2016. "Scribes in a Circumscribed World: From Esther to Me." *My Jewish Learning* (blog). 23 February. https://www.myjewishlearning.com/the-torch/scribes-in-a-circumscribed-world-from-esther-to-me/

Jobling, J'annine, and Roughley, Alan. 2009. "The Right to Write: Power, Irony, and Identity in the Book of Esther." In *Sacred Tropes: Tanakh, New Testament, and Qur'an as Literature and Culture*, edited by Roberta Sabbath, 317–33. BibInt 98. Leiden: Brill.

Kanarek, Yael. 2021. "I Reversed the Genders of Every Person in the Torah – and it Finally Feels Complete." *The Forward*, 27 September. https://forward.com/opinion/475974/i-reversed-the-genders-of-every-person-in-the-torah-and-it-finally-feels/

Karkov, Catherine E. 2015. "The Scribe Looks Back: Anglo-Saxon England and the Eadwine Psalter." In *The Long Twelfth-Century View of the Anglo-Saxon Past*, edited by M. Brett and D. A. Woodman, 289–306. London: Routledge.

———. 2016. *The Art of Anglo-Saxon England*. Woodbridge, Suffolk: Boydell Press.

Kogman-Appel, Katrin. 2018. "Books for Communal Liturgy and Domestic Worship: Structure, Function, and Illustration of the Mahzor and the Haggadah." In *Liturgische Bücher in der Kulturgeschichte Europas*, edited by Hanns-Peter Neuheuser, 101–37. Wiesbaden: Harrassowitz.

Koller, Aaron. 2014. *Esther in Ancient Jewish Thought*. Cambridge: Cambridge University Press.

Kondemo, Maleke M. 2021. "In Search of Biblical Role Models for Mongo Women: A Bosadi Reading of Vashti and Esther." *Old Testament Essays* 34(2): 554–72. https://doi.org/10.17159/2312-3621/2021/v34n2a14

Kraemer, Ross Shepard. 1991. "Women's Authorship of Jewish and Christian Literature in the Greco-Roman Period." In *"Women Like This": New Perspectives on Jewish Women in the Greco-Roman World*, edited by Amy-Jill Levine, 221–42. EJL. Atlanta, GA: Scholars Press.

Krauss, Anna, Jonas Leipziger, and Schücking-Jungblut, Friederike, eds. 2020. *Material Aspects of Reading in Ancient and Medieval Cultures: Materiality, Presence and Performance*. Materiale Textkulturen 26. Boston, MA: De Gruyter.

Langer, Ruth. 1998. "From Study of Scripture to a Reenactment of Sinai: The Emergence of the Synagogue Torah Service." *Worship* 72(1): 43–67.

———. 2013. "Constructing Memory in Jewish Liturgy." In *Toward the Future: Essays on Catholic-Jewish Relations in Memory of Rabbi Leon Klenick*, edited by Celia Deutsch, A. James Rudin, and Eugene Fisher, 117–28. New York: Paulist.

Larson, Jason T. 2013. "The Gospels as Imperialized Sites of Memory in Late Ancient Christianity." In *Iconic Books and Texts*, edited by James W. Watts, 373–88. Comparative Research on Iconic and Performative Texts. Bristol, CT: Equinox.

Lerner, Myron B. 2006. "The Works of Aggadic Midrash and the Esther Midrashim." In *The Literature of the Sages, Second Part*, edited by Shmuel Safrai, Zeev Safrai, Joshua Schwartz, and Peter Tomson, 133–229. Assen: Gorcum.

Lied, Liv Ingeborg, and Lundhaug, Hugo, eds. 2017. *Snapshots of Evolving Traditions, Jewish and Christian Manuscript Culture, Textual Fluidity, and New Philology*. Berlin: De Gruyter.

Lowe, Bryan D. 2017. *Ritualized Writing: Buddhist Practice and Scriptural Cultures in Ancient Japan*. Kuroda Institute Studies in East Asian Buddhism 27. Honolulu: University of Hawaii Press.

Mahmood, Saba. 2005. *Politics of Piety: The Islamic Revival and the Feminist Subject*. Princeton, NJ: Princeton University Press.

Malley, Brian. 2004. *How the Bible Works: An Anthropological Study of Evangelical Biblicism*. Cognitive Science of Religion. Walnut Creek, CA: AltaMira Press.

Martini, Annett. 2017. "Ritual Consecration in the Context of Writing the Holy Scrolls: Jews in Medieval Europe between Demarcation and Acculturation." *European Journal of Jewish Studies* 11(2): 174–202. https://doi.org/10.1163/1872471X-11121052

———. 2019. "The Ritualization of Manufacturing and Handling Holy Books by the Hasidei Ashkenaz between Halakah and Magic." In *Ritual Dynamics in Jewish and Christian Contexts: Between Bible and Liturgy*, edited by Claudia D. Bergmann and Benedikt Kranemann, 56–84. Jewish and Christian Perspectives 34. Leiden: Brill.

Morgan, David. 2018. *Images at Work: The Material Culture of Enchantment*. New York: Oxford University Press.

———. 2021. *The Thing about Religion: An Introduction to the Material Study of Religions*. Chapel Hill, NC: University of North Carolina Press.

Najman, Hindy. 2003. *Seconding Sinai: The Development of Mosaic Discourse in Second Temple Judaism*. JSJSup 77. Leiden: Brill.

———. 2004. "The Symbolic Significance of Writing in Ancient Judaism." In *The Idea of Biblical Interpretation: Essays in Honor of James L. Kugel*, edited by James L. Kugel, Hindy Najman, and Judith H. Newman, 139–73. JSJSup 83. Leiden: Brill.

Ochs, Vanessa L. 2007. *Inventing Jewish Ritual*. Philadelphia, PA: Jewish Publication Society.

O'Donnell, Emma. 2015. *Remembering the Future: The Experience of Time in Jewish and Christian Liturgy*. Collegeville, MN: Liturgical Press.

Ostriker, Alicia Suskin. 1997. *The Nakedness of the Fathers: Biblical Visions and Revisions*. New Brunswick, NJ: Rutgers University Press.

Parmenter, Dorina Miller. 2013. "The Iconic Book: The Image of the Bible in Early Christian Rituals." In *Iconic Books and Texts*, edited by James W. Watts, 63–92. Comparative Research on Iconic and Performative Texts. Bristol, CT: Equinox.

———. 2018. "How the Bible Feels: The Christian Bible as Effective and Affective Object." In *Sensing Sacred Texts*, edited by James W. Watts, 27–37. Comparative Research on Iconic and Performative Texts. Bristol, CT: Equinox.

Plaskow, Judith. 1990. *Standing Again at Sinai*. New York: Harper & Row.

Polaski, Donald C. 2018. "'And Also to the Jews in their Script': Power and Writing in the Scroll of Esther." In *Reading and Teaching Ancient Fiction: Jewish, Christian, and Greco-Roman Narratives*, edited by Sara Raup Johnson, Rubén R. Dupertuis, and Christine Shea, 107–22. WGRWSup 11. Atlanta, GA: SBL Press.

Polish, Daniel F. 2018. "Purim and her Sisters." *CCAR Journal*, 140–53.

Reimer, Gail Twersky. 1998. "Eschewing Esther/Embracing Esther: The Changing Representation of Biblical Heroines." In *Talking Back: Images of Jewish Women in American Popular Culture*, edited by Joyce Antler, 207–19. Waltham, MA: Brandeis University Press.

Riegler, Michael, and Baskin, Judith R. 2008. "'May the Writer be Strong': Medieval Hebrew Manuscripts Copied by and for Women." *Nashim: A Journal of Jewish Women's Studies & Gender Issues* 16: 9–28. https://doi.org/10.2979/nas.2008.-.16.9

Rosen, Norma. 1996. *Biblical Women Unbound: Counter-Tales*. Philadelphia, PA: Jewish Publication Society.

Rubenstein, Jeffrey. 1992. "Purim, Liminality, and Communitas." *AJS Review* 17(2): 247–77. https://doi.org/10.1017/s0364009400003688

Schleicher, Marianne. 2011. "Artifactual and Hermeneutical Use of Scripture in Jewish Tradition." In *Jewish and Christian Scripture as Artifact and Canon*, edited by Craig A. Evans and H. Daniel Zacharias, 48–65. LSTS 70. London: T&T Clark.

———. 2018. "Engaging All the Senses: On Multi-Sensory Stimulation in the Process of Making and Inaugurating a Torah Scroll." In *Sensing Sacred Texts*, edited by James W. Watts, 39–56. Comparative Research on Iconic and Performative Texts. Bristol, CT: Equinox.

Segal, Eliezer. 2007. "Crowning Achievement." In *In Those Days, at This Time: Holiness and History in the Jewish Calendar*. Calgary: University of Calgary Press.

Shemesh, Yael. 2002. "גלגוליה של ושתי: מקרא, מדרש חז"ל, הפרשנות הפמיניסטית והמדרש הפמיניסטי המודרני [The Metamorphoses of Vashti: Bible, Aggadah, Feminist Exegesis, and Modern Feminist Midrash]." *Beit Mikra* 47(4): 356–72.

Shoham, Hizky. 2014. *Carnival in Tel Aviv: Purim and the Celebration of Urban Zionism*. Israel: Society, Culture, and History. Boston, MA: Academic Studies Press.

Shoham, Oshrat. 2022. "The Woman's Scream: Cover-up and Tikkun." In *Dirshuni: Contemporary Women's Midrash*, edited by Tamar Biala, 168–69. HBI Series on Jewish Women. Waltham, MA: Brandeis University Press.

Singer, Ross. 2004. "Women and Writing the Megillah." *Edah* 4(2): 1–13. https://library.yctorah.org/files/2016/09/Women-and-Writing-the-Megillah.pdf

Sirat, Colette. 2002. *Hebrew Manuscripts of the Middle Ages*, translated by Nicholas de Lange. Cambridge: Cambridge University Press.

Smith-Christopher, Daniel. 2018. "Sleeping with the Enemy? Reading Esther and Judith as Comfort Women." In *Women and Exilic Identity in the Hebrew Bible*, edited by Katherine E. Southwood and Martien A. Halvorson-Taylor, 99–127. LHBOTS 631. London: Bloomsbury T&T Clark.

Solomon, Anna. 2020. "The Other Queen of Purim." *Tablet Magazine*, 9 March. https://www.tabletmag.com/sections/community/articles/the-other-queen-of-purim

Soloveitchik, Joseph Dov. 2017. *Megillat Esther: Mesorat Harav*, edited by Simon Posner, Eliyahu Krakowski, and Moshe Genack. Jerusalem: Koren.

Somekh, Simone. 2019. "Illuminating the Book of Esther." *Tablet Magazine*, 19 March. https://www.tabletmag.com/jewish-life-and-religion/281552/illuminating-the-book-of-esther

Song, Angeline. 2010. "Heartless Bimbo or Subversive Role Model? A Narrative (Self) Critical Reading of the Character of Esther." *Dialog* 49: 56–69. https://doi.org/10.1111/j.1540-6385.2009.00502.x

Sperber, David. 2020. "Contemporary Orthodox Jewish Feminist Art in Israel: Institutional Criticism of the Rabbinical Establishment." *Shofar: An Interdisciplinary Journal of Jewish Studies* 38(2): 191–227. https://doi.org/10.1353/sho.2020.0027

Stanton, Elizabeth Cady, and Chandler, Lucinda B. 1895. "Esther." In *The Woman's Bible*, 2: 84–92. New York: European Publishing Co. https://ecommons.cornell.edu/handle/1813/2585.

Stern, Elsie. 2012. "Concepts of Scripture in the Synagogue Service." In *Jewish Concepts of Scripture: A Comparative Introduction*, edited by Benjamin Sommer, 15–30. New York: New York University Press.

Sudilovsky, Judith. 2022. "Rare 255-Year-Old Scroll of Esther Acquired by Israel Museum." *The Jerusalem Post*, 8 March. https://www.jpost.com/archaeology/article-700664

Tamber-Rosenau, Caryn. 2020. "A Queer Critique of Looking for 'Male' and 'Female' Voices in the Hebrew Bible." In *The Oxford Handbook of Feminist Approaches to the Hebrew Bible*, edited by Susanne Scholz, 479–93. Oxford: Oxford University Press.

Times of Israel. 2021. "Rare 18th-Century Esther Scroll Penned by Teenage Italian Girl Unveiled in Jerusalem." 17 November. https://www.timesofisrael.com/rare-18th-century-esther-scroll-penned-by-teenage-italian-girl-unveiled-in-jerusalem/

Walfish, Barry Dov. 2002. "Kosher Adultery? The Mordecai-Esther-Ahasuerus Triangle in Midrash and Exegesis." *Prooftexts* 22(3): 305–33. https://doi.org/10.2979/pft.2002.22.3.305

Watts, James W. 2018. "Scripture's Indexical Touch." In *Sensing Sacred Texts*, edited by James W. Watts, 173–84. Comparative Research on Iconic and Performative Texts. Bristol, CT: Equinox.

———. 2019. *How and Why Books Matter: Essays on the Social Function of Iconic Texts*. Comparative Research on Iconic and Performative Texts. Bristol, CT: Equinox.

Wechsler, Michael G. 2015. *The Book of Conviviality in Exile* (Kitāb al-Īnās Bi-'l-Jalwa)*: The Judaeo-Arabic Translation and Commentary of Saadia Gaon on the Book of Esther*. Biblia Arabica 1. Leiden: Brill.

White, Sidnie Ann. 1989. "Esther: A Feminine Model for Jewish Diaspora." In *Gender and Difference in Ancient Israel*, edited by Peggy L. Day, 161–77. Philadelphia, PA: Fortress.

Wood, Sorrel. 2021. "Writing Esther: How do Writing, Power and Gender Intersect in the Megillah and its Literary Afterlife?" *Open Theology* 7(1): 35–59. https://doi.org/10.1515/opth-2020-0146

Yardeni, Ada. 2002. *The Book of Hebrew Script: History, Palaeography, Script Styles, Calligraphy and Design*. London: British Library.

Zaeske, Susan. 2014. "Esther's Book: A Rhetoric of Writing for Jewish Feminists." In *Jewish Rhetorics: History, Theory, Practice*, edited by Michael Bernard-Donals and Janice W. Fernheimer, 180–97. Waltham, MA: Brandeis University Press.

Zion-Waldoks, Tanya. 2015. "Politics of Devoted Resistance: Agency, Feminism, and Religion among Orthodox Agunah Activists in Israel." *Gender and Society* 29(1): 73–97. https://doi.org/10.1177/0891243214549353

About the Author

Joanna Homrighausen is Adjunct Lecturer for Judaic Studies and Religious Studies at William & Mary, Williamsburg. She holds a PhD in Religion from Duke University, writes and teaches on sacred words, sacred texts, and how individuals and communities reproduce, ritualize, and revere them through lettering arts and scribal crafts. Her recent dissertation, *Writing Esther*, unpacks the materiality of the Esther scroll in Judaism and shows how Jews have used the written artifact to think through pivotal theological questions raised by the Book of Esther. She also writes on religion and art, including *Planting Letters and Weaving Lines: Calligraphy, the Song of Songs, and The Saint John's Bible* (Liturgical Press, 2022).

6

"I Left My Bible At Home...": Evangelical Women's Bodies as Biblical Text in the Workplace during the 1980s

Rachel E. C. Beckley

Abstract

Evangelical affiliated periodicals serve as an important source to document how evangelical women coped with the absence of material markers of evangelicalism once they entered secular workplaces in the United States during the 1980s. In these affiliated periodicals, women writers legitimize their entry into the workforce with parable writing and story-telling that exemplify to their female readers how they can exhibit their evangelical identity and engage in evangelization by embodying motifs and narratives from the Bible. Theoretically, the article leans on Judith Butler and Karen Barad's understandings of performativity, which is why the article asks: what acts did evangelical women engage in, how did affiliated periodicals intra-act with and thus have an effect on the construction of evangelical women's identity, and how did these acts relate to the Bible? These questions are directed at evangelical affiliated periodicals from the 1980s, especially Shirley Schreiner Taylor's parable "God Protects His Sheep among the Wolves" from the February 1989 issue of Word and Work.

Keywords: United States evangelicalism, evangelical womanhood, affiliated periodicals, devotional literature, embodiment, Bible

Introduction

Most political and historical scholarship on US evangelicalism post-1940 utilizes similar empirical sources. These sources include best-selling evangelical books, like the *Left Behind* series or *The Late Great Planet Earth,* as well as the publications of large institutions such as the ecumenical flagship magazine *Christianity Today* or the conservative *Focus on the Family* (see for instance: Dochuk 2021; Kobes du Mez 2020; Ridgely 2017; Kruse 2015; Smith 2015; Dochuk 2011; Vaca 2019; Wuthnow 2015; Phillips-Fein 2009; Gilgoff 2007; Frykholm 2007; Hatch 1989). While these sources may be important to the development of American evangelicalism, most of them are either written, or run, by evangelical men. Thus, the majority of scholarship produced about US evangelicalism is from a male practitioner's perspective.

But women are writing. Affiliated periodicals are magazines written for and by denominational members. These magazines are less concerned with profit-making strategies because they run on volunteer labour, and their budgets can sometimes be supplemented by the denomination itself (Waters 2001, 308). The articles for affiliated periodicals come in the form of parables, memorials, remembrances, Bible studies, sermons, prayer requests, and other types of devotional literature, and they are often written by evangelical male pastors, but also by pastors' wives and other female parishioners. Unlike centrally managed flagship publications, these affiliate periodicals capture a greater diversity of voices in intimate, conversational articles. Consequently, their unique production allows me to access women's writing to other women, instructing them on how to bring evangelicalism into the world.

Using affiliated periodicals, I ask how women writers utilize biblical texts in devotional articles. I shall argue that women writers do not simply reference Bible verses or make intellectual or theological arguments. Instead, women writers focus on parable writing or story-telling to exhort women readers to perform evangelical womanhood by embodying submission, integrity, and trust in God from Bible stories as a way to evangelize, especially in a secular environment such as the workplace.

My work leans on Judith Butler's understanding of gender as processual, that is, that gender and other forms of identity emerge from the acts that one engages in (1990). I supplement Butler's notion with Karen Barad who argues that the emergence of identity through performativity needs to take account of the effects of materiality and how matter 'intra-acts' (Barad 2007, 141) in identificatory processes. An analytical consequence of Butler and Barad's understandings of performativity is to examine the acts that evangelical women engage in, how affiliated periodicals intra-act with and thus influence the construction of evangelical womanhood, and how their acts also intra-act with the phenomenon of "sacred text."

The devotional literature in these affiliated periodicals purposefully evokes sacred texts through allusion rather than through citing chapter and verse (Smith and Watson 1996, 3–4, 16–17; Bartlett and Bestul 1999, 2-3; Craig 1997, 89; Tompkins 1986, ix). Because they evoke elements of a sacred text, the devotional stories and parables provide familiar examples that a female reader can replicate in her own life, with her own body, thus embodying shards of a sacred text in her behaviour and activity. In using parable or story-telling in this way, evangelical women writers call for women readers to express evangelical womanhood through the active embodied performance of the biblical text so that their behaviour may be "read" by observers.

The material that I shall analyse stems from the 1980s. I shall bring a short overview of different statements before I go into detail about the article "God Protects His Sheep among the Wolves" by Shirley Schreiner Taylor from the February 1989 issue of *Word and Work*. This material provides insights into a significant change that took place in the 1980s. Previously, middle-class evangelical women remained at home, whereas in the 1980s evangelical women went to work (Collins 2009). Work was and is often situated in secular contexts where the presence of a physical Bible would be out of place. Transitioning from a home that women could line with all sorts of overt markers of their evangelical identity to a secular workplace devoid of evangelicalism required evangelical women to rethink how to signal their identity. This article argues that bodily allusions to the Bible and evangelical characteristics became the answer. Rather than exhibiting a material biblical text with ink and paper, women's bodily references to the Bible became not only a demonstration of their own religious identity, but also a primary mode of evangelizing in a workspace.

Analysis: "God Protects His Sheep among Wolves" in *Word and Work*

In the 1980s, affiliated periodicals within American evangelicalism shift from deploring the absence of material religiosity markers in the workplace, to presenting stories and parables about women workers like the parishioner and nurse Becky Brodin, who proudly states in the *Discipleship Journal* from 1988 that, when she goes to work, "I leave my bible at home!" (Brodin 1988). Instead of carrying a Bible, she tells her reader that she demonstrates her Christianity through her behaviour and excellence at her job. Another 1988 article in the denominational periodical *Gospel Herald and the Sunday School Times* even goes so far as to tell readers to *stop reading a Bible* on company time, because to do so is to steal time from an employer and produce a poor witness (Halsey 1988).

Witnessing with a material Bible is no longer the only way to evangelize in the workplace.[1] Instead, showing "proper" work ethic is the best way to evangelize. As Jessie Sandberg describes in the magazine *Joyful Woman*, to be an effective Christian witness, a worker must be the best and most faithful employee, "Let's face it ladies: bosses are not always fair," Jessie laments. However, to be an evangelistic tool in the workplace – that is, to be a text that can be read to proclaim the Gospel – Jessie describes how a woman should behave in more detail:

> [Y]ou have to be the best employee ... faithful, honest, hardworking, genuinely caring about the success of your job ... don't be critical of others, quarrelsome, moody, easily offended otherwise the Gospel will not be attractive to others. (Sandberg 1988)

G. Roger Schoenhals, a writer in *Alliance Life*, the organ of the Christian and Missionary Alliance denomination, declares that some people can be offended by "holier-than-thou and sanctimonious evangelization." Instead, he says, workers can evangelize through their behaviour: "Work among others in a natural, personable manner" (Schoenhals 1989).

In the February 1989 issue of the *Word and Work* magazine, Clarence Trowbridge writes: "While you do your regular work, you can make those eight-hour office days the occasions when you are 'read' as a living epistle," referencing 2 Corinthians 3:2–3.[2] The person becomes the text. How *they* touch, feel, and smell, how they dress, how they comport their bodies, how they behave, how they respond and interpret the world around them becomes a textual source for others who are constantly reading/watching. Much like John 1:14 when "The Word became flesh," I see in the 1980s a substantial shift in Christian magazine workplace discourse in which the materiality of the text switches from the book (evangelization with a

1. The Bible itself remains an important iconic text for many practitioners. As Dorina Parmenter points out, Protestants, especially evangelicals, eschew icons, but they still carry the material book. She argues persuasively that this relationship can be better described as an indexical relationship. See Parmenter 2019; cf. Watts 2012 [2017]. My article expands on Parmenter's analysis, showing more nuance of evangelical practice. I argue that women in the workplace maintain this indexical relationship with the biblical text. But, in this particular case, the physical biblical text is removed completely so that the only indication of the Bible is the practitioner's embodiment. She will still reference the biblical text, but does not have the physical Bible in hand. The body becomes the Bible.

2. "Ye are our epistle written in our hearts, known and read of all men: Forasmuch as ye are manifestly declared to be the epistle of Christ ministered by us, written not with ink, but with the Spirit of the living God; not in tables of stone, but in fleshy tables of the heart." King James Version. Note: I use the KJV because *Word and Work* only uses the KJV translation.

material biblical object) to the flesh (evangelization with the body and behaviour). Far from the absence of the material, instead the materiality of the sacred text is ensconced in the body of the practitioner.

The question is, *how* did this get incorporated? How did the evangelical gendered identity of "woman" possibly merge with a "woman-at-work" so that her material body could be read as an evangelical text? To analyse and reflect on this process, I shall go into detail with one example of these devotional parables from the February 1989 issue of *Word and Work.* Published in 1908 by a Church of Christ in New Orleans, *Word and Work* ended their printed publication in 2008 and became an e-magazine in 2011. It continues to be published today, affiliated with the Church of Christ denomination and all archived articles are available online.[3] The title of the article I will analyse is "God Protects His Sheep among the Wolves." The author, Shirley Schreiner Taylor, is writing to women in the workforce in 1989 concerning her own experience in the workforce when she first got a job, before she was married.

The theme of *Word and Work* from February 1989 was "Christians in the Workplace". Shirley's article is one out of six, all centred around how Christians should comport themselves in the workplace. The articles are all meant to be read together and are well edited to mirror each other. I have chosen to focus only on Shirley's article because it differs from the others in two main ways: first, it is the only article written by a woman and second, it is written in the form of a parable. The other articles are written by men and are in the style of essays or sermons. Shirley's parable is a first-person narrative of an actual occurrence in her life (as she claims). Her article is reminiscent of biblical parables and stories, which *Word and Work's* readers are primed to interpret dialectically, looking for timeless lessons to use in everyday life.

Shirley's parable represents a common narrative pattern found in evangelical affiliated periodicals.[4] First, it begins with a worker, often a woman, who must stand against a common worldly problem because of her own interpretation of Christian morality. Second, it always takes place in a secular, generally non-Christian and dangerous workplace. This is clearly outlined in a previous article in the same *Word and Work* written by a man named Martin Brooks. A former grocery industry manager, Brooks started

3. http://www.wordandwork.org/about/; accessed 2 June 2020. Archived issues from 2010–20 can be found at http://www.wordandwork.org/archived-issues/. Back issues from 1908 to 2008 can be found at https://www.therestorationmovement.com/ journals/ww.htm.

4. For a similar pattern, see Brooks 1989; Tamasy 1991.

a "preaching ministry" at the Cherry Street Church of Christ in New Albany, Indiana. Brooks asks his reader pointedly, "How should the Christian respond to a heathen work force?" (Brooks 1989). Indeed, the whole issue of *Word and Work*, including Shirley's article, is riddled with examples of Christians dealing with the temptations of "heathenness" in the workplace. Examples of heathenness include swearing while at work, lying, "stealing" work time, talking about sex or pornography with co-workers, drinking and doing drugs, and not standing up for "Christian ethics" when discussing the big issues of the day from abortion to racial discrimination.

Martin Brooks points his reader to 1 John 2:6, "Whoever claims to live in him must *walk as Jesus did.*" Thus, the Christian-at-work must ask "What would Jesus do if He were in my place? Then act accordingly" (Brooks 1989). Buford Smith points to Colossians 3:23, "Whatever you do, work heartily *as unto the Lord.*" "The theory is simple:" he exclaims, "work as unto the Lord ... Jesus provides the sustaining power" (Smith 1989). The editor of *Word and Work* Alec V. Wilson, after telling his own parable about an executive officer praying for a junior officer under his direction, offers this view of work because, in the end, "God [cares] about every-day, 'secular' life" (Wilson 1989). Kenneth J. Preston drives this point home by quoting John 3:21, "He that *doeth* the truth cometh to the light, that his works may be manifest, that they have been wrought in God." He jokes that "many feel that this has only a spiritual connotation." But Preston, with his preaching and business career from Parkville Church of Christ in Kentucky, argues that this verse "applies to one's entire lifestyle, whether at work or play." Preston advises his reader that a Christian should "handle our business affairs in such a manner that they are always above reproach. Remember, we Christians are being scrutinized today more closely than ever by those who would see to justify their non-Christian activities." He goes on to give examples of "doing the truth" (Preston 1989). Belonging to this common narrative pattern, Shirley's parable addresses workplace-related challenges.

Shirley's parable recounts her experiences when she worked at the Navy Department in Washington, DC, prior to her marriage. Here, she worked as a substitute for the Captain's personal secretary at the Navy Department in Washington, DC. The Captain is by all accounts a cruel and overpowering man. Shirley references the fact that this Captain "was a rather rough, tough kind of guy" (Taylor 1989, 41). She notes that even the other officers walked on ice around him. "He was known to dismiss an individual for no reason at all" (Taylor 1989, 41) she remembers. Central to her parable is Shirley's moral dilemma of how best to express her Christian womanhood in a secular work environment.

To navigate the narrativization of this dilemma, Shirley does not reference any biblical story explicitly. However, implicitly she expects her reader to recognize the obvious parallels between her experiences and those of biblical characters and events in the books of Esther, Daniel, and Acts. Similar to Daniel in the house of the Babylonian king Nebuchadnezzar,[5] or to Esther in the court of the Persian king Ahasuerus, Shirley's reader will know that her employment could be taken away on a whim. She has no protection as a temporary worker and the Captain, like Nebuchadnezzar and Ahasuerus, is unpredictable and toxic. Shirley is in a dangerous secular place. She is a woman, outside the protection of her Christian home. The question for Shirley is: how can she be loyal to, and express, her evangelical womanhood in a secular environment?

Shirley's process toward an answer emerges once she is asked to do something that goes against her personal moral code. The captain calls her into his office. "As I walked in," she recounts, "he threw a quarter on his desk ordering me to go and get him some cigarettes" (Taylor 1989, 41). Shirley faces a dilemma that may not be apparent to readers outside the *Word and Work* interpretive community. As a conservative evangelical in the Church of Christ, Shirley believes she would be a poor witness for anyone who saw her buying the cigarettes. If she did so, Shirley would consider herself guilty by association, helping someone else engage in a vice. Shirley describes her terror, but she also says that she "prayed silently for guidance."

Next in the narrative, Shirley gives a description of how she stood up for herself on the job. This is a critical part of the narrative because Shirley's example is meant to be generalized. Reminiscent of a parable, Shirley describes her actions in hopes that her reader can reproduce her actions in a similar situation. Interestingly enough, however, she begins by sharing incorrect ways of standing up before she presents the correct alternative of what to do to be read as an evangelical woman in the workplace.[6] In her description of how she first failed, she describes how she became

5. Even though Daniel is male, his story can still be used in magazines for women to mimic. In a Christian framework, women as well as men are expected to copy the saints. All people, women and men, are supposed to "be like Jesus"; men as well as women can learn from the story of Martha and Mary; all people can learn from Peter's blunders or Thomas's doubt. It is not odd for women to look to male biblical figures for guidance and enlightenment. This is especially the case for evangelical women as those denominations often elevate male biblical characters over female characters.

6. In Trowbidge's article in the same issue of *Word and Work*, he lists a process for standing up in a correct way: "1. Make an open stand for Christ 2. Adopt an uncompromising attitude 3. Temper all your actions with love" (Trowbridge 1989, 45).

mealy-mouthed and unequivocal. "I tried to say as nicely as I could that I would rather not" (Taylor 1989, 41). The Captain responded in a verbally abusive manner, "As he shouted out several oaths demanding an explanation it was obvious I was in trouble." She then explains to the reader how she felt: "I felt so insignificant, and just knew that comment would mean my job" (Taylor 1989, 41). Here, the reader is meant to be concerned for Shirley: will she give in on her moral stand, or will she be made a martyr? In this case, of course, the martyrdom does not refer to Shirley losing her life but instead losing her job, which can amount to a social and economic death, especially living as an unmarried woman in Washington, DC. Shirley made a second attempt to stand up as the tension rose. She says, "In a fumbling way I tried to explain I was a Christian and had strong convictions against smoking and even buying cigarettes" (Taylor 1989, 41). Notice her description: she is "fumbling". She has not spoken directly and simply said, "no." Shirley even describes her third failed attempt as the boss yells at her again, trying to explain away her moral concerns. Shirley recounts:

> God helped me stand firm as I explained to this officer that he and I knew [the cigarettes would be for him], but that the people I would be buying them from or anyone around watching would not know that, and my witness to them by action would not be good. Then with God's boldness I said, "Sir, I know that you can fire me and that is okey [sic], for God is my protector and He will take care of me and see that I get another job." I left. (Taylor 1989, 41)

Notice that her statement still respects the Captain's authority over her: she calls him "sir" and also acknowledges his power by saying "I know that you can fire me." While she acknowledges this boss's power over her, she then appeals to a heavenly boss, that is God, who is also male. If this earthly boss will fire her for standing on her conscience, then her heavenly boss, God, will care for her. Lastly, Shirley vacates the space, ceding her own right to be present, and in that way shows submission to an authority figure.

It would not be lost on the reader that Shirley is tempted three times. Shirley does not use the number three randomly. Jesus was tempted three times in the Wilderness (Matt 4:1–11), Peter had the opportunity to claim Jesus but instead betrayed him three times (Matt 26:69–75; Mark 14:66–72; Luke 22:54–62; John 18:15–18, 25–7), and Jesus asked if Peter loved him three times (John 21:15–17). To be tested three times is a common trope in the New Testament text especially with regards to declaring Christ's divinity. By using the trope of three, Shirley equates standing up for a moral principle as a form of declaring, or evangelizing, the Gospel. She laments that she did not perform this evangelism properly the first and second time. As we shall see, "proper" evangelism not only has to do with what the practitioner says but also the way she comports her material body.

Shirley also assigns her boldness to God, and believes that God (that is, the Spirit) spoke through her in this moment of testing. Trembling, Shirley goes back to her desk after confronting the Captain, absolutely terrified that she would still lose her job. She prays. Then, she waits. This is the climax of Shirley's narrative. The devotional reader is left interpreting the protagonist as a possible martyr figure after having stood so bravely against this lion of a Captain.

This leads us to the final part of the narrative sequence. Rather than becoming a martyr and losing her job, Shirley instead mirrors the heroism of Old Testament figures like Daniel or Esther whom God saves from trouble or death. As Shirley tells it, "Several days later as I was again sitting in for his secretary, this same Captain made his way out to [my] desk where I was typing. (Usually he just yelled from his office when he wanted us.) As I looked up my heart started pounding – but he was smiling" (Taylor 1989, 41).

In these magazine stories, the protagonist will not lose the job. Instead, the protagonist's boss and/or co-workers admit to feeling a deeper respect for a person willing to stand up for her morals and integrity in the face of intimidation. "[My boss] told me how much he appreciated and admired me for taking a stand" (Taylor 1989, 41). This returns us to the basic premise of a heathen workforce. Even the "heathen" Captain acknowledges that integrity and honesty are rare commodities in the workforce. It is not that Christians are not good workers because they appeal to a higher authority. On the contrary, Christians are the best workers because that higher authority also insists on certain types of behaviour as a worker, such as honesty, thriftiness, timeliness, and integrity. The Captain admires and appreciates Shirley because she disobeyed him, owing to her higher moral conscience. In fact, the Captain promises Shirley to support and protect her in the office from damaging her integrity. This new protecting behaviour serves to "convert" the very workspace itself. Shirley recounts,

> Not only did he apologize, he also told me to come to him immediately if anyone, employee or visitor, made any kind of pass at me or off-color remark to me. He ... became a very good friend and "protector." I praised my God for guiding me again through a tough situation and holding me with a strong Hand. (Taylor 1989, 41)

Shirley's parable shows how a woman can construct her evangelical womanhood to enable her to enter the workforce without bending her morals. One important way to do so is by finding inspiration from and embodying biblical narratives like those of Esther or Daniel on standing up for one's cause. In addition, when the narrative portrays God as intervening to save Shirley, the heroic believer, her behaviour of words and acts manifests the sacred text and thus enables evangelization. The biblical text can be mirrored through the life of the person. If the Christian enacts the Bible in a convincing way, people will recognize them as Christians. Material evidence of Christianity is shown through embodied acts in the workforce, not through objects such as a Bible or a cross. As an alternative, Shirley demonstrates her evangelicalism by making her words and bodily behaviours activate associations to biblical motifs and narratives.

The Christian Bible contains many texts whose motifs and narratives invite embodied mirroring. Here, it is noteworthy to see that Shirley reaches for Old Testament exemplars rather than New Testament ones. In my own experience and knowledge of evangelical theology, characters in the Old Testament and the New Testament perform very different functions. For evangelicals, the Old Testament contains heroic figures whom God saves in miraculous ways. Generally, those in the New Testament, on the other hand, hinge on martyrdom or a willingness to die as a vital part of the evangelical message. For example: Christians are "buried" with Christ in baptism and "made alive" again, symbolizing sacrificing the self; Stephen the first martyr is stoned; and the writer of Acts tells the reader of Saul, soon to become Paul, who has made it his mission to kill Christians. The lives of martyrs mimic the lives of Jesus in their death. But, as evangelicals interpret it, the stories of the Old Testament occur prior to Jesus's death. Therefore, not death/resurrection but rather salvation in the present life is the way that God demonstrates power in the world.[7]

Shirley's narrative mimics Old Testament stories like Daniel in the Lion's Den, encouraging the reader to read these articles devotionally. Shirley's situation is general enough to be recognizable to readers, who have likely been asked to do things that made them uncomfortable. Shirley sets herself up as an Old Testament hero whom God "saves." Here, it is important to notice how her weakness is typical of Old Testament heroes. If Shirley and the Old Testament heroes had been self-sufficient and strong, they could have overcome whatever obstacle they faced on their own with no need for divine intervention. By admitting to their weakness, both Shirley and

7. Note that the separation of heroic figures from martyr figures is entirely contrived by scholars. Evangelicals do not always interpret a difference between *risking* death and *actual* death. In my own youth, raised in an evangelical household, Esther and Daniel were both described to me as martyrs because they *risked* death and punishment.

the Old Testament heroes emphasize their being as miraculous. Accordingly, Shirley states that she stood "with God's boldness." Her weakness demonstrates that only a miracle could have softened the Captain's heart.

Shirley's appeal to "God's boldness" is an echo of Acts 4 as Peter and John go before the Sanhedrin. Once again, in the Acts story, these men are in a dangerous position. The story states that Peter and John were arrested and then brought before the Sanhedrin and there they preach about their belief in Jesus as a messiah. When they are released, in verse 23, Peter and John return to their people and they are afraid that the Sanhedrin will punish them, perhaps with death. Together the group prays to God to deliver them from the danger. After quoting from a Psalm, they say in verse 29, "And now, Lord, behold [Herod's, Pontius Pilate's, Gentiles', and the Sanhedrin's] threatenings: and grant unto thy servants, that with all boldness they may speak thy word ..." The story in Acts 4 ends with the Holy Spirit descending on Peter, John, and the others and "they spake the word of God with boldness" (verse 31). This proceeds to the last section in Acts 4 in which the early church is first formed.

The language of "boldness" here is attributed to the Holy Spirit and is specifically related to declaring who Jesus was. By using this exact language, Shirley depicts herself in the place of a member of the early church, in which God/the Holy Spirit provides her boldness to speak and declare the "gospel." Evangelicals in particular, who see the biblical text as a complete whole and *only* understandable with the revelation of the Christ in the New Testament, would also read this Holy Spirit-given boldness to figures in the Old Testament. The boldness of Esther speaking before her King, or the miraculous closing of the lion's mouths in Daniel is interpreted through the New Testament lens as foreshadowing the coming of the Holy Spirit, enabling Christians to speak with divine authority.

Through their trials, Shirley, Esther, and Daniel all made their spaces more rightoous. Shirley's lion became more kind, constantly offering her protection against other integrity challenges in her time at the naval department. In doing so, unwittingly, the captain is making the environment more Christian, or at the very least, less heathen. The evangelical witness is critical for the story. Shirley not only saves herself, but also evangelizes to the captain and to the entire workplace as a result of her bodily performance of an Old Testament hero.

Practically, Shirley's narrative implicitly argues that a Christian woman may enter the workforce without compromising her conservative morality, thereby potentially validating the trend of women entering the workforce.

However, while providing a new place for women to work, her narrative also maintains a number of conservative viewpoints: 1) the interpretive framework maintains the hierarchy of the company and the male boss, specifically eschewing collective strategies or producing systematic change; 2) it confirms a paternalistic view of the employee, especially the female employee – the boss should "take care of" or protect their employees as a result of their own righteousness, not because of a list of workplace laws; 3) Shirley argues women can retain domesticity and femininity even when in the workforce and that doing so is a vital aspect of performing the evangelical "woman-at-work."

Shirley writes this devotional parable for the *Word and Work* interpretive community to reflect on their own lives and apply the parable in the same way they would apply biblical stories. In this moment of change, when even conservative evangelical women are trying to find their way in the workforce, Shirley demonstrates how women can use biblical stories as a guide for their own behaviour, retaining their femininity, their protection, and their witness. And this witness is best given through behaviour and action, the performance of biblical stories, rather than through material items like a physical Bible.

Shirley represents the importance of seeing evangelical womanhood as processual. Evangelicalism did not define womanhood as a "woman who works." Quite the contrary, an evangelical woman was expected to be a Christian homemaker. Yet, evangelical women intra-acted with their workspace through embodied enactments of biblical motifs and narratives and thereby transformed the secular workplace into a potential place for evangelical women. Certainly, there were expectations of what these women should wear, how they should hold themselves, and how they should stand up for their personal integrity at work. Likewise, evangelical women were expected to be submissive to male authority. In performing biblical narratives, they could navigate, and implicitly uphold, the patriarchal system in the workplace. The boss could take on the position of a father or a husband. Still, the legitimizing power that follows from having replaced material markers of evangelicalism such as physical copies of the Bible with embodied enactments of biblical motifs and narratives enabled an important expansion of evangelical women's mobility into the workplace, including the expression of their religious identity.

Conclusion

Evangelical authors wrote more than just best-selling books post-1940 in the United States. Much of their most intimate writing took place within their own interpretive communities, sent out in monthly periodicals. As women entered the workforce, women writers pushed back against circumscribed evangelical womanhood as including only women-in-the-home. Instead, they argued, evangelical womanhood could include women-at-work. However, if a woman was going to maintain her evangelical womanhood in a secular, and even heathen, work environment, she needed to do it in a very particular way. There needed to be rules and guides for how a woman should behave. I found that, in these affiliated periodicals, women writers tended to reach for Old Testament exemplars to guide their at-work behaviour and the maintenance of evangelical integrity in a secular space. As a result, once women were allowed to enter the workforce, these affiliated periodicals document a pivotal moment in the becoming of evangelical womanhood.

This article documents how evangelicals during the 1980s could replace material copies of the Bible with bodily performances of biblical motifs and narratives as markers of their evangelical identity and also as means to evangelization. Here, evangelical women's bodies became the sacred text to be read by those around them, even in secular spaces like the workplace. Like Becky Brodin, they left their physical Bible at home, but they showed up at work as heroic biblical figures, continually re-enacting miraculous stories.

Acknowledgments

I would like to thank Dr Marianne Schleicher for all her support and editing expertise on this article. I would also like to thank Patrick Robbins of the J. S. Mack Library at Bob Jones University.

References

Barad, Karen. 2007. *Meeting the Universe Halfway: Quantum Physics and the Entanglement of Matter and Meaning.* Durham, NC: Duke University Press.

Bartlett, Anne Clark, and Bestul, Thomas H., eds. 1999. *Culture of Piety: Medieval English Devotional Literature in Translation.* Ithaca, NY: Cornell University Press.

Brodin, Becky. 1988. "What Makes You so Different?" *Discipleship Journal* 47: 13–15. Folder: Work, Fundamentalism File, Bob Jones University, Accession No. 48469.

Brooks, Martin. 1989. "Serving God in the Workplace." *Word and Work*, February. Folder: Work, Fundamentalism File, Bob Jones University, Accession No. 515254.

Butler, Judith. 1990. *Gender Trouble: Feminism and the Subversion of Identity.* New York: Routledge.

Collins, Gail. 2009. *When Everything Changed: The Amazing Journey of American Women from 1960 to the Present.* New York: Little, Brown & Co.

Craig, Terrence L. 1997. *The Missionary Lives: A Study in Canadian Missionary Biography and Autobiography*. New York: Brill.

Dochuk, Darren. 2011. *From Bible Belt to Sun Belt: Plain-Folk Religion, Grassroots Politics, and the Rise of Evangelical Conservatism*. New York: W. W. Norton & Co.

———, ed. 2021. *Religion and Politics Beyond the Culture Wars: New Directions in a Divided America*. Notre Dame, IN: University of Notre Dame Press.

Frykholm, Amy Johnson. 2007. *Rapture Culture: Left Behind in Evangelical America*. Oxford: Oxford University Press.

Gilgoff, Dan. 2007. *The Jesus Machine: How James Dobson, Focus on the Family, and Evangelical America are Winning the Culture War*. New York: St Martin's Press.

Halsey, Michael D. 1988. "Labor: Rat Race or Blessing?" *Gospel Herald and the Sunday School Times*. Folder: Work, Fundamentalism File, Accession No. 476416.

Hatch, Nathan O. 1989. *The Democratization of American Christianity*. New Haven, CT: Yale University Press.

Kobes du Mez, Kristin. 2020. *Jesus and John Wayne: How White Evangelicals Corrupted a Faith and Fractured a Nation*. New York: Liveright Publishing Corporation.

Kruse, Kevin. 2015. *One Nation Under God: How Corporate America Invented Christian America*. New York: Basic Books.

Parmenter, Dorina Miller. 2019. "Being the Bible: Sacred Bodies and Iconic Books in Bring Your Bible to School Day." *Postscripts* 10(1–2): 53–69. https://doi.org/10.1558/post.38256

Phillips-Fein, Kim. 2009. *Invisible Hands: The Businessmen's Crusade Against the New Deal*. New York: W. W. Norton & Co.

Preston, Kenneth J. 1989. "On the Job." *Word and Work*, February. Folder: Work, Fundamentalism File, Bob Jones University, Accession No. 515254.

Ridgely, Susan B. 2017. *Practicing What the Doctor Preached: At Home with Focus on the Family*. Oxford: Oxford University Press.

Sandberg, Jessie Rice. 1988. "When Your Boss is a Bear." *Joyful Woman*. Folder: Work, Fundamentalism File, Bob Jones University, Accession No. 446088.

Schoenhals, Roger. 1989. "Christians in the Workplace." *Alliance Life Magazine* August: 9–10. Folder: Work, Fundamentalism File, Bob Jones University, Accession No. 545020.

Smith, Buford. 1989. "At Work: Practicing What We Preach." *Word and Work*, February. Folder: Work, Fundamentalism File, Bob Jones University, Accession No. 515254.

Smith, Erin A. 2015. *What Would Jesus Read? Popular Religious Books and Everyday Life in Twentieth-Century America*. Chapel Hill, NC: University of North Carolina Press.

Smith, Sidonie, and Watson, Julia, eds. 1996. *Getting a Life: Everyday Uses of Autobiography*. Minneapolis: University of Minnesota.

Tamasy, Robert J. 1991. "Integrity in the Workplace." *The Church Herald and Holiness Banner*. Folder: Work, Fundamentalism File, Accession No. 664664.

Taylor, Shirley Schreiner. 1989. "God Protects His Sheep among the Wolves." *Word and Work*, February. Folder: Work, Fundamentalism File, Bob Jones University, Accession No. 515254.

Tompkins, J. P. 1986. *Sensational Designs: The Cultural Work of American Fiction, 1790–1860.* Oxford: Oxford University Press.

Trowbridge, Clarence. 1989. "Dilemmas in a Factory." *Word and Work*, February. Folder: Work, Fundamentalism File, Bob Jones University, Accession No. 515254.

Vaca, Daniel. 2019. *Evangelicals Incorporated: Books and the Business of Religion in America.* Cambridge, MA: Harvard University Press.

Watts, James. 2012 [2017]. "Scriptures' Indexical Touch." *Postscripts* 8(1–2): 123–84. https://doi.org/10.1558/post.32671

Waters, Ken. 2001. "Vibrant, But Invisible: A Study of Contemporary Religious Periodicals." *Journalism and Mass Communications Quarterly* 78(2): 307–20. https://doi.org/10.1177/107769900107800207

Wilson, Alex V. 1989. "Theme: Christians in the Workplace." *Word and Work*, February. Folder: Work, Fundamentalism File, Bob Jones University, Accession No. 515254.

Wuthnow, Robert. 2015. *Inventing American Religion: Polls, Surveys, and the Tenuous Quest for a Nation's Faith.* Oxford: Oxford University Press.

About the Author

Rachel Schwaller [publication name: Rachel E. C. Beckley] is a Multi-term Lecturer at the University of Kansas in the Departments of History and Religious Studies. She received her Ph.D. in American Studies from the University of Kansas in 2019 with a focus on religion in the United States. Rachel's dissertation focused on conservative evangelical Christianity in America with a particular interest in scriptural interpretation, race, colonialism, and economics. She uses a mixture of archival and ethnographic methodologies to uncover how people have made scriptures active in their everyday lives. (rschwallr@ku.edu)

7

Doing Piety through Care: Embodied Enactments of the Qur'an and Gender Perceptions in Muslim Families in Contemporary Denmark

Abir Mohamad Ismail

Abstract

This article takes the practice of elderly care as a starting place to discuss how Muslim men and women "do" piety when doing elderly care in their everyday lives. It introduces and analyses central passages in the Qur'an and the Ḥadīths that deal with birr-al- wālidayn (filial piety), 'awra (the intimate body parts that must be covered), and 'ayb (shame/shamefulness) since they all appear as central concepts in the Islamic tradition of elderly care. With a focus on the embodied enactment of these concepts, the article turns to the analysis of two ethnographic cases to look at how Muslims "do" care for their elderly parents and at the same time strive to embody their sacred text, the Qur'an, and the Ḥadīths in everyday life. The article aims to show that "doing" elderly care enables a domain of pious doings that matters to how Muslim men and women perform and understand gender.

Keywords: Qur'an, self-cultivation, Embodiment, Performativity, care, gender

Introduction

This article takes the practice of elderly care as a starting place to discuss how Muslim men and women "do" piety when doing elderly care in their everyday lives. It specifically looks into the correlation between the Islamic concepts of *birr-al- wālidayn* (filial piety), *'awra* (the intimate body parts that must be covered), and *'ayb* (shame/shamefulness) to discuss them as forms of embodied enactments of the Qur'an and Ḥadīths, the Muslim sacred texts, as well as how these influence gender perceptions in Muslim families in the context of the contemporary Danish welfare state.

In Denmark, like other Scandinavian countries, the number of elderly citizens with Muslim backgrounds is increasing. However, despite the free access to care and health services provided by the Danish welfare state via taxation (Andersen 2008, 4), Danish Muslims with ethnic minority background have a relatively dismissive attitude towards municipal health care services. When dealing with institutional care of ethnic minority elders with a Muslim background, gerontological and healthcare perspectives have dominated the research field in attempts which primarily have sought to address the challenges that healthcare professionals experience (Whitfield and Baker 2013). A few gerontological and healthcare studies have also addressed how the ideals of culturally appropriate care among the ethnic minority elders may clash with the institutional elderly care offered by the welfare state (Hooyman and Kiyak 2008; Whitfield and Baker 2013). Only recently, a few anthropological studies on everyday practices of elderly care in Muslim families have been made (Ismail 2021; Rytter et al. 2021). These studies identify culture and religion as dominant factors that explain why most Muslim families undertake the caring task themselves in their own homes. The studies in question provide well-founded anthropological insights into the experiences and expectations of Muslim minorities in relation to care and filial piety as well as the challenges and changes in gender and intergenerational relationships in Muslim families (Ismail 2021, 226; 2022, 1). Other important insights from these include the lived experiences of how and to what extent religious background influences perceptions and behaviour regarding filial piety, care for the elderly, and gender relations (Ismail 2022, 1). Yet, there is a lack of knowledge about how "doing" elderly care in a religious context functions as an opportunity to become a pious Muslim. Often overlooked is how embodied enactments of the Qur'an regulate how one is to lead a pious life in a field where norms and structured ideals for both elderly care and gender interact. This article takes the Islamic practice of elderly care as a starting place to offer insights into the effects that follow when a sacred text, Muslim pietistic practices, and gender perceptions interact.

After a brief introduction to the theories, methods, and data used in this article, I shall introduce and analyse central passages in the Qur'an and the Ḥadīths that deal with *birr-al- wālidayn, 'awra,* and *'ayb,* since they all appear as central concepts in the Islamic tradition of elderly care. With a focus on the embodied enactment of these concepts, I shall then turn to the analysis of two ethnographic cases of Um Ali, an Arab-Danish Muslim woman who takes care of her elderly mother, and Salim, an Arab-Danish Muslim man who takes care of his elderly parents. I will look at how Muslims "do" care for their elderly parents and at the same time strive to embody their sacred text, the Qur'an, and the Ḥadīths in everyday lives. The article aims to show that "doing" elderly care enables a domain of pious "doings" that matters to how Muslim men and women perform and understand gender.

Theories, Methods, and Data

Theoretically, this article is informed by Judith Butler's theory of performativity (Butler 1990) according to which identity reflects a process of becoming that rests on participation in iterative acts within a culture; that is, the acts one has access to engage in. Accordingly, I speak of "doing" care because care implies many culturally loaded acts where one's intelligibility as a carer to a high degree depends on a loyal repetition of how one has seen others perform them. When it comes to my perception of sacred texts, I lean on James Watts and his address of the performative dimension of scriptures, especially with regard to the contents in drama and art (Watts 2008, 2). He emphasizes the inspiring effect that such performance may have. However, Watts is primarily focused on the performative dimension as it can be witnessed in liturgical and public contexts. I therefore supplement his insights with Marianne Schleicher's work on artefactual uses of sacred texts, on how the handling of sacred texts activates associations to the physical sacred texts where the artefactual use itself becomes a hub that ties the user to the sacred text which again connotes potentially infinite meanings (Schleicher 2017), just as I welcome her editorial role in this volume to broaden the implications of artefactual use to include pious "doings" that activate associations to contents and structures of a sacred text. For the analysis, this means that I shall look for performances of the content in the private homes of lay users and investigate how "doing" a sacred text interacts with iterative acts of "doing" gender.

My method for gathering data for this article is based on fieldwork exploring practices of elderly care in multigenerational Arab Muslim families living in Denmark, and how care for the elderly as a religious tradition is negotiated, changed, and adapted in these families.[1] In total, sixteen families consisting of elders, adult children and their spouses, and children participated in my project. Most of the multigenerational families were stateless Palestinian refugees who came to Denmark during the Lebanese civil war in the late 1980s and were housed in Gellerupparken, Aarhus, along with just under 3,000 other Palestinian refugees (Johansen and Jensen 2017, 297). Access to the families was attained through the Municipality of Aarhus, who provided me with contact information.

In addition to the formal and informal interviews, the ethnographic fieldwork consisted of participant observation, where I observed the families over time, visiting them in their homes and taking part in everyday practices and ordinary family activities such as family gatherings, celebrations, doctor's visits, and shopping activities. Most of the interviews and informal conversations were conducted in Arabic, as it gave my interlocutors the freedom to freely narrate their life story. In this context, I asked questions about their everyday care routines and the sources of their religious knowledge, sources of support in caring for their elderly parents, how the caring arrangements had evolved, how caring responsibilities were distributed in their families, and why responsibilities were shared in certain ways. The interviews lasted approximately two hours and were recorded and transcribed for analysis.

In this article, I focus primarily on the two cases of Um Ali,[2] a 61-year-old Arab-Danish Muslim woman who takes care of her elderly mother, and of Salim, a 57-year-old Arab-Danish Muslim man who takes care of his elderly mother and who also used to provide care for his now late father. I choose to focus on these two particular cases to provide in-depth narratives (one female and one male) on caring for an elderly person, and to exemplify embodied performances of the Islamic sacred texts that are entangled with the gendered nature of elderly care in Arab-Danish Muslim families in complex ways.

1. The data were collected as part of my PhD project, but the analysis presented on the interaction of sacred texts, doing care, and doing gender has been developed uniquely for this article. For further research findings, see my PhD project which is part of the larger project AISHA (https://pure.au.dk/portal/en/projects/aisha--ageing-immigrants-and-selfappointed-helper-arrangement(4fc3883a-3ecf-4a26-a0ed-bfe8f1112abf).html). Accessed 28 March 2023.

2. Pseudonyms as real names are anonymized.

Elderly Care According to Muslim Traditions and Islamic Sacred Texts

In a general perspective, elderly care figures as a religious obligation and tradition in the everyday lives of Muslims around the world. Although not all the families I worked with in Denmark would identify themselves as particularly religious, they were nonetheless all driven and/or informed by the religious obligation to care for their elders. This religious obligation regulates the relationship between adult children and their elderly parents.

There is certainly a difference between being *driven* and *informed* by religious traditions. Sometimes this difference appears relevant, at other times less so, depending on the family in question. For some of the families I worked with, the practice of elderly care was driven by the Islamic duty of caring for one's elders and by the values and morals that this duty symbolizes and represents. These families took the religion of Islam as the fundamental moral engine (Mattingly et al. 2017) for why they "did" elderly care in the way they did and perceived it as essential and necessary in the maintenance of their religion, culture, and family relations. For other families, this religious duty only informed the practice of elderly care and its practices. They acted as they did because it had always been a family tradition and now the surrounding community expected them to engage in repetitious patterns of care informed by Islam. My ethnographic material shows that families can both be driven or informed by religion. Whatever the case, the religion of Islam is present in the everyday lives of the interviewed families and plays a role to differing extent.

In Islam, care and nursing are justified and legitimized, partly in the Qur'an itself and partly in the Sunnah (traditions) and Ḥadīth (accounts) of what the Prophet Muhammad said and did during his life. For Muslims worldwide, the Prophet Muhammad has the status of "the perfect human being" and is an example that everyone must try to follow in their lives (Juynboll and Brown 2012). Thus, for a practising Muslim, it is not an individual choice whether one wants to care for or nurture one's old parents. The religion of Islam prescribes *birr-ul-wālidayn* (filial piety); therefore, regardless of whether Muslims live in nuclear families, extended families, or separately, parents can expect to be taken care of by their children in their old age (Ahmad and Khan 2016, 831). The Islamic concept of *birr-ul-walidāyn* consists of two words, *birr* meaning "good deeds," and *wālidayn* meaning "parents." *Birr* is a Qur'anic term meaning "pious goodness" (Gardet 2012) and is a synonym for the word *iḥsān*. In Arabic, *iḥsān* means an intricate range of qualities and virtues, including goodness, righteousness, benevolence, propriety, moderation, perfection, and acting in a moral and appropriate manner. The term has a historical significance and rests not only on its moral and sacred meaning within the context of its Qur'anic use, but also on its importance as a construct within ethical, theological, and ascetic discourses.

The Qur'an on *birr* and *iḥsān*

Etymologically, the form *iḥsān* is the verbal noun derived from the fourth form of the verb *aḥ sana*. The verb *aḥsana's* base triliteral root is the verb *ḥasuna*, meaning to be good and beautiful (Mustafa 2020). A study of the usages of the word *iḥsān* in the Qur'an shows that it is used in the sense of doing good and carrying out an "action" in the best way. Concerning elderly care, *birr* and *iḥsān* are generally used interchangeably and indirectly regulate how to take care of one's parents, doing them good, being loyal towards them, and fulfilling their needs (Hidayat and Sukroni 2017, 21). Both exegetical literature and etymological literature are full of glosses of *iḥsān* linking it with the themes of righteousness, kindness, and morality.

Several verses of the Qur'an prescribe filial piety and respect for both parents. The importance of this command is emphasized by its intratextual position right after the command to worship God alone, cf. the concept of *tawḥīd* (God's unity),[3] thus juxtaposing respect of God and parents despite all differences.

Your Lord has commanded that you should worship none but Him, and that you be kind to your parents. If either or both of them reach old age with you, say no word that shows impatience with them, and do not be harsh with them, but speak to them respectfully. And lower to them the wing of humility towards them in kindness and say, "Lord, have mercy on them, just as they cared for me when I was little." (Qur'an, Sura 17:23–4)[4]

> ... Worship God; join nothing with Him. Be good to your parents, relatives, to orphans, to the needy, to neighbours near and far, to travellers in need, and to your slaves. God does not like arrogant, boastful people. (Qur'an, Sura 4:36)

Even if both parents do not worship Allāh but are polytheists, Muslims are not allowed to behave badly towards them. As the following verses

3. In Islam, the belief in one God and one God only is central. *Tawḥīd* is the belief in the oneness and unity of Allah as expressed in the first of the Five Pillars of Islam, the *Shahādah*.

4. All quotations from the Qur'an are rendered in M. A. S. Abdel Haleem's translation from 2008.

emphasize, it is not permissible to obey sinning parents, yet a child is still obliged to show them kindness and display a good attitude to them.

> We have commanded people to be good to their parents: their mothers carried them, with strain upon strain, and it takes two years to wean them. Give thanks to Me and to your parents – all will return to me. If they strive to make you associate with Me anything about which you have no knowledge, then do not obey them. Yet keep their company in this life according to what is right, and follow the path of those who turn to Me. You will all return to Me in the end, and I will tell you everything that you have done. (Qur'an, Sura 31:14–15)

While alive, a Muslim must show devotion to their mother and father. However, filial piety expressed in acts involving both parents comes in different forms, among other things by visiting them, caring for them, not hurting them with words and deeds, praying for their kindness, and providing a decent living and living facilities if both are categorized as poor. Alive or dead, the opportunity to serve both parents is always open. As the following verses state, neglecting this obligation is considered a great sin; hence, it can hinder a Muslim's access to paradise.

> We have commanded man to be good to his parents – his mother struggled to carry him and struggled to give birth to him; his bearing and weaning took a full thirty months – and when he has grown to manhood and reached the age of forty to say, "Lord, help me to be truly grateful for Your favours to me and to my parents; help me to do good work that pleases You ; make my offspring good. I turn to You; I am one of those who devote themselves to You." We accept from such people the best of what they do and We overlook their bad deeds. They will be among the people of Paradise – the true promise that has been given to them. But some say to their parents, "What? Are you really warning me that I shall be raised alive from my grave, when so many generations have already passed and gone before me?" His parents implore God for help; they say, "Alas for you! Believe! God's promise is true," but still he replies, "These are nothing but ancient fables." (Qur'an, Sura 46:15–17)

The Ḥadīths on *birr* and *iḥsān*

The usage of the word *iḥsān* in the Sunnah[5] and the body of the Ḥadīth (prophetic traditions) resembles the Qur'anic usage. The mention of *iḥsān* and *birr* occurs in the Ḥadīth where the following is recounted about the Prophet: "Abdullah bin Amr narrated that the Prophet said: 'The Lord's pleasure is in the parent's pleasure, and the Lord's anger is in the parent's

5. Sunnah means the "way" of the Prophet Muhammad and includes everything he said, did, and approved of. The Sunnah is known from the statements called Ḥadīths.

anger'" (at-Tirmidhi 1899).[6] This Ḥadīth warns the Muslim of the consequence of not pleasing the parents. Again, the parents are mentioned not because the parents are equated with God, but the Ḥadīth underlines the almost vicarious role that parents have in reacting on behalf of God. If the parents fill in for God, the respect that God deserves must be extended to the parents. "It is reported on the authority of 'Abdullah that the Messenger of Allah observed: The best of the deeds or deed is the (observance of) prayer at its proper time and kindness to the parents" (Muslim n.d., 155).[7] This Ḥadīth accentuates kindness to parents as a main Islamic act together with time-bound prayer, which shows how important filial piety is.

'*Awra* and '*ayb* – two gendered Islamic norms

The many verses in the Qur'an and examples from the Ḥadīths that mention *birr* and *iḥsān* do not distinguish between the parents. Both parents must be respected equally. The Qur'an and the Sunnah do not distinguish between men and women's obligations in elderly care. In practice, however, perceptions of gender pertain to agency and make "doing" care a complex matter. The sacred texts instruct both Muslim men and women to care for their elderly parents, but it does not come with a manual that instructs how care should be done in practice. While this gives the Muslim a relative amount of freedom to interpret, choose, and negotiate care tasks and options, it can simultaneously form a challenge. In a recent ethnographic study on elderly care in Muslim families in Denmark, Ismail discusses gender in its performative dimension and argues that when Muslim women and men "do" care, they simultaneously "do gender" (Ismail 2022). The study shows that elderly care is surrounded by intertwined gendered, cultural, and religious norms that underlie and reinforce widespread perceptions of women as "natural caregivers" and most often discourage men from providing elderly care on an equal footing with women. This explains why Muslim women dominate as the direct care providers in Muslim communities. I identified the intimate sphere of elderly Muslims as regulated by the norms of '*awra* (precautions to cover someone's body parts) and '*ayb* (shame/shameful) in line with various studies (see e.g. Al-Heeti 2007; Hansen 2014; Liversage and Jakobsen 2016; Naldemirci 2013) to explain why Muslim families have a dismissive attitude towards municipal care services and nursing homes. In my study on care arrangements in Muslim families,

6. Quotations from the Ḥadīths collected by Abu `Isa Muhammad at-Tirmidhī are rendered in Abu Khaliyl's translation.

7. Quotations from the Ḥadīths collected by Muslim ibn al-Hajjaj al-Naysaburi are rendered in Abdul Hamid Siddiqui's translation.

'awra and *'ayb* are identified as interrelated norms that are not always distinguishable regarding elderly care and intimate support (Ismail 2021).

Etymologically, the term *'ayb* stands for shame or shameful in Arabic, which is closely linked to what is deemed morally wrong in culture and by society. The word is commonly used in everyday conversation to condemn a behaviour that violates social and moral norms. The word is often less attributable to a behaviour being *ḥarām* (a sin or religiously forbidden) as to the fear that it will lead to gossip and therefore public disdain. The theological interpretation of *'ayb* is "fault" or "defect"; yet, it is rarely used as such in everyday language.

In the plural, *'awra* or *'awrāt* derives from the root *'awr*, a term which means a hidden and secret place, but can also mean "nakedness," "blemish," "defect," "fault," "imperfection," or "incompleteness" (Cambridge Dictionary 2023). In Islamic terminology, a person's *'awra* must be kept hidden. It also refers to everything that causes shame when exposed. Thus, the *'awra* of a person is the area of the body that "normally" causes embarrassment if exposed to others. In English, the most common translation is "nakedness," or the "area of the body that must be concealed" and covered with appropriate clothing.

> Children of Adam, We have given you garments to cover your nakedness and as an adornment for you; the garment of Godconsciousness is the best of all garments – this is one of God's signs, so that people may take heed. (Qur'an, Sura 7:26)

The covering of one's nakedness (*'awra*) is of great importance for men and women in Islam. Thus, the Qur'an[8] and Sunnah lay emphasis on this topic:

> And tell the believing women to lower their eyes, guard their private parts, and not display their charms beyond what [it is acceptable] to reveal; they should draw their coverings over their necklines and not reveal their charms except to their husbands, their fathers, their husband's fathers, their sons, their husbands' sons, their brothers, their brothers' sons, their sisters' sons, their womenfolk, their slaves, such men as attend them who have no desire, or children who are not yet aware of women's nakedness; they should not stamp their feet so as to draw attention to any hidden charms. Believers, all you, turn to God so that you may prosper. (Qur'an, Sura 24:31)

When defining a woman's *'awra* it entails the concept of *maḥram*. The term *maḥram* comes from the word *ḥarām* that means something which is prohibited. Based on the *tafsīr* (interpretation) of the verse above, the *'awra* signifies the parts that a woman must cover when she is with non-*maḥram* members of the opposite sex to prevent any arousal to protect herself from

8. See Qur'an, Sura 7:28; 24:31.58, 33:13.

sexual harassment and to reduce chances of becoming involved in a non-marital sexual relationship. A *maḥram* to a woman is a person with whom marriage is prohibited. From a social perspective, one could say that the concept pertains to close relatives where a sexual relation would be either incestuous or disruptive of relations in the extended family. Accordingly, a *maḥram* could be the father, grandfather, great-grandfather, or any other paternal ancestor. It also includes stepfather, sons, grandsons, great-grandsons, and any further male descendants she has from her children, brothers, or maternal or paternal uncles and nephews. Finally, a *maḥram* could also be half-brothers, foster-related (adoptive), or even milk-related men. A child that a woman breastfed at least five times before he reached the age of 2 becomes her son, which means that the boy eventually will become a *mahram*. Cousins and stepsiblings are considered non-*maḥram* (Al-Absi 2018). The part of the *'awra* that a woman must cover in front of all her *maḥram* but not for her husband, preteens, and the elderly, is the area from the chest to the knees. She can show her hair, wear short sleeves and shorts that reach her knees. Women can also show to other women the same parts of the *'awra* which they can show to male family members. However, she must cover the chest to the knees (Al-Absi 2018).

While the Qur'an, Sura 24:31, quoted above, clearly mentions *charms* (*'awra* in the Arabic version) of women as the nakedness/nudity of women, there are no Qur'anic verses that mentions the *'awra* of the man directly, while several Ḥadīths do so: "The Messenger of Allah said: A man should not see the private parts of another man, and a woman should not see the private parts of another woman, and a man should not lie with another man under one covering, and a woman should not lie with another woman under one covering" (Muslim n.d., 667). In another Ḥadīth, Abu Az-Zinad narrates that "Ibn Jarhad informed me from his father, that the Prophet passed by him while his thigh was exposed, so the Prophet said: 'Cover your thigh, for indeed it is 'Awra'" (at-Tirmidhi 1899, 2798).

The two major Islamic denominations, Sunni and Shia, have different interpretations of the *'awra* of a man, however, there seems to be a consensus that the *'awra* of a man refers to the part of the body from the navel to the knees. This to ensure that a man covers his genitals. The Islamic rule to cover one's *'awra* applies to a Muslim once he or she reaches puberty or is mentally mature. This, however, does not apply for people with developmental or mental disorders.

A man's *'awra* in front of another man is also the same as his *'awra* with non-*maḥram* and female family members, namely from the navel to the knees. A *maḥram* to a man is his mother, grandmother, great-grandmother, and any further maternal ancestors that he has. The stepmother, the daughter, granddaughter, great-granddaughter, and any further descendants he has from his children, sister, aunt on both sides, and nieces are also included. With the husband or wife, there are no limitations on which part of the *'awra* a person can and cannot show. A husband or a wife is permitted to get completely naked for the spouse. The description of the abovementioned rules for *'awra* in both the Qur'an and the Ḥadīths emphasizes that the concept of *'awra* functions to regulate the outward appearance of the individual Muslim. One could argue that when Muslims perform in accordance with these rules and adopt these regulations their performance becomes a matter of bodily enacting the sacred texts.

Piety through Elderly Care: An Ethnographic Insight

The Muslim families that I worked with lived by the tradition of *birr-ul-walidāyn* and were both driven and informed by it. In the lives of my interlocutors, the practice of elderly care is integrated in most of their daily tasks and care arrangements. Many of them strive to live up to the obligation of *birr* and *iḥsān* despite challenges and compromises.

Um Ali,[9] a 61-year-old Arab-Danish Muslim woman, is one of my interlocutors. She came to Denmark in the late 1980s together with her husband and children. Her parents and some of her siblings followed her to Denmark a few years later. Today, Um Ali lives with her husband and their youngest son. Her other children are married with children, but live close by. Besides being a wife, a mother, and a grandmother, Um Ali is together with her siblings responsible for taking care of their 83-year-old mother, who lives in the same block of flats as Um Ali. Before Um Ali's mother suffered a stroke a couple of years ago, she used to be strong and independent. Today though, the elderly mother is paralysed on one side of her body, hence, she requires extensive care and nursing. Since they have chosen not to entrust the care to the municipal home care, Um Ali shares the caretaking of her elderly mother with her siblings. The elderly mother receives care almost around the clock and is rarely left alone. While Um Ali's brothers and their families are responsible for domestic chores like the cooking, the cleaning, and the grocery shopping, Um Ali, her sister, and sometimes her daughter are responsible for the more intimate care chores. According to Um Ali, while it was not an easy nor comfortable task to take upon herself in the beginning, it got easier with time.

9. The prefixes "Um" and "Abu" are excessively and commonly used in Arab and Muslim societies. Abu is an Arabic word that means "father of" and Um means "mother of" followed typically by the name of the first-born son.

Like many of my interlocutors, Um Ali was well aware of the notions of *'awra* and *'ayb* when speaking about performing personal and intimate care on her elderly mother, including bathing her, washing her after a toilet visit, or helping change her underwear. In the families I visited, it was a norm that the female family members took care of such intimate care tasks for their female elderly, but when the elderly is a man, a male family member, if available, helps with the intimate care tasks.

> I bathe her, I apply moisturizing cream on her body, I wipe her after toilet visits, I do all those things ... when I'm not available, it's my daughter or my sister who does it ... the idea of others, you know strangers, helping her out with those things makes her uncomfortable, and frankly speaking, it makes me uncomfortable too ... when we started helping her out with the intimate tasks, she was very uncomfortable and unhappy, because she had a hard time being okay with revealing her *'awra* to us, but then we talked about it, and she understood that it is better to have us, her daughters, granddaughters, and daughters-in-law, than others, than strangers. (Um Ali)

Um Ali was very open and knowledgeable about the topic of intimate caregiving and *'awra*. When her mother fell sick, she and the rest of the family faced a new reality followed by sometimes-overwhelming care tasks, like those which are more intimate. On the one hand, Um Ali was very much determined to fulfil her duty by showing *birr* and *iḥsān* and to take on whatever care her elderly mother needed. On the other hand, she was concerned with the issue of *'awra*. Um Ali told me that she and her sister questioned whether they were "permitted" to be exposed to their mother's private parts when they helped her. To them, it was a dilemma because they feared that they were doing something *ḥarām* (prohibited) and crossing a line.

> In the beginning it was a very difficult situation. On the one hand, we wanted to be good Muslims and do what Allāh commanded us in the Qur'an, to be there for our mother in her need, to show her kindness, mercy and patience, but then with intimate care came a boundary we needed to cross but did not know how to until we sought after guidance (Um Ali)

At this point, the two female siblings decided to contact a local imam to ask him how to deal with their concerns. The imam advised them to do their duties as daughters and not be concerned with the issue of *'awra* because their mother could not take care of herself and depended on their caregiving. Although their dilemma could be considered one that should concern the family as a unit, the two female siblings did not share their concern regarding the issue of *'awra* with their male siblings. Neither did they discuss the matter with the males in the family.

> Of course, we did not share our concern with the rest of the family, because my brothers should have nothing to do with these kinds of care tasks as long as we [females] are available, plus it will make my mother truly uncomfortable and embarrassed to be wiped or bathed by her sons or grandsons. We will never subject her to that kind of humiliation … but of course, it would have been different if my mother had not had daughters. She would be left with no other choice but her sons to help her out … but thank God my mother does have daughters and my brothers have us, sisters, so we save them the embarrassment and the *'ayb* [shame]. (Um Ali)

When Um Ali and her sister went to the local imam for advice regarding the question of *'awra*, they had no intention of asking him about whether his advice applies to the males in the family. According to Um Ali, not only would that have been unnecessary, but a shameful question too. The notion of *'ayb* (shame) not only manifests itself if care is assigned to strangers; it also manifests itself if an enabled female leaves specific intimate care tasks to a male relative to perform.

This point suggests that, in addition to the fact that *'awra* and *'ayb* as religious and cultural norms are not opposites, but interrelated, they are also entangled with gendered norms. On the one hand, *'awra* and *'ayb* can serve as an excuse for men to resist more active involvement in care and sometimes even domestic tasks. On the other hand, they can serve as norms by which Muslim women monopolize the caregiving and create social barriers for men assuming caregiving roles (Ismail 2022; Peacock 2003). Note here how Um Ali under no circumstances would allow a male relative to do the intimate care that she herself performs for her elderly mother "unless there are no other options."

"Unless there are no other options" is a phrase I have heard several times during my fieldwork not only from women, but from some of my male interlocutors as well. One of those men is my 57-year-old interlocutor Salim. Like most of my interlocutors, Salim came to Denmark in the late 1980s together with his parents and siblings. Today Salim is married and has four children. He works in an electronic company. Salim is the eldest among his siblings. Salim's father died in 2017 at the age of 89, but his elderly mother is still alive. Despite her weak and poor health, she is an active and important part of his and his siblings' family life. Like his other siblings, prescriptions in sacred texts constitute a driving force in Salim's determination to take an active part in caring for his mother.

> I do as much as my brothers and sisters do. We have divided the care tasks between us. My sisters are responsible for some of the domestic chores and the more personal and intimate care chores, while my brothers and I take care of everything else. This is our duty as her children and as Muslims. I would never

> be able to look myself in the mirror if not I am partaking in my mother's care, besides as the *ḥadīth* says she is my entry to *Jannah*[10] *inshā'allāh* [if God permits]. (Salim)

The division of the care tasks in Salim's family resembles that of Um Ali. However, according to Salim, he would not refuse to perform intimate care on his mother, but only if it was absolute necessary, and no other option was available.

> If both my sisters decide that they do not want to do the intimate part of the care chores, then I see it as my duty as her son to step in. But I would ask my wife or my daughters first, but if they are reluctant to do it then I would do it myself of course ... It would be very difficult, awkward, embarrassing for my mother and for me as well ... because of the *'awra* you know ... it was easier with my father, because he was a man, not completely easy but easier for me to do. It would be a much more difficult situation with my mother ... but again thank God we are a big family, some of the other women in the family would probably be able to step in, I do not know. (Salim)

Salim also reflects on the personal and intimate care that he provided to his now late father. The father was poorly in the days before he died and needed help to wash, to bathe and to do the *Wuḍū'*[11] before prayer.

> It crossed a boundary for both of us. May he rest in peace, he was so embarrassed, I could clearly see that in him, but I tried to be as respectful as possible ... there were no other options. After all, he would never allow my sisters to give him the needed intimate care, I would not either, because I was there, my brother was there, so no need to involve the women, and I think my father was grateful for that ... I mean I would be ... I would definitely not be comfortable with receiving intimate care from my daughters when I reach old age. (Salim)

Still, Salim considered his ability to do the caregiving and provide it to his father was a "priceless privilege" – priceless with regard to religious merit.

> Although it was awkward and at times difficult, I was really happy to do it, because I know that Allāh was watching, and I genuinely hope that I fulfilled my duty as a son and Muslim but more importantly that my doings to my father would be counted as *ḥasanāt*[12] in the Day of Judgment. (Salim)

Although *birr* and *iḥsān* are not gendered per se (according to the sacred text), gender, *'awra* and *'ayb* interact in practice and construct care as a

10. Salim is referring here to the following ḥadīth "'O Messenger of Allah! I want to go out and fight (in Jihad) and I have come to ask your advice.' He said: 'Do you have a mother?' He said: 'Yes.' He said: 'Then stay with her, for Paradise is beneath her feet.'" (Sunan an-Nasa'i 3104).

11. Wuḍū' is the Islamic procedure for ritual purification or ablution of parts of the body before prayer. It is an important part of ritual purity in Islam.

12. Good deeds.

highly gendered way of "doing" one's Muslimness. Both of the interlocutors noted above strive to live out what the Qur'an and Ḥadīths command concerning filial piety when "doing" elderly care, which emphasizes the performative dimension of these very texts (Watts 2008). However, the way they choose to divide the care tasks and how they constantly reconsider and negotiate the effect and implications of *'awra* and *'ayb* on what they claim as "pious doing" (filial piety) indicate an artefactual use involving manipulation (Schleicher 2017) and an embodied enactment of the sacred texts within the private sphere, often without a human public other than the human cared for. The gendered division of care tasks itself does not derive from Qur'anic verses or Ḥadīths guidance. Yet their daily performance of *'awra* and *'ayb* are central concepts in Um Ali's and Salim's intentions and hopes of becoming pious Muslims. It is not immediately obvious if Um Ali's and Salim's intention is to establish a legitimizing reference to the Qur'an and the Ḥadīths to excuse their transgression of the limits of bodily intimacy, if it is visually to embody the sacred texts in ways that make them recognizable as pious Muslims, or if it reflects an effort to earn salvific merit. Still, it is evident that their bodily enactments of prescriptions in the Qur'an and Hadiths concerning filial piety interfere with, challenge, and sometimes overrule expectations to consider *'awra* and *'ayb.*

Conclusion

This article introduced and analysed central passages in the Qur'an and the Ḥadīths that deal with *birr-al- wālidayn,* along with *'awra* and *'ayb,* since they all appear as central concepts in the Islamic tradition of elderly care. With a focus on the embodied enactment of these concepts, the analysis used the two ethnographic cases of Um Ali and Salim to look at how Muslims "do" care for their elderly parents and at the same time strive to embody their sacred text, the Qur'an, and the Ḥadīths in everyday life.

The stories of Um Ali and Salim represent lived examples of Muslims' identification within the religious dimension of practicing elderly care and the formation of their piety and self-cultivation. Here, Islam and its sacred texts constitute the dominant discourse by which Um Ali and Salim are subjected and enact their religious identity. Inhabiting *birr, iḥsān, 'awra,* and *'ayb* are techniques of the self through which they become better Muslims, sons and daughters. In Um Ali's and Salim's case, "being good Muslims" and hoping to achieve the afterlife means that they must continuously maintain their relationship with God by "being good at" caring for their parents, who are not only the receivers of the caregiving but also the link between them and God. Furthermore, this article has attempted to show that "doing" elderly care enables a domain of pious activities that matters to how Salim and Um Ali perform and understand gender.

As showed above, the access to care as a pious practice rests on an artefactual use (Schleicher 2017) of the sacred text in its performative dimension (Watts 2008), which serves to legitimize Um Ali's and Salim's pious practice. The stories of Um Ali and Salim show that they work to interpret the sacred texts in such a way as to legitimize their way of doing their piety through elderly care. The negotiation, rationalization, and argumentation they offer regarding *'awra, 'ayb*, and their gender roles can be perceived as part of the formation of their moral and religious selves. They do feel challenged by the norms of *'awra* and *'ayb* and express a reluctance towards performing intimate care on a parent of the same or the opposite sex. Yet the religious commandment to do care for one's parents and the religious reward that follows from it outweigh the embarrassments – and also, as in Salim's hypothetical considerations, establishes a willingness to break with norms of *'awra* and *'ayb* if no alternative solution is at hand. Here, the central emphasis on *birr* and *iḥsān* in the Qur'an trumps the norms pertaining to the naked body and makes both Um Ali and Salim struggle with and navigate the boundaries of intimacy to access what is more important for their piety, namely "doing" care.

Acknowledgments

A special thanks goes to my former colleague Marianne Schleicher for seeing the potential in my ethnographic material and whose work and insights inspired me to write this article.

References

Abdel Haleem, M. A. S., tr. 2008. *The Qur'an*. Oxford: Oxford University Press.

Ahmad, M., and Khan, S. 2016. "A Model of Spirituality for Ageing Muslims." *Journal of Religion and Health* 55: 830–43. https://doi.org/10.1007/s10943-015-0039-0

Al-Absi, M. 2018. "The Concept of Nudity and Modesty in Arab-Islamic Culture." *European Journal of Science and Theology* 14(4): 25–34.

Al-Heeti, R. M. 2007. "Why Nursing Homes Will Not Work: Caring for the Needs of the Aging Muslim American Population". *Elder Law Journal* 15, 205.

an-Nasāʾī,, Aḥmad. n.d. *Sunan an-Nasa'i*. Translated by Nasiruddin Al-Khattab. https://sunnah.com/nasai. Accessed 29 March 2023.

Andersen, H. T. 2008. "The Emerging Danish Government Reform: Centralised Decentralisation." *Urban Research & Practice* 1(1): 3–17. https://doi.org/10.1080/17535060701795298

at-Tirmidhi, Abu 'Isa Muhammad. n.d. *Jāmi' at-Tirmidhī*, translated by Abu Khaliyl. Riyad: Darussalam. https://sunnah.com/tirmidhi. Accessed 29 March 2023.

Butler, J. 1990. *Gender Trouble: Feminism and the Subversion of Identity*: New York: Routledge.

Cambridge Dictionary. 2023. Arabic–English translator. https://dictionary.cambridge.org/translate/arabic-english. Accessed 30 March 2023.

Gardet, L. 2012. "Birr." In P. J. Bearman, T. Bianquis, E. J. v. Donzel, C. E. Bosworth, and W. Heinrichs, eds, *The Encyclopaedia of Islam*. 2nd ed. online: Leiden: Brill Academic Publishers. https://referenceworks-brillonline-com.ez.statsbiblioteket.dk/browse/encyclopaedia-of-islam-2

Hansen, E. B. 2014. "Older Immigrants' Use of Public Home Care and Residential Care." *European Journal of Ageing* 11(1): 41–53. https://doi.org/10.1007/s10433-013-0289-1

Hidayat, A., and Sukroni, A. 2017. "The Value Inheritance of Family System in Islamic Tradition: Birr-ul-Walidayn." *Ulum Islamiyyah*.

Hooyman, N. R., and Kiyak, H. A. 2008. *Social Gerontology: A Multidisciplinary Perspective*. London: Pearson Education.

Ismail, A. M. 2021. "Care in Practice: Negotiations Regarding Care for the Elderly in Multigenerational Arab Muslim Families in Denmark." *Contemporary Islam* 15(2): 215–32. https://doi.org/10.1007/s11562-020-00458-8

———. 2022. "'Doing Care, Doing Gender': Towards a Rethinking of Gender and Elderly Care in the Arab Muslim Families in Denmark." *Journal of Religion, Spirituality & Aging*, 1–19. https://doi.org/10.1080/15528030.2022.2145413

Johansen, M.-L. E., and Jensen, S. B. 2017. "'They Want us Out': Urban Regeneration and the Limits of Integration in the Danish Welfare State." *Critique of Anthropology* 37(3): 297–316. https://doi.org/10.1177/0308275x17719990

Juynboll, G. H. A., and Brown, D. W. 2012. "SUNNA." In *Encyclopaedia of Islam*. 2nd ed. Leiden: Brill Academic Publishers. https://doi.org/10.1163/1573-3912_islam_COM_1123

Liversage, A., and Jakobsen, V. 2016. Ældre fra Tyrkiet: Hverdagsliv og vilkår. Frederiksberg: Roskilde Universitetsforlag.

Mattingly, C., Dyring, R., Louw, M., and Wentzer, T. S. 2017. *Moral Engines: Exploring the Ethical Drives in Human Life* 5. Oxford: Berghahn Books.

Muslim, ibn al-Hajjaj al-Naysaburi. n.d. *Sahih Muslim*, translated by Abdul Hamid Siddiqui. https://sunnah.com/muslim. Accessed 29 March 2023.

Mustafa, S. 2020. "Iḥsān." In *Encyclopaedia of Islam*. 3rd ed. Leiden: Brill Academic Publishers. https://doi.org/10.1163/1573-3912_ei3_COM_32381

Naldemirci, Ö. 2013. *Caring (in) Diaspora. Aging and Caring Experiences of Older Turkish Migrants in a Swedish Context*. Göteborg: University of Gothenburg, Department of Sociology and Work Science.

Peacock, D. 2003. "Men as Partners: Promoting Men's Involvement in Care and Support Activities for People Living with HIV/AIDS." Paper presented in the conference "The role of men and boys in achieving gender equality," Brasilia, Brazil.

Rytter, M., Sparre, S. L., Ismail, A. M., and Liversage, A. 2021. *Minoritetsældre og selvudpegede hjælpere: Kommunal velfærd og omsorg i forandring.* Aarhus: Aarhus Universitetsforlag.

Schleicher, M. 2017. "Engaging All the Senses: On Multi-Sensory Stimulation in the Process of Making and Inaugurating a Torah Scroll." *Postscripts: The Journal of Sacred Texts and Contemporary Worlds* 8: 39–56. https://doi.org/10.1558/post.32694

Watts, J. W. 2008. "The Three Dimensions of Scriptures." *Postscripts: The Journal of Sacred Texts and Contemporary Worlds* 2(2–3): 135–59. https://doi.org/10.1558/post.v2i2.135

Whitfield, K. E., & Baker, T. A. 2013. *Handbook of Minority Aging.* 1st ed. New York: Springer Publishing Co.

About the Author

Abir Mohamad Ismail is a Postdoctoral Researcher at Aarhus University's Department of the Study of Religion. She earned her PhD in Anthropology and holds a Master's degree in Arabic and Islamic Studies from the same university. Her research focuses on care, aging, family and intergenerational relations, gender dynamics, and the experiences of Muslims in Western societies. Ismail's work also explores religious individualization, secularization, and the intersections of religion, politics, and society. Additionally, she is involved in projects addressing integration, migration, majority-minority relations, transnational Islam, and the teaching of Arabic as a foreign language. (ami@cas.au.dk)

Index

www.ingramcontent.com/pod-product-compliance
Lightning Source LLC
Chambersburg PA
CBHW062027270326
41929CB00014B/2348